£29

AVAILABLE ON
DISKETTE

D1806969

EDUCATION AT A GLANCE: THE OECD INDICATORS

This interactive data diskette presents a set of international education indicators compiled by the OECD in response to the growing need for comparative data on the quality and performance of educational systems. The indicators, covering the period 1985-1991, offer information on the demographic and economic context of education, characteristics and features of education systems, and the outcomes of education.

Not only does the diskette software allow rapid consultation of the data, but it also offers the possibility of having instant access to information, constructing tables, producing a large variety of diagrams/graphs and creating charts/maps.

(Descriptive leaflet available on request from OECD Electronic Editions.)

In order to benefit from the special price of:

FF 1 200 £ 135   US$ 215   DM 365 (instead of FF 1 500 £ 165 US$ 270 DM 455)

please return the order form below *now* to the OECD in Paris at the address below, one of OECD's Publications and Information Centres in Bonn, Tokyo or Washington, or the OECD Distributor in your country.

OECD PUBLICATIONS OCDE
Electronic Éditions Électroniques
2, rue André-Pascal, 75775 Paris Cedex 16, France

- -

ORDER FORM

☐ I wish to order
EDUCATION AT A GLANCE: THE OECD INDICATORS
☐ 5 1/4" diskettes   ☐ 3 1/2" diskettes
at the special price of: FF 1 200 £ 135 US$ 215 DM 365

☐ Send invoice: official order attached ☐ Payment is enclosed

Signature _____ Date _____

Name _____

Address _____

_____

Country _____

CERI / 94 / 01

OECD HISTORICAL SERIES

EDUCATION
1960-1990
THE OECD PERSPECTIVE

by George S. Papadopoulos

ORGANISATION FOR ECONOMIC CO-OPERATION AND DEVELOPMENT

ORGANISATION FOR ECONOMIC CO-OPERATION AND DEVELOPMENT

Pursuant to Article 1 of the Convention signed in Paris on 14th December 1960, and which came into force on 30th September 1961, the Organisation for Economic Co-operation and Development (OECD) shall promote policies designed:

— to achieve the highest sustainable economic growth and employment and a rising standard of living in Member countries, while maintaining financial stability, and thus to contribute to the development of the world economy;

— to contribute to sound economic expansion in Member as well as non-member countries in the process of economic development; and

— to contribute to the expansion of world trade on a multilateral, non-discriminatory basis in accordance with international obligations.

The original Member countries of the OECD are Austria, Belgium, Canada, Denmark, France, Germany, Greece, Iceland, Ireland, Italy, Luxembourg, the Netherlands, Norway, Portugal, Spain, Sweden, Switzerland, Turkey, the United Kingdom and the United States. The following countries became Members subsequently through accession at the dates indicated hereafter: Japan (28th April 1964), Finland (28th January 1969), Australia (7th June 1971), New Zealand (29th May 1973) and Mexico (18th May 1994). The Commission of the European Communities takes part in the work of the OECD (Article 13 of the OECD Convention).

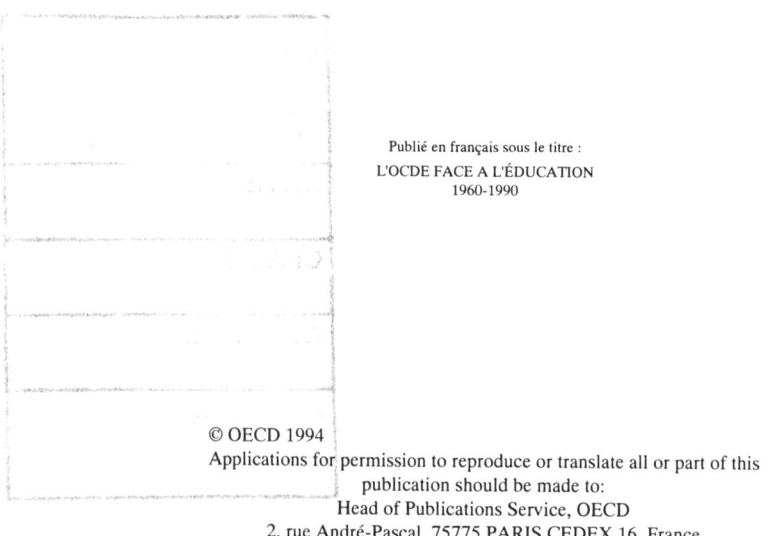

Publié en français sous le titre :
L'OCDE FACE A L'ÉDUCATION
1960-1990

PREFACE

by the Secretary-General of the OECD

OECD societies are moving rapidly towards becoming "learning societies". Learning, the very stuff of education, is pivotal to their economic prosperity. This learning takes place in a variety of settings: in schools and colleges, but also in families, communities, enterprises and political institutions. Formal education cannot realise its full potential unless it is seen as part of this overall learning effort in society. And such is the pace of change that, more than ever, education must help *all* individuals to develop the inclination and ability constantly to learn afresh: learning becomes a life-long process. Education can best assist in this process if it is firmly rooted in its wider economic, social, cultural and political environment, but recognising at the same time that it has its own dynamics directed to each individual's development.

Of the many policy areas that are dealt with at the OECD, Education is one which is par excellence a *national* concern but it is an area where the OECD has worked to assist its Member countries to think, and often work, together in their search for solutions to the problems confronting their educational systems during a period of unprecedented economic and social change. As demonstrated in this book, the Organisation – the Secretariat working closely with national administrations and the research community in Member countries – has been able to identify major current and emerging problems in this particular area, and bring to bear on them innovative thinking and approaches. It exemplifies the value of the catalytic role of the Organisation in influencing national policies, but without intervening in the internal affairs of individual countries.

In relating education to other sectors of policy, economic, social and environmental, the OECD has developed an approach to its work that distinguishes it from other international organisations. Education is seen as a major partner of such policies, with which it interacts, both contributing and responding to them. By relating education to the socio-economic realities within which it operates, the Organisation has, I believe, rightly emphasised the role which education plays in the total polity.

The author of this book, George S. Papadopoulos, has drawn on his rich experience over thirty years at the OECD to provide an invaluable insight into the way in which work on education at the OECD has made major impacts on educational thinking and policy development in Member countries. The work, to which he made such a considerable contribution before retiring at the end of 1990, of course, continues. It was given

3

additional impetus by the conclusions of the 1990 OECD Ministerial Meeting on Education. The tasks ahead are as challenging as they are vital to the well-being of our economies and societies undergoing rapid change in terms of technology, employment and community life. Education, and the human qualities it helps develop, will be increasingly required to contribute to the generation and management of such change, while, at the same time, maintaining its role of ensuring the continued stability of democratic societies and the preservation of what is best in their values and cultures.

Jean-Claude Paye

TABLE OF CONTENTS

Chapter IV

EDUCATIONAL GROWTH AND ITS LEGACIES
(mid-sixties-early seventies)

Chapter V

EXPERIMENTING WITH CHANGE: PROBLEMS OF EDUCATIONAL
DEVELOPMENT (early and mid-seventies)

Chapter VI

EXPERIMENTING WITH CHANGE (continued): EDUCATIONAL
STRUCTURES AND STRATEGIES FOR EQUALITY

Chapter VII

EDUCATION AND SOCIETY: THE SEARCH
FOR NEW LINKS (the seventies)

Chapter VIII

RECESSION AND ITS CONSEQUENCES
(mid-seventies-early eighties)

Chapter IX

EDUCATION AND STRUCTURAL
CHANGE (the eighties)

Chapter X

CONCLUSION ....

Chapter I

INTRODUCTION

Purpose and scope

Over the last thirty years, the OECD has come to be recognised as having played an important role in educational co-operation among the industrialised democracies of the world which constitute its membership. Its educational activities are highly regarded by the educational community, both policy-makers and researchers, within Member countries and more widely. They have constantly received support by governments, largely at the instigation of senior officials in the Member countries with direct responsibilities for administration, planning and policy-making in education who judge these activities as directly relevant to their current preoccupations and interests; and who also look to OECD work in education for the contribution it can make to the identification of new or emerging problems, their clarification and possible approaches to how they can be tackled.

The primary purpose of this book is to try to record and explain how this unique venture in international co-operation in education has come about. It will attempt to do this by providing a historical overview of the educational activities of OECD, from their inception and origins around 1960 and how they developed over the following thirty years, a period which coincides with the thirtieth anniversary of the Organisation itself. It is an insider's account of what the OECD did in education during this period, and how and why it did it. The accent will be on how these activities relate to the evolution of educational policies and policy thinking, and of their practical implications and consequences, and on how they endeavoured to both respond and contribute to broader policy trends and developments during a period of unprecedented educational expansion in the OECD countries matched by equally significant social and economic change.

The substantial volume and variety of OECD educational activities during this period precludes any attempt at an exhaustive account of them. The presentation will rather take the form of an evolutionary analysis relating OECD work to broad themes which can be observed in the evolution of national educational policies, themselves reflecting broad chronological cycles – or pendulum swings – in educational thinking and fashions and the different perceptions which accompany them as moulded by changes in the broader social, economic and political environment of education. It is recognised thatthe fit between themes and chronology does not always work, but on the whole it does provide a meaningful structure within which this historical account can be put together. A retrospective view of this kind, with the advantages deriving from hindsight, makes it possible to offer, where necessary, a critique of approaches and activities which were conjuncturally designed, as well as to suggest lessons and pointers for the future.

The analysis leans heavily on the impressive record of the OECD educational output during the last thirty years, embodied in its reports and publications. The bibliographical references to each chapter provide ample testimony to this and indicate the specific sources which have been drawn upon, often textually, in putting the OECD educational story together.[1] It also draws on the author's personal experience and memory as someone who has been closely associated with this work over the whole of the period under review. References to individuals have been kept to a minimum, in line with the collective nature of OECD work.

The plan of the book is as follows. This first introductory Chapter is rounded off with a brief description of the main characteristics of the OECD approach to education and explains the distinctive features which give this work its specificity vis-à-vis that of other international bodies dealing with education. Chapter II traces the origins and early stages of the work, embedded in the preoccupations of the predecessor Organisation – the OEEC (Organisation for European Economic Co-operation) – with productivity, scientific research and scientific and technical personnel. It records how these initial efforts at improving the human skills infrastructure in order to sustain the momentum of economic recovery, achieved with the aid of the Marshall Plan, evolved into a broader concern for improving and expanding the educational system as a whole, culminating in the 1961 Washington Conference on Economic Growth and Investment in Education. The OECD response to the massive expansion of education during the sixties is dealt with in Chapter III, with particular attention to the significant and, in many respects, original contribution which the Organisation made to the development of educational policy/planning, its theoretical and methodological underpinnings and its practical application to country situations.

The three chapters that follow cover the period from the late sixties to the mid-seventies. Chapter IV takes up the consequences of growth and its legacies, in terms of unresolved problems and new challenges and the main bottlenecks standing in the way of their solution, particularly resources, structures, disparities in educational participation and the planning and management of vastly expanded educational systems. The 1970 Conference on Policies for Educational Growth was a useful stocktaking exercise of the momentous decade that followed the 1961 Washington Conference. It also helped identify the key areas in educational development – teachers, school building, innovation, equality, needed changes in overall educational structures and within the various levels of the educational system, as well as the need for new approaches to educational policy and planning – which were then tackled within the OECD programmes, as recorded in Chapters V and VI.

Throughout the seventies, the turmoil of educational change was accompanied by an upsurge of new social concerns and growing anxiety about the capacity of social policies to respond to these concerns. Inter-sectoral approaches were called for, and education, as a major sector of social policies, was looked to for the contribution it could make to such approaches. Chapter VII is devoted to the variety of activities that were undertaken in the effort to forge closer links between education and society, at both policy/planning and institutional levels.

Chapter VIII recounts how the promise held by this growth-led process of educational change and innovation came to be stultified by the onset of stagnation, and then contraction, beginning around the mid-seventies and resulting from the combined effects of economic downturn, the consequent rise in unemployment and the reversal of demographic trends. It then deals with the different responses that his new situation called for, particularly its impact on new approaches to educational policy and planning and to the setting of objectives and priorities, on financing, and the more effective use of resources and on the relationship between education and working life, especially for the young. These problems were compounded by the new economic imperative of the eighties, with its twin demand on education to contribute to structural change in the economy and improve its own standards and quality, while, at the same time, becoming more responsive to the needs of special groups in the population – the handicapped, the socially disadvantaged, ethnic and cultural minorities.

How the OECD educational activities responded to this new social and economic context is taken up in Chapter IX, which also sets the scene for the definition of an educational agenda for the nineties, as it emerged from the third OECD Education Ministerial Meeting (November, 1990). A brief concluding chapter indulges in some general reflections inspired by this history of education at OECD.

The OECD approach to education

There is no explicit reference in the OECD Convention to Education being among the concerns and purposes of the Organisation. The nearest it comes to getting such a reference is in Article 2(b), on policies designed to promote the development of Member countries' resources in science and technology, encourage research "and promote vocational training". Yet the Preamble to the Convention talks of economic strength and prosperity as essential to "the preservation of individual liberty and the increase of general well-being" and of the determination of Member countries "by consultation and co-operation to use more effectively their capacities and potentialities so as to promote the highest sustainable growth of their economies and improve the economic and social well-being of their peoples". In fact, the dominance of economic concerns within OECD has always been tempered by recognition of the social dimension and purposes of economic growth and development, reinforced by equal, if only gradually evolving awareness of the importance of human capital, and more generally of the "residual factor", in the process of economic growth.

There is, thus, an inferred role for education, both for the contribution it can make to economic growth and as means by which the purposes of such growth, namely an increase in general well-being, can be given reality; which, in turn, implies that education has its own proper dynamics and must be handled as such if it is to fulfil its role adequately.

It is important to note this dyarchy of concepts about education in its OECD context, for it has provided the hallmark of the Organisation's approach to its educational work throughout its history.

The distinctive feature of this approach, and the one for which OECD educational activities have been particularly valued by Member countries, is to be found in the policy-oriented nature of the work, in which education is related to its broader social, economic and cultural environment and in which the interplay between education policies and policies in these other sectorsis constantly brought out. It must be stressed from the outset that this linking of education to other sectors of policy has never been seen as a one-way process, subordinating education to other sectors. It provides rather an effective means of analysing the constituents of educational policies in their interaction with the social and economic realities around them, a complex process of reciprocal influence and of cause and effect, in which educationcontributes as much as it responds to broader developments in the polity.

Admittedly, in a setting like that of the OECD in which the economic dimension dominates, it is tempting to see education as a mere instrument of economic policy. And there has often been a tendency, both within certain parts of the Organisation itself, but also among sections of the educational establishment and the public more generally, to hold such a view. It has taken many years of effort, for example, and many a heated debate before Teacher Organisations came to be convinced that this is not the case. Nonetheless, there is a sense in which education within OECD has had to be "protected" against narrow economic and instrumentalist perceptions of its role– a task, it must be admitted, which was greatly facilitated by the expressed views of successive Secretaries General that education cannot be meaningfully organised, planned or even discussed merely in response to economic cycles or other conjunctural phenomena.

Integrating education into the central objectives and mainstream activities of the Organisation was, in fact, never an easy task. It was easy enough at the level of general concepts, as already explained. Difficulties often arose when it came to translating these concepts into specific activities, targeted, as they had to be, to the problems and needs of the educational sector, in its wider connotations, and to those responsible for it in the Member countries, *i.e.* essentially Ministries or Departments of Education and Training and key institutions operating in these areas. It was the perceived relevance of the activities to the direct interests of the educational constituency which gave the educational programmes the necessary country support at Committee level, which in turn got translated into political support at the level of the Council.[2]

But it was not always possible for members of the Council, even if they had the time, to devote enough attention to specific activities, or see the relevance of some of them, even if they recognised their intrinsic value, to the central preoccupations of the Organisation. It was partly a question of perceptions, but also of language, and this often imposed a delicate mediating role on the Secretariat. In actual practice, it has been extremely rare, even in times of sharp budgetary constraints and the painful process of priority setting within the overall annual programme/budget of the Organisation, that an activity agreed by the Committees was thrown out by the Council. Here, again, the mediating role of the Secretariat is in evidence: as Committee decisions are made on the basis of proposals by the Secretariat, the latter had to be sensitive to the budgetary and political realities which prevailed at any particular time in putting forward its proposals. This is a process common throughout the structures of the Organisation, as is the consensus basis on which decisions are made. In the case of education, it must be noted that the degree of political support has been constantly sustained by the interest shown in this sector by a significant core of Member countries, particularly among the smaller ones.

The primacy of the educational constituency as the source and target of the activities must in no way be interpreted as serving the narrow interests of an educational lobby, of encouraging isolationism. On the contrary, seen in the OECD context outlined above, it has proved useful in demonstrating to educationists the importance of relating to other sectors of policy and leading them to understand how their own interests, and those of education as part of the body politic, are best served by greater appreciation on their part of these inter-relationships. This has been done through the substance of the work itself, linking the analysis of educational policy issues to the realities of broader policy making, thus bringing out the inter-relationships, or "horizontality", of sectoral policies which increasingly came to dominate the overall OECD approach to its work. It proved a more subtle and effective way of passing the message than would have been the case with direct exhortation or prescription and helped allay the fears that "horizontality" was merely an astuce for imposing the views of one branch of government, *e.g.* Ministries of Finance, on other sectors of policy. In this sense, it has been an educative function in its own right and one which has been particularly valued by Governments who have often seen OECD educational activities as a useful training ground for their officials.

What has been said above is but one illustration of how OECD educational activities operate and the kind of influence they have on Member countries. A basic precept in the whole approach is recognition of the fact that education policies are *par excellence* national policies reflecting the specific circumstances, traditions and cultures of individual countries. The notion of an international education policy – even if such a thing existed, which has not been the case, at least so far – is altogether foreign to this concept. This goes hand in hand with a second basic precept, common to the bulk of OECD work, namely that the Organisation has no prescriptive role for countries, individually or collectively. Its influence, therefore, must be sought in terms of a catalytic role, through a process of which the following are the main features.

The starting point is the identification of major new policy issues which emerge on the educational horizon, and which might call for priority attention in the countries. These are issues which are somewhat ahead of actual country developments and thinking, but not so far ahead as to appear unrealistic or irrelevant. They must also be neutral, *i.e.* must not reflect particular ideological positions or viewpoints, although a minimum of normative thinking is unavoidable. These issues are then put together within a structured framework, leading to a number of questions which arise for policy-making. Arriving at a convincing statement of such issues and questions, of how and why they arise, and of their implications, is already half the work done. It involves a dialectical process of Secretariat and country thinking and exchange, including a strong dose of advice from experts, and provides the basis for subsequent programme planning and the designing of specific activities and plans for their implementation.

An essential component and often the point of departure of this implementation is the proven capacity of the Organisation to carry out solid and objective analysis of the problems, both quantitative and qualitative. Such analyses bring to bear on the problems the collective experience of Member countries, in terms of concepts and actual policy and practice, and endeavour to marry these to insights and findings deriving from research. The OECD very rarely undertakes fundamental research of its own, but the kind of analytical work that it does, geared as it is to policy and problem-solving concerns, can be classed as policy research in its own right.

The process by which such analyses are done is as important as their outcome. It is designed to facilitate ongoing and meaningful discussion and exchange within and across countries, leading ultimately to general conclusions which serve as guidelines for policy development. These are then fed back to individual countries to be followed up according to national circumstances, and, of course, interest and capacity, matters on which countries differ widely. This whole task is greatly facilitated, and made more manageable, by the limited and more-or-less homogeneous market economy based country membership of OECD, with clearly identified shared problems. The fact that all the members, in varying degrees, belong to the category of advanced industrial democracies enables these problems to be handled at a level of sophistication which would not have been possible if membership were more widely spread.

In addition, the OECD educational work has greatly benefited from the Organisation's flexibility in programming and methods of work. In this, the role of the Secretariat has been crucial. It is a Secretariat recognised for its professionalism, enjoying a relative independence within the rules set by the Organisation, and encouraged to bring creative thinking to bear on the work. It has the responsibility for initiating proposals for programmes and activities and, more generally, for putting up issues for discussion by Member country representatives. As programmes are decided on an annual basis, the Secretariat is constantly kept on its toes – a poor quality programme would be reflected in correspondingly poorer levels of budgetary allocations! The pressure on high quality is reinforced by the fact that the very existence of the educational programmes within the Organisation comes up for review every five years or so, with no guarantee that they would be automatically renewed. This places a premium on substance, which is always more important than bureaucratic formalities. Moreover, preoccupations with protocol, which pester many other international organisations, are mercifully minimal in OECD work.

The fact that there is no mandatory role for education in OECD has meant that continuing, service-type of functions have been purposefully avoided, the only and very recent exception being the annual report on basic educational statistics. The Country Educational Policy Reviews, which have been a permanent feature of the programme, do not come under this category: they are done on a voluntary basis and follow a *sui generis* pattern in terms of their methods of investigation, coverage and periodicity. They have proved, however, invaluable over the years as a source of programme inspiration, over and above their direct impact on the country under review and the contribution which the review process makes to a sharing of experience among all Member countries.

Thus, the Secretariat has to operate on the basis of programme targets which are constantly moving in response to newly emerging policy concerns. The normal life-span of an activity is 2-4 years, even though, as is natural, major themes within which specific aspects are investigated may last much longer. This need for programme renewal is a permanent challenge to the Secretariat, compounded by client expectations that the work should lead to forward-looking analyses and conclusions rather than the reproduction of conventional wisdom. In this, the Secretariat has built up very close working relationships with the Member countries, not only with Governments, but also with the research community, local and institutional leaders and other networks. In turn, this ensures an adequate level of conceptual and analytical respectability for the work and at the same time encourages the development of a progressive climate of opinion in the countries, spreading well beyond administrative and governmental structures. The importance of country participation and contributions at all stages of the work cannot be overstated. That they are prepared to do this, and the high degree of their involvement, is a sign of the relevance to their own problems and predicaments which countries see in the necessarily conceptual generalisations developed by the Secretariat, themselves deriving from the collective experience of the OECD membership, but raised to a minimum level of abstraction so as to make international discussion possible.

Structures and means

Nothing is more indicative of the flexibility of the OECD in its approach to international co-operation in education than the structures and means it has developed to enable Member countries to work together. Co-operation is not seen as an end in itself, enshrined in given structures and processes; it only comes about if there is a need for it, *i.e.*, in relation to clearly identified problems on which such co-operation is felt to be useful. It is this problem-oriented, *à la carte* approach to co-operation, as opposed to any preconceived or mandatory requirements, that has largely determined the instruments set in place, rather than the other way round.

The way in which these instruments have evolved over time, at the intergovernmental and Secretariat levels, will be dealt with in the appropriate place in subsequent chapters. But it would be helpful at this point to outline their main features as they currently exist.

The educational activities of OECD come under four distinct programmes. Two of these – that of the Education Committee (EDC) and that of the Centre for Educational Research and Innovation (CERI) – are the core programmes which deal with the full range of educational issues and are controlled by intergovernmental bodies in which all Member countries participate. The other two are more specialised programmes, one dealing with Educational Building (PEB) and the other with problems of Institutional Management in Higher Education (IMHE), with more limited country membership, in the case of PEB, and mainly institution-based membership and finance in the case of IMHE. They originated as decentralised programmes, offshoots of EDC and CERI respectively, largely in order to relieve the budgetary pressure on the core programmes. They operate within the normal management structures, rules and procedures of the Organisation, though, for reasons which will be explained later, they no longer appear in the annual OECD programme and budget.

They provide a remarkable illustration of the organisational flexibility of OECD, mentioned above, including its capacity to attract additional resources without burdening its central budget.

Between the two main programmes, EDC and CERI, there are important differences in terms of functions and governance which are not always easily understood. They operate largely within the same areas (their annual programmes of work are presented together in a single two-part document to ensure transparency), but at different levels of concern, as reflected in their respective mandates: EDC dealing with educational policies and specific structural and resource questions pertaining thereto, as opposed to the more operational activities of CERI focused on research, experimentation and innovation which help elucidate as well as feed such policies. The Education Committee and the Governing Board of CERI, as plenary bodies of the Organisation, share equal status, even though the former, as the body through which the policy implications of all the work, including that of CERI, are put to Governments, operates under Part One of the budget while the latter comes under Part Two – an arrangement designed to give Part Two programmes greater flexibility in membership, methods of work and the procurement of additional finance beyond that provided by the normal national contributions according to the scale applicable throughout the Organisation. In this, CERI has been eminently successful, in as much as its core budget has been significantly augmented by voluntary contributions throughout its existence. (An essential condition for the acceptance of such contributions is that they must be related to the objectives of an activity as defined in the agreed programme of work; and this to avoid possible distortions to the programme brought about by outside interventions.) Moreover, while the Education Committee is composed of senior officials from national Ministries of Education, CERI Governing Board members sit as individual experts, nominatively appointed by the Council on the basis of proposals put forward by governments. Though it is a fact that over the years, with all countries participating in CERI and its financing, this distinction has tended to erode, it is equally true that the Governing Board has succeeded in maintaining a healthy balance in its membership as between experts and officials.

In education, as in other social fields, it is never easy to distinguish between what is policy and what is research; the choice of research that governments support, and often of the people who will carry out the research, is in itself an aspect of policy. It is, therefore, understandable that the boundaries between the two symbiotic programmes have at times appeared less than clear-cut, and this has been, on and off, a subject of worry among some administrations. But overlap must not be interpreted as duplication or substitution between different jurisdictions; and, by and large, countries have been content to leave it to the Secretariat to ensure the necessary co-ordination among all the four programmes, allowing, within a reasonable interpretation of principles, initiatives to flourish wherever the best competence and capacity were to be found. Moreover, countries were aware that any strict rationalisation or streamlining of programmes could lead to a diminution of the total resources available for education within the Organisation, operating, as it has been over so many years, within a zero growth budgetary ceiling with ever increasing new demands made upon it.

Co-ordination among four discrete programmes, each with its own staff and budget, and between these and other programmes of the Organisation, particularly Manpower and Social Affairs, would not have been possible without the joint Secretariat management under which all the educational activities of the Organisation have always functioned. This was so in the early days when education was within the ambit of the Directorate for Scientific Affairs. It was further reinforced in 1975 since when education came to be located within the new Directorate for Social Affairs, Manpower and Education (SME), recently renamed as the Directorate for Education, Employment, Labour and Social Affairs, (DEELSA). The DEELSA Director is also Director of CERI, with a Deputy Director for Education overseeing all the educational programmes. This ensures proper co-ordination at the programming as well as the implementation stages, encourages staff to work together as colleagues rather than indulge in inter-programme rivalries, facilitates inter-Committee co-operation and provides a coherent channel of communication with national administrations and the outside world more generally. Though somewhat of an exacting task, as I can personally testify, this management structure has proved extremely effective, even though, in its relaxed and collegial ethos, it deviates from some of the basic precepts of management and organisation theory not unknown within the OECD itself.

It is an ethos, it must be added, that extends well beyond the Secretariat and colours its relationships with Committees, working groups and the wide spread of national and international networks involved in the OECD educational activities, thereby encouraging among all participants a sense of personal commitment to the work at their respective levels of responsibility. Plenary bodies deal with the general lines of the programmes of work and discuss the results of their activities, usually on the basis of the conclusions of specially convened intergovernmental conferences of senior officials, occasionally with the participation of ministers. Detailed implementation of the activities is handled within more specialised meetings of country representatives and experts, usually a combination of the two. This working together within a climate of congenial professionalism has been an important factor behind the effectiveness of the OECD work in education, and if I may be allowed a personal remark, one of the most satisfying features which I have myself experienced over my long involvement with this work.

It would be in order at this point to refer briefly to the resources which are made available for the educational activities of the Organisation. Those coming from the OECD budget itself, Part One and Part Two, are relatively modest. Their bulk is taken up by the core staff which operates the programmes, and this has remained constant at about twenty-five professionals, with a corresponding number of support staff. In addition there is an annual allocation of about 3.5 million francs, which has also remained constant (in real terms), to cover operational expenditures, such as fees for outside experts, meetings, editing, etc. (This applies to EDC and CERI only, PEB and IMHE having their own separate funding, covering both staff and operational expenditures, deriving directly from Governments, in the case of PEB, and from Member institutions in the case of IMHE.) But the function of these resources is in effect merely catalytic – used mainly in the conceptualisation and preparatory stages of the activities – compared to the significantly larger costs which are borne by the countries themselves in orchestrating their participation in these activities. The level of such costs varies from country to country, according to the intensity of their involvement. They cover representation in international meetings, the organisation of national meetings around an OECD activity to which foreign participants are also invited, and the preparation of country studies or reports as a contribution to activities for which common guidelines had been agreed at the planning stage. Very often, and increasingly so in recent years, activities are designed with a strong element of country-based components which feed directly into national policy making and benefit from the corresponding policy related financing. In the case of a Country Educational Policy Reviews, the total cost to the Organisation (Secretariat and Examiners) would be in the region of 120 000 FF, whereas the country in question would incur costs (preparation of the Background Report, special delegation to the Review meeting, etc.) amounting to between four and five times that figure. In addition, specific educational activities, particularly in CERI, have benefited from additional voluntary contributions from Governments, research institutes and Foundations, often, as in the case of the CERI project on the Handicapped, considerably more significant than those provided in the normal budget.

Finally, a few words about relations to other international organisations and bodies. The special membership of the OECD and the specificity of its approach to education, as described in this chapter, have shielded the educational sector of the Organisation from any serious accusations, so often voiced elsewhere, of duplicating the work done in other international forums. Relations have been particularly close with the Council of Europe, especially in the context of the Standing Conference of European Ministers of Education, in whose work the OECD has consistently participated, and often contributed. Co-operation with UNESCO has been more sporadic, except in the area of educational statistics where the two Organisations worked closely together in developing the joint ISCED questionnaires. The Commission of the European Community participates in OECD work and has direct access to its results, but a reciprocally beneficial relationship has still to be worked out. OECD has no programme of relationships to non-governmental organisations other than with its two statutory consultative committees, BIAC and TUAC, representing employers and trade unions interests respectively. Both these bodies have set up Education Committees to facilitate consultation at both Secretariat and Committee levels. These consultations have proved increasingly valuable and constructive. They have, in particular, helped the two sides, on the basis of OECD work, to clarify their respective viewpoints on major issues of educational policy, leading to a remarkable degree of convergence as evidenced in the joint statement which they submitted to the 1990 Meeting of the Education Committee at Ministerial Level.[3]

Notes and references

1. In a very real sense, this book can be regarded as a distillation of, and commentary on, the OECD work in education reflected in its reports and publications. Hopefully, it will encourage the reader to have recourse to these sources and the useful bibliographies they contain for more detailed information.

2. *Committees* are specialised bodies made up of senior officials from each Member country charged with guiding and supervising the work programme of the Organisation in individual sectors, *e.g.* Education, Science, Trade, etc. The *Council* is the supreme governing body of the Organisation composed of the heads of National Delegations, usually at ambassadorial level, accredited to OECD. It is chaired by the Secretary-General of the Organisation.

3. Reproduced in the report of the Ministerial Meeting: *High Quality Education and Training for All*, OECD, 1992.

Chapter II

THE FORMATIVE YEARS

(late fifties – early sixties)

The origins of the Organisation's interest in education and the early stages of its work in this area are of more than purely historical interest. Underlying them are concerns, and approaches to their solution, which represent perennial features of the role of education in modern societies and which together have exerted a continuing influence in the shaping of OECD work over the years. As such, they deserve to be recounted in some detail, and this is the purpose of the present chapter. It deals, firstly, with the background and origins of the educational concerns of the Organisation, reaching back into OEEC days; secondly, it recounts the main directions and achievements of the initial programme of work, dominated by the quest for scientific and technical personnel; and it concludes with the quantum leap forward, in the first years of OECD, whereby this specific concern got merged into the much broader question of investing in overall educational expansion and development.

Origins and background

Set up in 1948, as an integral part of the post-war arrangements directed at helping the economic revival of Western Europe, the Organisation for European Economic Co-operation (OEEC) rapidly evolved into an effective instrument of multi-facetted co-operation among its Members, reaching well beyond the immediate purposes for which the Organisation was set up, namely the distribution of the generous American aid – totalling about $12 billion from 1948 to 1952 – made available under the Marshall Plan. Indeed, developing such co-operation – which, it must be remembered, was something new in the habits of international economic relations – was inherent in the very purposes of the Organisation, inscribed in its Convention. Under the terms of this Convention, Member countries agreed, in particular,

> "...to join together to make the fullest collective use of their individual capacities and potentialities, to increase their production, develop and modernise their industrial and agricultural equipment, expand their commerce, reduce progressively barriers to trade among themselves, promote full employment and restore or

maintain the stability of their economies and general confidence in their currencies.''

More specifically, Article 8 of the Convention stipulated that "the Contracting Parties will make the fullest and most effective use of their available manpower".

It was an essential function of the formative years of OEEC to develop the machinery for putting this far-reaching programme of co-operation into effect. Building on the initial requirement for countries to provide detailed reports on the state of their economy and the joint scrutiny by all Member countries of such national economic reports as a basis for the allocation of Marshall Aid to individual countries, a whole series of instruments and procedures for mutual consultation and co-operation gradually evolved covering a variety of other, more specific areas. Many of these instruments were inherited, adapted and further developed by the successor Organisation, the OECD, set up in 1961.

By the mid-fifties, the initial objective of the OEEC – European economic recovery – had been achieved, so that as early as 1955 one could already speak of a "return to normality".[1] Thenceforth, attention shifted to structural issues, certainly less dramatic than the major bottlenecks tackled in the recovery period, but nonetheless crucial in building up capacity to sustain the momentum of the economic take-off.

Among these issues, increased productivity, and the factors and methods behind it, became a primary concern, reflected in the creation in 1953 of the European Productivity Agency (EPA) within OEEC. Facilitated by a grant from the United States of a sum of $100 million (on the initiative of Senator Blair Moody of Michigan), and working in conjunction with National Productivity Centres created in most Member countries on the recommendation of the OEEC Council, the Agency played a leading role in fostering the spread and development of productivity concepts and of managerial skills and techniques, drawing heavily on US experience. The adjustment of training to the requirements of modern economies came to be seen as a fundamental condition of progress and considerable effort went into improving training at all levels and in all sectors of activity, particularly technical and vocational training.[2]

In this way, the human factor in economic development began to appear centre stage. It was essentially seen, in these early days, in the narrow sense of needs in scientific and technical manpower; and there were as yet no specific structures or mechanisms within OEEC to deal with it as a separate issue in its own right. Its twin links were to science and applied research, on one side, dealt through the Committee for Applied Research (serviced by the EPA, of which Alex King was co-Director) and, on the other side, to the training and utilisation of technical manpower handled jointly by the EPA, as indicated above, and by the Manpower Committee. The latter body concentrated in particular on initial surveys of the supply and demand of highly qualified scientists and engineers (two such surveys were completed in 1955 and 1956), on the supply of technicians and on vocational training in specific sectors of industry.

On the science side, the work was more forward-looking from the beginning. Pointing to the increased dependence of the economy, and of national prosperity more generally, on science and technology, it highlighted the growing gap between the highly developed, science-based industries of the United States and the explosive development of Soviet technology on one side, and, on the other, the stagnant scientific and technological status of Europe which, in spite of its rich traditions, remained a prisoner of its ageing institutions and ill-adjusted systems of education. It was thus imperative for European countries to expand their capacity in scientific research and technical development.

At the same time, the growing costs of scientific research and its applications made it difficult for individual countries to match the immense and rapidly growing scientific resources of the US and the USSR. A sharing of scientific resources and efforts on a European scale was thus called for. Out of these considerations ultimately evolved the practice of international scientific co-operation, more systematic and better organised than had been the case in earlier periods, and also the concept of a coherent national science policy, so far foreign to the thought of many European countries, both of which were vigorously taken up when the OECD was set up, through its Committee for Scientific Research and its new Directorate for Scientific Affairs (DAS), under the leadership of Alexander King. Inherent in these developments was the realisation that progress in improving the scientific and technical potential of European countries and, more particularly, in resolving the problem of shortage of well-qualified scientists and engineers, had long-term consequences for the educational system itself: these objectives could not be achieved without major changes in both general education and university education and training.

In this way, the scene was set for a broader and more concerted approach by OEEC to its work on scientific and technical manpower. This was reflected in the decision, in May 1958, to establish the Office for Scientific and Technical Personnel (OSTP), with its corresponding Governing Committee, thus bringing together the various strands of the work in this area so far dealt with disparately by a number of agencies within the Organisation, as already indicated. It is clear that the determining factor behind this decision was the incipient faith in scientific advance as the driving force for progress, of which Alexander King was one of the pioneering protagonists. He was named Director of this new agency, with Ronald Gass as his Deputy. These arrangements were subsequently enshrined in the new OECD structures, with OSTP attached to DAS and the Governing Committee renamed the Committee for Scientific and Technical Personnel (CSTP) – a name under which it operated during the momentous decade of the sixties until it was transformed into the Education Committee in 1970.

While the ground within OEEC had been well prepared for the establishment of OSTP, the decision itself came about under almost emergency circumstances. As in the earlier case of the EPA, the initiative came from the US, but this time as a direct consequence of the Sputnik shock. Russian success in space was attributed to the quality of Soviet scientific and technical personnel and of the educational system behind it. It was imperative, in the US view, to redress the balance and this became part of the strategy of the cold war.[3] This was already evident in the "new curriculum" movement in the US which, with strong financial support from the Department of Defence, was devoting massive efforts and resources for the reform and updating of the curriculum and the preparation of new teaching materials in the natural sciences and mathematics. Stimulated by a US offer of an initial grant of $500 000, to match a similar sum to be contributed by Member countries, the OEEC Council agreed, in the record time of about six months, on a detailed programme of activities "in regard to shortage of scientific and technical manpower" which was then formally embodied in the decision to establish OSTP.

It must be emphasised that it was the offer of the US grant which was the decisive factor in the expeditious setting up of the new programme. Half a million dollars was quite a large sum of money in those days and, together with the matching contribution which European countries agreed to make, it provided a solid financial basis, backed by political commitment, for the programme to take off. It must also be recalled that the US, which was not a member of the OEEC, committed itself to participate fully in the activities of the programme, thus inaugurating a new era of transatlantic co-operation and heralding, in this sense, full US membership in the OECD when it was set up three years later.

The initial STP programme

The programme of activities which the Council agreed in May 1958 was based on the detailed recommendations of Working Party 25 which had been charged to: *i)* examine the problems of basic education, university and technical high school education and training, and recruitment and utilisation of scientific and engineering personnel in Member countries in relation to existing and future needs; *ii)* work out a programme of action to help Member and Associate countries to solve these problems.

As defined by the Working Party, the purpose of the programme was "to help to increase the number, quality and maximum use of scientists and engineers trained in Member countries, in order to meet the present and future needs of the economy of Western Europe". This sounds like a narrow and limited objective. Yet it concealed a whole series of underlying problems that needed to be tackled, the magnitude and variety of which were explicitly spelt out from the beginning. It was, in particular recognised that the fundamental problem was one of modifying educational systems, and that this was a matter of long-term adjustment and growth rather than of quick solutions. It was one which required the understanding and approval of public opinion, the removal of social and economic obstacles to higher education and training, changes in the nature of educational curricula, etc. Above all, it required greatly increased financial resources and, hence, the political will to make these resources available among competing claims from other sectors of policy.

Thus, from its inception, the programme was essentially directed at improving the quality of educational systems and expanding their capacity – quality and numbers. The first task of the new Committee – CSTP – was to draw up a series of major objectives to guide its work in this direction. They included:

- more accurate data on the long-term needs and on the existing and potential supply of scientific and technical personnel;
- improved public knowledge and appreciation of the educational needs of science and technology, including measures to arouse and develop the interest of young people;

- adequate basic education in science (so as to provide a firm foundation for subsequent scientific and technical training), with improved methods of teaching, curricula and supply of teachers;
- opportunities for secondary and higher education for all who could benefit, in order to improve the flow of talented individuals into scientific and technical careers;
- expansion of facilities for scientific and higher technical education, bearing in mind the possibilities of international co-operation to meet the needs which exceeded the capacity of individual countries;
- freer exchange of personnel as a basis for future scientific and technical co-operation between Member countries;
- more effective use of the existing corps of scientific and technical personnel in Member countries.

Over the next three to four years a vigorous programme of activities was put in motion in pursuit of these objectives. Some of these activities, having served their initial purpose, faded away. Others opened up new and broader vistas which eventually consolidated the educational interest of the Organisation and shaped its future development, as will be evident from the brief description below.

Country Reviews

Drawing on the practice within the Organisation in the field of economic policy, annual reviews were initiated as from 1958/9 as a means of appraising in each Member country the general situation of scientific education and technical training, the particular problems arising and the various actions already taken or being planned towards their solution. The technique which was applied was to send to each country a small group of independent experts to discuss these matters with government officials and competent representatives of other interested circles. On the basis of these interviews they prepared a report which was then discussed at a "confrontation meeting" at the headquarters of the Organisation, at which high-ranking representatives of the examined country answered the various questions put to them by the "examiners" and members of the Governing Committee. Although at this early stage these reviews were fairly slender affairs, mostly of a descriptive rather than analytical nature, they soon showed their value in providing a useful channel for wide exchange of experience, and in stimulating, and sometimes guiding, national action. They also gave useful general background for the overall OSTP programme.

Over time, these reviews have evolved into a permanent and powerful instrument of the Organisation's educational work. Their techniques and function have remained practically the same, but their scope and coverage have been considerably enlarged. The turning point came in the early sixties with the spread of national educational planning, itself stimulated by the OECD, resulting in the preparation of national plan documents which provided a much more solid foundation for reviewing country policies. At an even later stage, when this particular type of planning went out of fashion, countries showed the value they attached to such reviews by their willingness to submit voluntarily to them and prepare for the occasion substantial background reports in lieu of the earlier planning documents. The quality of the reviews was enhanced by the readiness of outstanding professional or political experts to serve as members of the OECD examining team as well as by the interest of Education Ministers in personally leading their national delegation at the "confrontation" meeting. In this way "the OECD became a real factor in the national policies of Member countries, and the legitimisation of such policies through favourable reactions from the OECD became important for Governments".[4] An essential feature of the Educational Policy Reviews, and one which distinguishes them from those in economic policy, is the fact that the role of the Secretariat is less explicit and the responsibility for what is said in them rests with the group of independent "examiners" in their expert capacity and not with the OECD as such. In practice, this distinction does not alter the public visibility of the Reviews as OECD pronouncements; nor does it diminish their political impact.

The mapping of scientific and technical personnel

Getting a clear picture of the existing manpower situation and of the likely trends in the supply and demand of scientists, engineers and technicians was recognised as an essential need as far back as the early fifties. A couple of initial international surveys were undertaken. Their results, published in 1957[5], helped sensitise countries to the magnitude of the problems confronting their education and training systems, even though, as the surveys themselves fully recognised, no accurate picture could be given of actual and future needs because of inadequacies in the availability of data and of analytical methodologies, both still in their infancy. Not surprisingly, one of the principal recommendations emerging from these surveys was the need of more accurate fact-finding and more clearly defined assessment of supply and demand. This challenge was picked up and rigorously pursued as soon as OSTP was set up. It led to a line of investigation with far reaching implications going well beyond the narrow limits of needs in scientists and engineers. It ushered, as we shall see later on, the era of the economics of education and of educational planning.

The first major exploratory step was taken at an OEEC "Conference on Techniques for Forecasting Future Requirements of Scientific and Technical Personnel", held in the Hague in November 1959. Its report was published in 1960 under the title *Forecasting Manpower Needs for the Age of Science*. It was essentially a methodological investigation into how effective numerical comparisons could be made of the existing stock, output and future needs of scientific and technical personnel. Its central recommendation was "that an extension of comparative statistics was an essential prerequisite to better understanding and to effective examination of educational policies affecting the supply of scientists and engineers ... In carrying out the Third International Survey of Supply and Demand of Scientists and Engineers, the OEEC should endeavour to obtain such information on expenditure and educational structures as will permit a clearer understanding of policies for mobilisation of reserves of talent for training in science and technology".[6]

Over the next two years considerable Secretariat resources were devoted to this task. Focusing as it did on the capacity of educational institutions, the Survey became in fact a study of the secondary and higher education training systems in the Member countries. The major problem was the lack of satisfactory international standards of education and manpower classifications and statistics. Some useful work towards achieving greater comparability of technical qualifications in engineering had already been done in an OEEC/Ford Foundation sponsored report[7], prepared by the Conference of Engineering Societies in Western Europe and the United States of America (EUSEC). But the bulk of the problem remained, and this was tackled through lengthy negotiations with individual countries about the classification of various types of education, particularly in what concerned the definition of the level of secondary education attainment, qualifications for entry into higher education institutions and enrolments in and graduation from such institutions. The importance of this effort in arousing public interest in and building up capacity for comparative educational statistics cannot be overestimated. It laid the foundations for the more systematic work in this area subsequently undertaken within OECD and in Member countries themselves.

In the end, with all the reservations about the validity of international data in a first exercise of this kind, a broad comparative picture could emerge of the actual performance of education systems in the Member countries and of their likely development over the next decade.

The results of the Survey were widely publicised[8]. They showed a picture in which European Member countries, in spite of remarkable progress in education over the previous ten years or so, had little cause for complacency when compared to their North American counterparts. For example, while in 1959, 65 per cent of an age group qualified for admission to higher education in the United States and Canada, the corresponding European percentage was 7 per cent. For the same year, 32 per cent of the relevant age group entered higher education in the former countries against 5 per cent in the latter countries. Similar differences existed in the total number of students in higher education institutions, although European countries were at a qualitative advantage in the percentage of first degrees awarded to the relevant age group – 16 and 2.4 per cent respectively.

These figures must be seen against the background of rapid educational expansion in the OECD area as a whole during the fifties: the number of pupils qualifying for higher education increased by 40 per cent, the number of new entrants to higher education by 60 per cent, the number of students by somewhat less than 50 per cent and the number of first degrees by 25 per cent. Estimates for the 1960s indicated an even more rapid expansion: 100 per cent increase in those qualifying for admission to higher education, 80 per cent in the number of entrants to higher education and 100 per cent increase in the number of first degrees. In spite of a tendency towards a relative diminution in the difference between North America and Europe in the number of graduates, a comparison of absolute figures revealed clearly a growing difference between the two parts of the OECD area: while in 1952, the United States and Canada had 215 000 more first degrees in higher education than the European Member countries, this difference was estimated at probably 500 000 in 1970.

Equally marked differences appeared in the total stock of scientific and technical personnel, which in 1959 totalled between four and four and a half million in the OECD area as a whole, corresponding to slightly above 2 per cent of the total employed in this area. This average, however, covered a marked difference between North America and Europe, the corresponding percentage being of the order of 3 per cent in the former and 1.5 per cent in the latter countries.

These differences have been noted at some length because this was the first time, at least at an authoritative international level, that the educational gap between North America and Europe was revealed in its full amplitude. It was a gap which was compounded by the results of a parallel OECD analysis, also done within DAS a couple of years later, of differences in the scientific and technological capacity of the two regions, revealing an even more glaring, and politically more sensitive, "Technological Gap".[9] Up to now, catching up with the Russians had been the leitmotiv of the Western Democracies, as dramatised in an early OSTP report,[10] which pointed to the clear lead which the Soviet Union had gained in the annual output of graduate engineers over the past five years, and which was not expected to be greatly changed over the following five years. Thenceforth, in the minds of many Europeans, attention shifted to catching up with their North American partners in the new competitive economic environment, stimulated by the liberalisation of trade. And this, together with the limits to how far the American model could be emulated, became part of the hidden, and at times, explicit, agenda of the education and science policies of the more advanced among the European OECD countries, which was not without its influence on the relevant OECD programmes themselves.

The school science revolution

Macro studies of the kind described above went hand-in-hand with intensive efforts at expanding and improving the educational infrastructure for science and technology, recognised from the beginning as a *sine qua non* for meeting the long-term manpower needs of the economy. The attention focused on science and mathematics teaching at the secondary school level, largely inspired by the "new curriculum" movement in the United States, as already mentioned. In the space of a few years, these efforts developed into a veritable campaign for the comprehensive reform of school science whose effects, in varying degrees, were felt throughout the OECD area.

It was a campaign led on many fronts, all covering on the ultimate objective of convincing governments, and Ministers of Education in particular, of the need for a coherent policy for school science. It was recognised that such policies, in this as in other areas, would be conditioned by the stage of development of educational systems in individual countries. A distinction was made, therefore, between countries with advanced systems of education – North America and Central and Northern Europe – and those with "special problems of basic educational development" – the Mediterranean Member countries, including the southern region of Italy. For this latter group of countries a special programme of Technical Assistance already operated within the Organisation and some of its resources could be, and were in fact, used for educational purposes.

On the basis of this distinction, policies for school science were discussed at two separate intergovernmental seminars, in 1960 and 1961.[11] In both cases, the same central constituents of such policies were identified: improvement of science and mathematics curricula; the availability of appropriate teaching equipment and materials; recruitment and training of teachers; a more active role by industry in assisting science and technical education; improved systems of orientation of pupils to facilitate the search for talent. In each of these areas, specific recommendations were made to Governments and it is in these that the differences between the two groups of countries were reflected. While those addressed to advanced countries were couched in terms of general exhortation for a revamped system of science teaching as an integral part of a more systematically planned total educational provision, those directed at developing countries dealt with specific measures of how immediate needs could be met. They were in particular urged to set up Central Planning and Statistical Offices within Ministries of Education for overall educational planning purposes, together with a "strong" Council for Scientific and Technical Education whose duties would include: the planning and equipment of school laboratories; the design of scientific apparatus and equipment; the design and provision of teaching aids, including film and television programmes; the supervision of National Centres for Science Equipment; the organisation of refresher courses and in-service training of science and technical teachers; science curriculum reforms.

This list is in itself a good summary of the enormity of practical probelms facing these countries at the time. In attempting to tackle them, they received direct support through their participation in the Organisation's programmes, drawing on the generosity of special funds made available by the US, designed to promote country projects in this area on a cost-sharing basis. This applied, in particular, to the setting up of national teams on educational planning (under the Mediterranean Regional Project, which we shall discuss later), pilot projects in the reform of science curricula, refresher courses for teachers and the provision of teaching aids and equipment. It was in this way, for example, that Greece and Turkey were helped to build up their National Centres for Science Equipment and that "Mobile Units" for science teaching were set up in these countries and in Italy (Sicily) as a demonstration of how the lack of properly equipped laboratories in schools could be economically overcome by a well-equipped perambulating facility, serving a group of schools. It is sad to record that many of these projects came to an abrupt end once the outside funding dried up by the mid-sixties.

There were other imaginative initiatives in these creative early days which were also not pursued beyond their experimental stage. Two of these were directed at expanding training and research facilities in the new specialised fields of science and technology through the international pooling of resources. One was built around the "Growing Points" concept, whereby individual national centres were recognised for their excellence and were jointly supported to provide advance training for other Member countries. The other was the "Senior Visiting Fellowships" scheme, designed to facilitate the exchange of qualified specialists among higher education institutions, both to learn from and contribute to the development of specific new techniques in teaching and research.

As was to be expected, policies for the reform of school science were seen to rest on two fundamental pillars: teachers – and teaching more generally – and curricula. On teachers, there was little that the Organisation as such could do in terms of practical measures other than support a series of refresher courses across the European Member countries. It did, however, make sure at a very early stage that the totality of the problems involved, in terms of supply, recruitment and training, were brought to the attention of Governments. This was done in a report prepared by a small group of experts, based on a detailed investigation of the situation, actual and prospective, in the Member countries.[12] Its conclusions pointed to the dramatic disparity which existed between supply and demand and to the enormous effort, and investment, that would be needed if the shortages were to be overcome over the next ten years, particularly in view of the rapid growth of the school population. It equally pointed to serious deficiencies in teacher training and to the danger of countries having to resort to inadequately trained teachers in order to meet the pressure of numbers. It made a series of recommendations concerning both long-term and short-term and emergency measures, many of which have remained valid ever since.

One of these recommendations advocated more intensive use of media of mass communication such as television, films and radio. This would help not only alleviate the shortage of teachers, but also keep the content of courses up to date. Possibilities in these areas had already been investigated by the OEEC, which had taken the initiative for the production of a series of films for the teaching of science and technology. This led to the building up of a sizeable educational film library within the Organisation, with an efficient system of distribution to countries on a lending/borrowing basis. Parallel with this, and based on a survey of television teaching in the Member countries, particularly the experience of France, Italy and the United Kingdom,[13] the educational status and potential of the medium, and related audio-visual aids, were discussed in detail at the Ashbridge (England) Seminar in July 1960. The recommendations of the Seminar[14] were followed up over the next few years in a series of country-based activities, drawing on the enthusiasm of a wide educational TV network which this work had generated. A major problem was how to get teachers themselves to be convinced of the potential value of this innovation and overcome their instinctive resistance to change. Unfortunately, this message did not get through, with the result that for many years to come teachers, and their organisations, remained in the majority suspicious that the objective was to replace them rather than provide enrichment to their tasks.

We come, finally, to the modernisation of the curricula in mathematics and the natural sciences, the linchpin in the whole complex area of the school science reform movement. This was by far the most systematically attacked problem and the one in which the Organisation played a – if not *the* – leading role and whose impact had the most direct and lasting effects, particularly on the European scene. Largely inspired by the US, it was part of a general movement among the scientific community to ensure a proper place for their respective, rapidly advancing disciplines within the secondary school curriculum. In this, they found a propitious climate in the growing faith among education policy-makers and others concerning the role of the experimental sciences in sustaining the economy, a faith which had its pedagogical echoes in the shift towards a more ''scientific'' approach to teaching and learning.

The pace was set by the mathematicians, through the International Committee for Mathematics Teaching, under the presidency of Marshall Stone of he University of Chicago. As the guardians of the discipline of mathematics, they were worried about the difference in quality and status of mathematics teaching at university level, which they found adequate, and that still taught in secondary schools, and the methods used for its teaching, which they considered to be fully inadequate to the sweeping advances made in modern mathematics. The extent of this inadequacy was confirmed by the results of an OEEC survey of mathematics education in Member countries, carried out in 1959.[15] This in turn provided the basis for a prestigious seminar of eminent mathematicians and educators, held at the end of that year, at Royaumont (France). Its purpose was to define the content and methods of modern school mathematics education and to formulate suggestions and recommendations for a reform of its curricula. Out of this emerged the gospel of the "New Mathematics", widely publicised under the title *New Thinking in School Mathematics*.[16]

This is not the place to spell out the details of the new doctrine. In its emphasis on a more unified approach to mathematical patterns and structure as against the hitherto isolated subjects (algebra, geometry, trigonometry, analysis); on the introduction of modern concepts of sets, mappings, relations, functions and group theory to serve as unifying elements in the instruction; on the treatment of Euclidean space from a vectorial and algebraic viewpoint (*Euclid Must Go*); and on the introduction of probability and statistical inference, the New Mathematics represented nothing less than a revolution to the traditional teaching of the subject. It was realised that a mutation of this dimension could not be put into practice without sustained developmental work and the Seminar made specific recommendations on how this could be done in terms of the preparation of teaching material and textbooks, the re-appraisal of examinations, the re-education of teachers and of experimental programmes at national levels. Over the next few years, the Organisation devoted a lot of effort and resources (with the help of special US funds) to get such experimentation going in a large number of Member countries.

This pattern was followed in physics, chemistry and biology, more or less simultaneously. The physicists fired the first shots with an OEEC sponsored report – a real manifesto – which was presented to the International Conference on School Physics in 1960,[17] followed, a few years later, by a Teacher's guide.[18] Here the approach to implementation was somewhat different, as the requisite material was already available in the work done by the Physical Science Study Committee (P.S.S.C.) in the United States, and the problem was therefore one of assisting other countries to adapt it to their needs and special circumstances. *New Thinking in School Chemistry* was produced in 1961 and *New Thinking in School Biology* in 1963. In these latter two subjects, European initiatives and contributions were in greater prominence than had been the case with mathematics and physics.

It is a pity that the effects of this impressive work, to which the shere number of reports published bears testimony,[19] have never been properly evaluated. No doubt, the school science reform movement would have taken off in any case, under the sheer dynamics generated by the broader scientific movement. But it is doubtful whether its impact on national policies would have been as rapid and effective if it had not been for the more than catalytic role played by the Organisation in harmonising the interests of the scientific community, ensuring the necessary policy support and marshalling the resources for both the conceptual/analytical work and the pilot demonstrations of its applicability within individual national systems. What is less clear is the relative balance in the whole approach as between the interests of scientists, on the one hand, and those of pedagogues, on the other. This is particularly telling in the case of the "New Mathematics" which represented by far the most revolutionary departure from established concepts and educational practice and where pedagogical realities, including the capabilities of teachers and parents, may have been too abruptly sacrificed to the interests of the discipline itself.

From STP to Investment in Education

The concentration of the initial OSTP programme on the activities described above stemmed from the conviction that the rate of growth of the economy would be increasingly determined by the provision of education in science. But it was equally accepted from the beginning that the problem of producing an adequate supply of well qualified scientists, engineers and technicians was not one which could be examined independently from the output of the educational system as a whole, since such technical personnel represented only part of the apex of the educational structure. It was only logical, therefore, that a central objective of the programme would be to stimulate policies in Member countries for increased allocations of resources to education as part of their efforts to maintain an adequate rate of economic growth. Out of this simple idea emerged the "Economics of Education" which was to play such a prominent role in the work of the Organisation and, more generally, in providing political support for the massive expansion of education over the next ten years.

The concept itself had already been stimulated by the evolution of economic thinking on both sides of the Atlantic, reflected in the work of such people as Odd Aukrust (Norway) and Edward Denison and Gary Becker (USA). Drawing on this work, the American economist Theodore Schultz, in his 1960 Presidential address to the American Economic Association, was able to demonstrate that the traditional economic factors could not explain more than a small part of the actual growth of the national product and to show that the educational level of a country could be an important factor in this respect. Within the Organisation itself, this idea was echoed in a report on the "Prospects of Long-Term Economic Growth", prepared in 1959 by a Working Group of Economic Experts who concluded that "since the rate of growth of the labour force will tend to decline in the coming decade, and since the accumulated need for fixed investment has largely been eliminated, the role of educated manpower in the growth of output will become greater".[20]

From this point on, and in line with the vitality which characterised the OSTP programme, things moved rapidly. The first requirement was to produce a convincing argument on the relation between investment in education and economic growth, an argument which would be acceptable to economists and educationists alike and which could be sold to finance policy-makers. This was done at a first informal meeting of "distinguished" economists and educators, held in May 1960. Its brief report – *Investment in Education and Economic Growth* – laid the foundations for the significant volume of work which was undertaken over the next twelve months, leading to the Washington "Policy Conference on Economic Growth and Investment in Education" in October, 1961, which will be discussed in the next chapter. By identifying, in particular, the types of economic studies that were needed in order to better attack policy problems concerning investment in education, it provided the embryo for the constitution of the "Study Group in the Economics of Education", as we shall also see later on. It thus marks the beginnings of the consecration of the economics of education not merely as a new discipline, but as an area of direct policy relevance and concern.

One further, but closely related, significant development of these early days needs to be noted before we conclude this chapter. It is one which demonstrates the twin concern of the educational philosophy of the Organisation – economic growth and social progress – and the conviction that the one could not be achieved without the other. Incipient interest in the economics of education was parallelled with similar interest in its social dimensions. Beginning with the assumption that the vastly increased manpower needs of the economy could not be met without extending the pool of talent, the argument soon developed into the right of all individuals to have access to education and led to the consideration of measures that were needed – economic, social and educational – to give reality to this right. This brought into prominence, for the first time, the whole question of the social objectives of education and, indeed, the broader role of education as the major culture-forming instrument of society. Focusing as it did on the role of education for individual development, this line of reasoning, pushed primarily by sociologists and pedagogues, could not but bring out the potential conflict between the social and economic objectives of education, an issue which – somewhat artificial and largely generated in the disciplinary minds of academic analysts – became the battleground of apposing camps of educational planners for many years to come.

For the time being, the accent was on convergence rather than conflict. The social dimensions of education were still largely unmapped and it was primarily to provide a solid analytical basis for a more informed discussion of the issues that the first major *OECD* conference on education was organised in Kungalv (Sweden) in June 1961, *i.e.* at a time when the economics of education was becoming the dominant concept, around the theme of the search for talent. Eminent sociologists presented detailed analyses of the major barriers to the use of potential human abilities in education, specifically in terms of social class, rurality, school organisation and cultural inequalities, together with the problems of measuring reserves of talent and the use of relevant international statistics. The report of the Conference[21] remains a milestone in the sociology of education. The spirit that prevailed can be best summed up in the words of the rapporteur, A. H. Halsey:

> "...the greatest encouragement to countries that seek a society which is both educative and materially rich, is that the pursuit of this double aim involves a virtuous ascending spiral. Human ability is socially defined; the more complex the culture the greater the talent that a society demands of its people. But also, the more complex the culture in its application to the productive organisation of society, the greater are the resources available to convert potential into actual ability. Thus, economic growth may be said to create the very skills that it demands. Again, it is only with economic advance that a nation can afford to go beyond the ideal of formal equality of educational opportunity to the high ideal of substantive equality of opportunity for every individual to develop his latent ability."

The decade which followed provided ample opportunity to test the workings of this "virtuous circle" – and its limitations.

Notes and references

1. *OEEC at Work*, p. 20.

2. Years after the demise of EPA, its former Director, Roger Gregoire, wrote a special report on this topic: *Vocational Education*, OECD, 1967.

3. See Kjell Eide: *Thirty Years of Educational Collaboration in the OECD,* 1990.

4. Eide, *op. cit.*, pp. 18-19. See also Maurice Kogan, *Education Policies in Perspective: An Appraisal*, OECD, 1979 – the so-called "Review of Reviews". The value of this review technique is attested by its use outside the OECD membership. In the eighties, the government of Hong Kong, with the help of the OECD Secretariat, carried out a similar review which has provided the basis of its subsequent educational development policy. The Council of Europe has replicated the OECD review procedures for similar reviews of country Cultural Policies. More recently, a number of Central European countries have invited the OECD to review their policies in a similar way.

5. *The Problem of Scientific and Technical Manpower in Western Europe, Canada and the United States*, OEEC, 1957.

6. *Ibid.*, p. 115.

7. *Education and Training of Professional Engineers*, (3 vols., 1960).

8. *Resources of Scientific and Technical Personnel in the OECD Area*, OECD, 1963.

9. *Gaps in Technology: Analytical Report*, OECD, 1970.

10. *Producing Scientists and Engineers*, OEEC, 1960.

11. See *Policy for School Science – Countries with Advanced Systems*, OEEC, 1961; and *Policy for School Science – Countries with Special Problems of Basic Educational Development*, OECD, 1962.

12. *Supply, Recruitment and Training of Science and Mathematics Teachers*, OECD, 1961.

13. *Teaching Through Television*, OEEC, 1960.

14. *Television for School Science*, OEEC, 1961.

15. *Survey of the Present Status of Mathematical Education in the Member Countries of OEEC*, OEEC, 1960.

16. OEEC, 1961.

17. *A Modern Approach to School Physics*, OEEC, 1960.

18. *Teaching Physics To-day*, OECD, 1965.

19. In addition to the ones already mentioned, the following titles were produced in the *New Thinking in School Science* series, Mathematics occupying pride of place:

- *Mathematics To-day: a Guide for Teachers*, OECD, 1964.
- *School Mathematics in OEEC Countries: Summaries*, OEEC, 1960.
- *Synopses for Modern Secondary School Mathematics*, OEEC, 1960.
  (*See, also,* **Mathematical Education for Engineers**, OECD, 1966, and *Engineering Education in the Computer Age*, OECD, 1964).
- *Biology To-day: its Role in Education*, OECD, 1966.
- *Chemistry To-day: a Guide for Teachers*, OECD, 1963.
- *School Chemistry: Trends in Reform: Selected Topics*, OECD, 1964.

20. EC/EWP/59.1.
21. *Ability and Educational Opportunity*, OECD, 1961.

Chapter III

THE GOLDEN AGE OF EDUCATIONAL GROWTH
(the sixties)

The transformation, in 1961, of the OEEC into the OECD implied no discontinuity in its educational work, as the previous chapter has shown. However, the wider geographical coverage of the new Organisation – which eventually came to include Australia, New Zealand and Japan, in addition to the US and Canada (with Finland becoming a regular Member and Yugoslavia with special status) – gave new political impetus to economic collaboration among the Western industrialised countries. The need for such collaboration had already been amply demonstrated under the OEEC, but there was now a new accent on economic *growth,* an objective cherished by all OECD governments. At its very first meeting, in November 1961, the Ministerial Council of OECD set a growth target of 50 per cent in the Gross National Product of its Member countries for the decade 1960-1970. In addition, the extended mandate of the Organisation brought in new fields of co-operation, particularly the co-ordination of the policies of Member countries towards the third world. Together, these two new features had profound effects on the objectives of the Organisation and its methods of work which could not but be felt in its educational activities as well.

The new accent on economic growth as a primary objective was particularly relevant. It was to dominate the political scene for the major part of the sixties; and it was one which was most congenial for education in propagating its own growth and in locating itself in the mainstream of policy thinking. How this came about, and the role which the OECD played therein, in a decade which was to leave its permanent mark on the educational landscape of OECD societies, constitute the substance of the present chapter.

Economic growth and investment in education: the Washington Conference

Under the enterpreneurial leadership of Alex King and Ron Gass, the CSTP was quick to cash in on the new opportunities opened up by the economic growth objective. The rapid shift in programme priorities towards the economics of education, which was initiated even before the OEEC disappeared, was in fact an inspired, intentional move designed to secure a lasting place for education within the new Organisation. For this to be done, it was essential to move quickly and convincingly drawing on the best available expertise on both sides of the Atlantic and capitalising on the political interest, particularly in the United States, in meeting the Soviet technological challenge. Thus, neither the timing nor the location of the OECD Conference on Economic Growth and Investment in Education, held in Washington D.C. in October, 1961, was fortuitous. Its political pay-off was as rapid as it was substantial.

The Conference, which brought together an impressive mix of people with policy responsibilities for education and national budgets as well as professional economists and experts, was designed to address two central questions:

i) the nature and the magnitude of the task facing education in the next decade to meet the needs of social and economic progress in the OECD area;

ii) in addition to meeting their own needs, what should the OECD countries do to respond effectively to the requests of the underdeveloped countries whose needs for educational expansion were relatively even greater than their own.

Discussion of these issues was supported by a series of analytical reports specially prepared for the Conference by leading economists and educationalists, published separately at the time[1] and conveniently put together in a subsequent omnibus publication.[2] Of these, the star performer was the paper by Professors Svennilson, Edding and Elvin on *Targets for Education in Europe in 1970*. It represented the most sophisticated attempt so far to spell out the relationship between education and the economy in all its complexity, stressing the view that, in addition to being an investment, education must be regarded as current consumption as well as a desirable consumption asset. It also underlined the impact of education on future consumption patterns as well as the fact that, though all indicators showed that social and private returns on investment in education were expected to be high, these represented only part of the additional social return. Rejecting the assumption that there is an immutable relationship between the development of education and the economic level of a country, the paper stressed the preponderant influence, at a certain income level, of tradition and belief in the value of education as against the income level itself. It concluded that any methodology for the setting of educational targets must be founded ''on the basic belief and assumption that more and better education for more people is desirable in itself and is at the same time one of the most important factors in economic growth''.[3]

Based on these assumptions, the paper produced estimates of the needs for expansion in the OECD area in terms of pupils, teachers, buildings and expenditure over the next decade. These were quite dramatic as illustrated by the following figures for the European OECD area.

Increase in the number of students:

Age 5-14 8   million or 18 per cent
''   15-19 . . . . 4.5   ''   '' 94 ''   ''
''   20-24 . . . . 0.8   ''   '' 83 ''   ''

Increase in the number of teachers:

For students aged **5-14** . . . . **400 000 or 28 per cent**
''   ''   ''   15-19 . . . . 280 000 '' 110 ''   ''
''   ''   ''   20-24 . . . . 50 000 '' 81 ''   ''

Such expansion, according to estimates in the report, meant not less than a doubling of educational expenditure from all sources. An expansion of the same relative order of magnitude was foreseen in Canada and the United States. As we shall see later, these targets proved to be by no means unrealistic and were even surpassed by the end of the decade.

It was evident, from the figures indicated above, that the expansion of education would be concentrated on secondary and higher education, *i.e.* the more expensive sectors of the educational system. These were also the sectors which presented the greatest difficulties in forecasting, involving as they did a complex combination of demographic, social demand and economic factors, as yet untested in planning methodologies still in their infancy. It is not surprising, therefore, that the planning of education was at the centre of the discussions, resulting in a strong plea for the creation or strengthening of the development and planning function within ministries of education, in "co-operation with the governmental and other groups concerned with research and having responsibilities for advising on the most economic allocation of national resources". This was seen as a *sine qua non* for giving effect to the equally strong plea for the establishment of medium and long-term objectives for university and school enrolments and for the creation of the necessary resources in teachers and buildings. The importance of the availability of improved statistical data in respect of pupils, teachers, buildings and finance was equally stressed as was the need for regular studies on all factors relating to future enrolments, including the manpower structure. All this provided the bases for the pioneering work on educational planning which was subsequently undertaken within OECD and the Member countries themselves.

Little need be said here on the second main theme of the Conference – assistance to the underdeveloped countries. The overwhelming nature of the task facing these countries was fully recognised and various strategies were discussed by which the advanced countries could make an improved contribution. Among these, the one that proved most operationally useful, at least as far as future work by the OECD was concerned, was to provide help to these countries, through experts and the transfer of experience, to assess their existing and long-term needs for education and to formulate strategies and priorities for the balanced expansion of education. Such assessments were seen to be necessary if the magnitude of the assistance required was to be realistically appraised and priorities for its use properly established. This was as true then as it is now. But, even though the practical effects were not immediately apparent, at least the analysis of the problem which was presented to the Conference and the discussion of aid strategies led to greater awareness of the enormity of the predicaments confronting the underdeveloped areas of the world and provided donor countries and agencies with broad guidelines for their future aid policies.

The Washington Conference stands out as a landmark in the OECD educational story. It set the agenda for much of the work which followed, within both OECD and Member countries themselves, on the future development of education, in terms of its growth, structures and planning instruments and methodologies. In retrospect, it is the political significance of the event that deserves to be underlined. It was the first OECD-sponsored Conference to be held in the United States; and this did not escape the attention of Dean Rusk, the US Secretary of State, who in his opening address to the Conference went out of his way to stress that "we in this country have great expectations about the possibilities of OECD. And we pledge that we shall give it our very strongest active support in the years ahead". It also marked the turning point in the attitude of some of the European Member countries which, like Germany, had earlier shown hesitations about letting OECD get involved in what they regarded as a cultural domain foreign to the objectives of the Organisation. But above all, the Conference, by providing professional legitimisation of the expansion of education, contributed significantly to convincing ministers of finance and other politicians of the interest they had in allocating the additional finance required to support this expansion.

Ministers of education themselves were of course easily convinced. But the OECD stamp to the conclusions of the Conference encouraged them to become more assertive in their claims on national resources. At their Third Conference, held in Rome in October 1962, the European Ministers of Education in their Resolution No. 9 on "Investment in Education", fully endorsed the outcomes of the Washington Conference which were presented to them by Dr. King:

> CONSIDERING that expenditure on education is not only designed for the functioning of a public service, but is increasingly acquiring the nature of an investment which would result in increasing the national income;

> REQUEST that expenditure on education and research be considered in relation to national incomes and so be financed by means similar to those used for important public works;

> PROPOSE to set up the necessary machinery for evaluating medium and long-term national requirements ... and to fix targets for the expansion of the educational apparatus based on estimates established in conjunction with all the ministries and organisations concerned.[4]

These were no empty words. Not only did they signal the political consecration of the investment approach to education; they also reflected and at the same time endorsed the reality that serious measures had already been set afoot, within the Secretariat and in Member countries, to give practical effect to the recommendations of the Washington Conference.

Rationalising somewhat – and this is the advantage of the historical perspective adopted for this report –, these varied measures, which went on concurrently during the best part of the sixties, can be presented as a two-front attack in the follow-up to Washington:
- Elaborating the theoretical bases and practical applications of the economics of education.
- Development of educational planning.

Each of these is dealt with below.

The Study Group in the Economics of Education

As indicated in the previous chapter, the origins of the Study Group, under whose aegis much of the theoretical work on the economics of education was undertaken, predate the Washington Conference. The Study Group was formally set up in 1960 and its members contributed to the Conference. It was to be a small group of professional economists and educators, designed to bring the resources of free academic thought to bear on the theoretical and practical issues involved in the relationship between education and enconomic development. Its Chairman was Henning Friis, Director of the Danish National Institute of Social Research, who was also Chairman of the parent Committee, the CSTP. The other members were Freidrich Edding, Seymour Harris, Raymond Poignant, Ingvar Svennilson and John Vaizey, subsequently joined by Michel Debeauvais, Selma Mushkin and Jan Tinbergen. The Group operated as a think-tank, organising its work around a series of Conferences for which it had no difficulty in attracting original contributions from other outstanding researchers. Over its brief life-span – effectively 1962-65, when the bulk of its work was produced –, the Group came, in fact, to be regarded as a focal point and a prime mover in the development of a new and exciting branch of economics, the economics of education.

A review of the Study Group's meetings and publications deriving from them shows how its deliberation ranged from global economic problems in educational development to specific substantive issues directly relevant to actual development planning for education – institutional, organisational, financial and social. Its first major Conference (June 1962) dealt with the economics of higher education, a subject of special interest as in many countries higher education was the most rapidly growing sector of the educational system, as documented at the Washington Conference. Problems of both theoretical and practical interest were discussed, such as admission practices, the demand for higher education, the internal efficiency of higher education systems and their financing, against a constant preoccupation with its high and rising costs. Not surprisingly, unit costs emerged as a problem calling for special study.[5]

At its next meeting, (May 1963), the Group focused on the state of research into the contribution of education to economic growth. Its report was published the following year under the title *The Residual Factor and Economic Growth*. It was in fact at this meeting that the "residual factor" came into prominence among economic growth theorists, dominated by Denison's presentation of the results of his work in the United States: "Measuring the Contribution of Education (and the Residual) to Economic Growth". The presentation gave rise to considerable controversy, particularly on the part of European economists. The main difference of opinion arose between those who rejected the underlying principle in Denison's analysis, the connection between income shares and marginal contributions to output, and those who accepted the principle, and were sympathetic to Denison's approach, viewing it at least as a first approximation.

But though the discussion remained inconclusive, at least the economics of education received at this meeting and those that followed the most authoritative review possible at the time; and the way was opened for further more detailed studies involving national comparisons based on macro-economic models. At the end of the day, what emerged from these studies was that the level of educational attainment in the population as a factor in economic growth varied strongly from country to country, and over time in individual countries. "We realised that we were facing an interplay between different growth factors which made it difficult to attach a specific degree of importance to each of them".[6] Similar conclusions were reached from parallel studies at the micro level, focusing especially on the "rate of return" to education.

In subsequent meetings the Study Group moved steadily away from academic type of analysis of the links between education and economic growth to consider key policy issues arising from that relationship and relevant instruments and approaches. It thus dealt successively with:

a) *Organisational Problems in Planning Educational Development* (November 1963[7] – a first attempt to spell out the need for changes in administrative and governmental structures if educational policy and planning were to be properly co-ordinated with broader, particularly manpower and economic, policies;

b) *Financing of Education for Economic Growth* (September, 1964)[8] – which dealt with the full range of the financial implications of educational expansion, in both developed and under-developed countries, and the instruments and mechanisms by which these expenditures could be handled;

c) *Social Objectives in Educational Planning* (discussed at the final meeting of the Group in March 1965[9] – which in essence picked up the theme of educational equality discussed at Kungalv four years earlier; and reached the obvious conclusion that the increase in the demand for education "arises from both economic and social development needs, which in practice call for an expansion of education of such proportions as to reinforce in practice the idea of a democratisation in educational participation" – a fitting epitaph to the work of a Study Group in the Economics of Education.

It will be clear from the above that the final phase of the work of the Group came to be merged with the more empirical, country-based educational planning activities of the CSTP which had developed rapidly and in parallel with the theoretical work of the Study Group. In fact, by the mid-sixties the Study Group had outlived its purpose, as the majority of Member countries had already established or strengthened educational planning bodies to deal with the hard problems of their educational development. This did not mean the end of research based activities within the Secretariat. But such activities were henceforth increasingly oriented towards building up a theoretical framework for the practical planning work in Member countries. In this, the foundations laid by the Study Group were seminal. Its work had been truly pioneering and, with all their limitations in providing conclusive, practical guidelines to policy, the approaches developed by the Study Group have had a lasting resonance among educational planners nationally and within various international settings.

The emergence and consolidation of educational planning

The Washington Conference, and subsequent work by the Study Group in the Economics of Education, provided legitimisation for the continuing growth of education systems, for reasons which were at the same time economic – linked, in particular, to manpower requirements – and social, linked to the escalating demand for education from all sectors of society. The relative weight of these two factors on the motivation of governments to support educational growth varied from country to country, according to their stage of development: while the "social demand" approach was more congenial to the situation and needs of the more developed, industrialised Member countries, the "manpower demand" approach was seen as more immediately useful to the less-developed ones, *i.e.* those around the Mediterranean fringe. But in both cases, the overall context of educational growth, and its inevitability, was provided by the realities of the rapid economic growth of the sixties, accompanied by the growing concerns of governments to spread the benefits of this growth more equally across all strata of society, exemplified by the "fair deal" policies of Presidents Kennedy and Johnson in the United States. There was thus created a virtuous circle of supply and demand, whereby manpower-hungry economies, together with rising expectations among the population, led to an upsurge of social demand for education fed by the post-war baby boom, and sustained by rising national and family incomes. These circumstances were unique to the sixties. They provide the backcloth to the equally unique development of educational planning which OECD countries experienced during the same period, and in which the OECD played a leading role.

This role is considered below in terms of four specific sets of activity:

- The Mediterranean Regional Project;
- The Educational Investment and Planning Programme;
- The Development of Educational Statistics and Quantitative Analysis Techniques;
- Training in Human Resource Development: The Fellowship Programme.

The Mediterranean Regional Project (MRP)

In the annals of the OECD operational activities no project was endowed with more extensive support – financial, intellectual and political – or received more sustained critical scrutiny, conceptual and methodological, or greater public attention, and publicity, than the Mediterranean Regional Project (MRP). The idea was simple enough: it was an attempt by the six OECD Mediterranean countries – Greece, Italy, Portugal, Spain, Turkey and Yugoslavia – to relate education to economic growth, and by extrapolation, to social advancement; and to do this not in terms of abstractions around questions such as how to calculate the rate of return to society on investment in education, but in the real conditions of planning and policy-making in individual countries. In more precise terms, the MRP was "a joint research project aimed at assessing the educational needs of each of the six countries, particularly those relating to scientific and technical manpower, in the context of economic growth for the target year 1975 or thereabouts, and formulating detailed plans, including financial estimates, for meeting these needs".[10]

The inception of the project goes as far back as 1960, when, after an OSTP Country Review of Portugal, the Portuguese Government sought the help of the Organisation for a project designed to set targets for educational development to meet the manpower requirements of the country's long-term economic objectives. The idea appeared attractive to the other Mediterranean Member countries who expressed their willingness to participate in a joint project of this kind. They all shared a number of common problems which set them apart from the rest of the OECD membership: lower incomes *per capita,* large percentages of the labour force still engaged in agriculture, with considerable disguised unemployment, great shortages in educational facilities, with low enrolment ratios and levels of educational expenditure and severe shortages of qualified manpower, particularly scientific and technical manpower – with the exception, of course, of the northern and other highly industrialised regions of Italy. There followed twelve months of bilateral negotiations between the six countries and the Secretariat and by the beginning of 1962 agreements were concluded setting out the purposes and working arrangements for the project. The MRP was operational.

Under the terms of the agreements, the project was to be carried out in each country by a national team of 5-6 members, composed of a director and of economists, statisticians and educationalists appointed by and reporting to the Government concerned. The main objective of the teams was to formulate, in the form of national reports, the needs for education over the next fifteen years (1961-1975) of each of the countries, and put forward proposals of the resources needed to meet the needs. The final reports were to be published by the OECD with the agreement of the Governments concerned. Finance was crucial to the whole operation and this was facilitated by the availability of substantial funds under the US contribution to the OSTP programme, making it possible for the national teams to be financed jointly by the OECD and the Government concerned. In addition, the OECD undertook to provide experts and arrange periodical meetings between the national directors of the teams and OECD staff and consultants to discuss the progress of the work, provide practical advice to the teams, deal with problems of programming and methodology common to the teams and, in general, ensure the organisation, co-ordination and administration of the project. Subsequently, the OECD also undertook to train specialists in human resource development. This liberal injection of foreign expertise, together with the very active role played by the Secretariat throughout the implementation of the whole project, drawing also on the facilities of the Technical Assistance Programme of the Organisation, proved a vital element in the work of the national teams and the sophistication of the methodology which was brought to bear on the preparation of the national reports.

It should be remembered that the political context within which the MRP was launched was shaped by the primary concern of OEEC/OECD with economic growth and development and the prevalent belief in central planning, into which education policy would need to be integrated. It was essential, therefore, that the work of the national teams should be so organised and located as to ensure the closest connections possible between national economic ministries and central planning bodies, on the one hand, and education ministries, on the other. In actual fact, it was the central economic and planning interest which became the dominant one. In three of the countries – Greece, Turkey and Yugoslavia – the teams were located within the newly established governmental planning organisations. In Spain, though the work took place within the Ministry of Education, the operative influence came from the Planning Group in the Prime Minister's Office. In Portugal and Italy the work was undertaken by independent research groups – a team of university researchers in the case of Portugal, and SVIMEZ, in the case of Italy – in close liaison with national planning agencies.

These arrangements no doubt enabled the teams to have access to a wide range of sources of information, such as national income projections, census data, manpower and educational surveys. On the other hand, they remained organically distant from the national ministries of education, even though contact was in principle maintained. There is no disguising the fact that ministries of economics and ministries of education often had different views and different perspectives on problems of educational development and that, in one sense, the strategy adopted for the project was to bring outside pressure to bear on reluctant and slothful educational administrations and establishments. Education was too important to be left to the educationists! In the end, however, this approach may have backfired, for by failing to secure the intimate involvement and commitment of ministries of education, it tended to reduce the direct impact which the work of the teams had on national education policies as such.

Over the next three years (1962-65), intensive work by the national teams, under the collaborative arrangements described above and with strong inputs from OECD consultants – mostly US specialists in human resource development, seconded by their universities – resulted in the completion of the six country reports, which were individually published by the Organisation.[11] This is not the place to analyse the detailed contents of these reports, nor the validity of their analysis and the reliability of their projections. But at least they do provide, for each of the countries concerned, as well a documented picture as available data and methodologies permitted at the time of the deficiencies of the existing educational systems, an assessment of future requirements for education in the light of economic needs and recommendations on the ways and means by which these requirements could be met. Their ultimate value lies not so much in the accuracy or otherwise of their quantitative analyses and predictions – these can be conveniently checked against a subsequent retrospective analysis carried out by the Organisation in the early seventies[12] – as in the stimulus they provided for a more systematic approach to educational planning and in sensitising public opinion to the reality that such planning cannot be done in isolation of broader economic and social planning. Above all, they identified in explicit terms the major bottlenecks inherent in their traditional educational systems which impeded economic and social advance and brought home to the countries concerned the urgency of measures to overcome them and of the priorities that needed to be set in doing so.

One example will suffice to illustrate this point. One general conclusion from all the reports was that the chief obstacle to economic growth lay in the lack of middle-level technicians and skilled craftsmen and workers. This pointed to the prime importance of the provision of more education in order to improve the supply of people with elementary and middle-level education. This, in turn, implied a minimum long-term objective of full-time education for everybody between the ages of about 6 and 14 years – an objective with little hope of being achieved within a decade, seeing that in most of these countries the legal duration of education was still only five or six years, with enrolment ratios, even within this age-group, well below that of other OECD countries. The problem was compounded by manifest imbalances within secondary education itself between the dominance of general education and the poor status of technical and vocational education, an imbalance which was exacerbated by a similar situation within higher education. Not surprisingly, one of the strongest recommendations in the reports was the need to build up capacity in technical and vocational education throughout the secondary and higher education systems. It was the one which was subsequently most fruitfully pursued in the majority of the countries concerned, leading eventually to the setting up, not without serious difficulties and opposition from the established systems, of new institutes or colleges of technology to channel demand away from the traditional, academically-oriented universities. In the rare cases where new universities as such were set up as direct offsprings of the MRP reports – as was the case of the University of Patras in Greece – these were based on detailed planning of regional needs and incorporated innovative features in the organisation and structure of courses and their overall management.[13]

The most original and striking feature of the MRP, and the one which attracted the most attention outside the OECD area, was its methodology. Although cultural and social factors were taken into account, the methodology used in the project was essentially the application of the ''manpower approach'' to educational planning, itself revolving around the central issue of forecasting future manpower requirements and their incidence on estimates of educational requirements. The project started virtually in a methodological void and the six Mediterranean countries provided a living laboratory for testing a number of manpower planning hypotheses and evolving from them the elements of a theory and a methodology.[14] The method was based on three principal considerations: i) forecasts as to the probable or desired growth of the economy; ii) an assumed relationship between the growth of the various sectors of the economy and the number of people holding certain qualifications; iii) an assumed relationship between educational qualifications and occupational ones. The main technical and methodological problems which are raised by this approach have been discussed extensively in the literature and there would be little point in taking them up here.[15]

It is easy, at this distance, to decry this method. Yet it is one which had strong appeal, and still has, to developing countries with ambitious economic growth rates, but sluggish educational systems. It was particularly appealing to the situation which then prevailed in Latin American countries, and the Ford Foundation provided generous financial aid to enable the MRP experience to be transferred to countries in that region. MRP-type of teams were thus established by OECD in Argentina and Peru which resulted in the preparation of national reports based on a refinement of the MRP methodology, taking into account the particularities of these countries.[16] An attempt was also made to transfer this experience to Arab countries through a seminar held in Beyrout.[17] This concluded the first phase of the MRP.

As a postscript, it should be noted that a second stage was envisaged for the MRP, aiming essentially at translating the long-term plans for educational development into medium and short-term *operational* programmes, in particular those concerned with the efficiency of the educational system. This never materialised in practice, for in the meantime outside funds had run out and the Organisation itself had switched its interests away from operational activities – a move which was not unrelated to the drying up of the special financial contributions which the US had been making in support of these activities. Without outside support, in logistics as well as in expertise and in political stimulus, the governments in the six countries found it difficult to gear up the necessary implementation effort.

In addition, by 1965 the educational planning scene came to be dominated by the rapid progress which the parallel EIP programme had made in the more advanced OECD countries. Gradually the MRP group began to be associated with the work of the EIP and it was becoming increasingly obvious that the paths of the two groups were converging, a convergence which was consecrated at a joint meeting of the two groups in December 1965. The record of that meeting[18] represents perhaps the most balanced view of the inextricable relationships between the manpower and social demand approaches to educational planning.

The Educational Investment and Planning Programme (E.I.P.)

Largely inspired by the MRP concept, the EIP was effectively set up at the end of 1962. It was designed to provide a framework of mutual assistance among the Member countries, working closely with the Secretariat, in their efforts to plan for educational development. Its immediate clients were the groups or authorities in each country directly responsible for educational planning, programming and development. The remit of the programme was to enable these groups to "conduct a systematic exchange of information, guide co-operative research into key policy issues, and study the planning work undertaken in the countries in this field". The programme had a long life, reaching well into the seventies, during which it came to play a dominant role in the evolution of the scope and perception of educational planning, the development of the educational planning functions and mechanisms in the Member countries and in the policy work of the STP Committee itself, In practice, it absorbed and broadened the functions of the Study Group in the Economics of Education and provided much of the analytical work which fed the policy discussions in the Committee, including a whole round of Country Educational Policy Reviews during the sixties and early seventies based on the planning reports of the national EIP groups.

The work of the EIP was grounded in the social, economic, political and administrative complexities of highly industrialised countries, with educational systems in full expansion. In contrast to the MRP, the setting of educational targets for educational development could not be derived simply from an assessment of future manpower needs; these would have to be woven into the broader nexus of the needs of society as a whole, including political objectives and concerns and with due consideration of factors affecting the performance of the education system and the consequences of educational policy decisions themselves – all of which is conveniently defined as the application of the "social demand" approach to educational planning. It follows from this – and this is the other major difference with the MRP – that educational planning activities had to be integrated into the established education policy and administration mechanisms, *i.e.* the planning groups had to be located within Ministries of Education. This, in fact, was adopted as a deliberate policy of the EIP programme and was an essential element in the success of the whole operation.[19]

Thus, the first, and by no means the least significant outcome of the EIP was the establishment of educational planning groups in individual Member countries, or the strengthening of such groups in the few cases where they already existed. The initial task of each group was to prepare, in the form of a technical report, a comprehensive framework for the deliberate development of education based on an assessment of the future needs of society, including, but not limited to, the economy. The preparation of these reports, and the international scrutiny to which they were subjected – often during the process of their preparation – within the EIP network and subsequently within the STP Committee, amounted to a sustained exercise of self-examination by each participating country of its educational policy objectives and of its planning methods and criteria, from which, of course, other countries also benefited. In this way, the EIP had considerable influence as a catalyst in the development of national policies for education and in stimulating the analytical techniques and scientific work to inform such policies.

The first country to move in this direction was Ireland and the decision by the Irish Government, in October 1962, to set up an interdisciplinary team to prepare the first national report under the EIP marks the effective launching of the programme. Completed in 1965,[20] the report was consciously conceived as a "Pilot Survey" to serve as a model for what came to be known as "first generation" educational planning. It was seen essentially as a technical study of trends in Irish education and of the use of human and material resources in tha system. It estimated the demands that were likely to be made on these resources and considered the extent to which the system seemed likely to meet future needs, including satisfactory participation in education by all sections of the community and an adequate supply of qualified persons. Arising out of these investigations, an examination was made of the effects of possible changes in the educational system and in the traditional use of resources. While the report did not directly recommend a large expansion in the Irish educational system, the impressive data which it assembled and organised clearly pointed in that direction. As such, it had a lasting influence on the future development of educational policy in Ireland.

Very soon, the Irish example was replicated in other countries, with Sweden (1967) and Austria (1968) taking the lead in producing similar reports; so that by the end of the sixties, educational planning groups or equivalent machinery were in active operation in the majority of the OECD membership, a movement which was sustained well into the seventies. The nature, pace and the precise manifestations of this movement varied from country to country, according to national administrative circumstances and traditions, but the pattern was everywhere the same: newly set up or reinforced mechanisms for the preparation of deliberate plans for the development of educational systems, or specific sectors of such systems, and the submission of these plans for discussion within the OECD procedures.

Thus, even countries like France, which had a tradition of self-sufficiency in this area, joined the process, leading to its Educational Policy Review in 1970.[21] A few other examples can be quoted to illustrate the impact of the programme. In Germany, the Bund-Lander Commission for Educational Planning was founded in 1970 and was instrumental in preparing the Background Report for the German review in 1972.[22] *The Educational Policy Review of Japan* (1971), with its particular flavour on culture and the quality of life, was similarly based on a planning document, interim versions of which had been discussed within the EIP group. An untypical example was that of the United States where central educational planning is constitutionally precluded. But even within this constraint the Department of Education found the means of participating extensively in the EIP programme. It made a special contribution to it by preparing a remarkably documented analysis of one aspect of educational policy – the role of research and development – which fell within the remit of the Federal Government, on which the *Educational Policy Review of the United States* was undertaken in 1969.[23]

Finally, an interesting, if somewhat *suis generis,* example is provided by the United Kingdom, more specifically England and Wales. There was no national EIP report as such, but participation in the programme was active from the beginning, encouraged by the spread of planning procedures and machinery within the overall governmental structures consequent on the 1961 Plowden Report on Public Expenditure Control, In addition, the analytical work of the programme was sustained by a constant flow of contributions by UK academics and experts. The National Plan of 1965 contained indicative statements about educational investment and a Planning Branch was created within the Department of Education and Science in 1967.[24] Subsequently (1971), the Planning Branch gave way to the Department of Planning Organisation in an attempt to bring together the different policy areas into a coherent whole without taking away the policy-making functions of the main branches. It was under these arrangements, serviced by a small Planning Unit, that the 1972 White Paper "Education: A Framework for Expansion" was prepared, which in turn served as the basic document for the OECD Review.[25]

The review focused heavily on the planning process itself, of which the examiners were very critical. They noted, in particular, that the political impact of the high quality analysis on which decisions were made was undermined by the absence of transparency and of consultative procedures. This was in sharp contrast to the participative doctrines which prevailed at the time, a contrast which was spectacularly demonstrated by the review of Norway[26] which took place at the same meeting of the Committee. An inadvertent leak of the examiners' report in the British press, at a rare time of shortage of other news, gave rise to considerable comment in the media, as a result of which the Education, Arts and Home Office Sub-Committee of the Expenditure Committee of the House of Commons decided to enquire into "Policy-Making in the Department of Education" and, in particular, to investigate the validity of the criticism in the OECD review. The Sub-Committee, after hearing evidence from a wide range of professional and other interest groups in the country, produced a voluminous report which by and large endorsed this criticism. It resulted in recommendations which eventually led to a serious shake-up of the concepts and practice of educational planning in the Department, themselves reviewed by OECD a few years later.[27]

The England and Wales Review was probably the last act in the first stage of the educational planning saga initiated by the EIP. Interest in planning as such was in decline and attention began to shift to key substantive issues with which planning should be concerned rather than with the techniques and mechanisms of planning, already well established in the countries. The germs for this were already evident from the start. The Swedish Review (1967), for example, had pointed to the concept of a "rolling reform" and the ways in which research and development could be harnessed to implementation. The Austrian Report (1968) had gone much further, in highlighting the fact that the changing quality of social life and the changing patterns of income and of social demands created new demands on the educational system too far reaching to be considered only on a quantitative basis. What was needed was a deeper understanding of educational process and social dynamism. There was, thus, gradually a noticeable shift in emphasis from quantitative to qualitative aspects, from short to long-term perspective planning and from para-educational variables to the education process itself. In addition, there was a shift in the perception of planning itself, away from viewing it as discrete expert activity, towards integrating it into policy and decision-making in the wide variety of settings where such decisions are made. All this constitutes the elements of "second generation" planning with which we shall deal in a subsequent chapter.[28]

Educational statistics and quantitative analysis techniques

As was the case with the Washington Conference, the educational planning work of the Organisation received strong endorsement and backing by the European Ministers of Education. They discussed this at their fourth Conference, held in London in April 1964. In their Resolution Number 2, on Planning and Investment in Education, Ministers recorded the necessity for individual governments "to embark forthwith on a forward-looking course of action [of educational investment and reform], based on as accurate an appreciation as possible of objectives and methods". They recommended, in particular:

> "...that OECD, whose work in this field is greatly appreciated, be invited to formulate clearly in a model handbook the various factors involved in effective educational investment planning, so that countries represented may have a basis for the compilation of comparable statistics."

With the subsequent endorsement by the STP Committee and the OECD Council, this Resolution provided the necessary additional political impetus in supporting the extension of the statistical and methodological work already in hand within the MRP and EIP groups.

The nature of this work was determined by two broad considerations, both essentially of a quantitative character. Firstly, and foremost, was the need, arising from the pressure of numbers, to devise reliable techniques for forecasting the size and patterns of future enrolment at various levels of the educational system. Secondly, the swelling fiscal implications of the education "explosion", particularly the ever-rising trend in enrolments in higher education, needed to be assessed and, increasingly, to be justified. Related to this was the growing concern to bring about greater efficiency in the use of resources in all areas of education. The chosen instrument for tackling these problems was the application of *mathematical models* to the education sector.

Mathematical methods had, of course, a long history in helping understand physical phenomena and were extensively used in theoretical and applied economics. Their use in other areas of the social sciences was of relatively recent origin and the circumstances surrounding education provided a propitious climate for testing their applicability to this sector. The OECD led the way and very rapidly an impressive network of mathematical model builders was in operation, on the earlier model, but at a more technical level, of the Study Group in the Economics of Education.

Beginning in 1965, the work progressed from macro-models linking the education system to other sectors, particularly the economic and manpower systems, to comprehensive models of the education system itself and to micro-models dealing with problems of individual sectors or institutions of the system, with the accent on management and resource utilisation in higher education, subsequently taken up in greater depth within the CERI programme. Details of this work can be followed in the series of OECD publications that ensued from this activity.[29]

Concurrently with this expert activity, Secretariat-based work resulted in the preparation of a large-scale computable model which related the education sector to the labour and production sector of the economy in terms of a series of input/output relations.[30] Also constructed by the Secretariat was a detailed computer simulation model of the educational sector for use as a tool by policy-makers.[31] The model permits an examination of a number of policy options in terms of future consequences and the dynamics of changes as a result of quantifiably defined conditions affecting the educational system.

The fashion in model-building went hand-in-hand with a parallel interest in systems analysis, operations research and related management techniques, and these were also reflected in the OECD work at the time.[32] An experimental programme in this area was subsequently tried out in Greece, Portugal and Spain. Designed as a joint project, with field applications, this faint attempt to revive the MRP focused on the suitability of existing decision-making mechanisms and administration set-ups for implementing educational policies. It paid particular attention to the adequacy of existing communication patterns within the educational sector and between this sector and other parts of the administration and society at large. As in the case of the MRP, the ultimate value of this work lay in its diagnostic function rather than its immediate policy applications. There is no doubt the three participating countries benefited from the empirical analysis of the actual functioning of their education systems, judged against the most sophisticated concepts of systems analysis; and some glaring gaps were brought home to them, particularly the gap between central decision-making and its applications and relevance to regional and local levels, a problem with which they have been struggling ever since.[33]

The work on mathematical model-building and on systems analysis, in addition to its epistemological difficulties, had come up against the major stumbling block of its distance from an effective system of educational data collection and classification. An attempt to bridge this gap was in fact made at the time by Professor Stone in his report on demographic accounting[34] which included a highly disaggregated pupil flow-matrix for direct computation of enrolments. But this also turned out to be abortive, for no country was as yet in a position, or even willing, to install a comprehensive demographic accounting system of the kind proposed in the report. At the end of the day, there was little more that could be done beyond attempting to draw the lessons from the totality of this endeavour. This was done in a critical evaluation of this work, involving some of the main proponents of mathematical model-building themselves. It resulted in a report[35] which, for the clarification it contains of the various types of mathematical models developed in the Member countries, the analysis of the technical problems confronting these various models and of the obstacles that stand in the way of their applicability, remains a useful source of reference to the present day.

The one general conclusion that stood out most clearly from this review was "the gap between the construction of formal mathematical models, on the one hand, and their use in educational decision-making and planning, on the other".[36] The road to modelling had thus turned out to be a *cul-de-sac*. Yet one must not underestimate the contribution which this work, with all its limitations, had made in infusing a more rigorous approach to the analysis of the relationship between educational objectives and means, between education and other sectors, and the identification of data, and their organisation, necessary for coherent and informed planning and decision-making in education.

The work on data collection and classification, which went hand-in-hand with and was fed by, the work of the MPR/EIP groups and that on mathematical models, proved to be much more immediately useful as well as of more lasting influence. Taking the European Ministers of Education at their word, the end-product was indeed a "model handbook" for the compilation of comparable statistics useful to educational planners.[37] The "Green Book", as it came to be known, has been generally recognised as having made an important contribution to the development of effective educational planning, of its methods and its statistical infrastructure. It definitely represents the most balanced testimony to the permanent value of the work of OECD in this area.

The impact of the Handbook was largely conditioned by the clarity of its limited objectives. These were to consider recent developments in the theory and practice of educational planning and out of these to set out systematically their statistical implications in the form of a series of tabulations which should be available to educational planners on a regular routine basis. In a second place, it was also to consider the utility of international comparisons to educational planners and make proposals for the collection of data from which a wide range of comparisons could be made. Thus, the essential remit of the Handbook was to address the information needs of educational planners, by reference, in the first place, to a more precise definition of the questions to which such planners are trying to provide answers. Recognising that the number of problems for which educational administrators require statistical data is almost infinite, the Handbook set explicit limits to its coverage, concentrating only on "primary" statistics, while noting that if these statistics are collected and presented properly, they would permit the derivation of a wide range of "secondary" statistics useful to the study of more specific educational questions.

The basic data required by educational planners were of two types. Firstly, statistics of the educational system itself – pupils, teachers, buildings, expenditures, etc. The planning problems which arose under each of these categories were clearly enumerated and analysed, and these constitute the bulk of the proposed tabulations. Secondly, it was recognised that there is a large amount of supplementary data – economic, demographic and social – required by educational planners for the calculation of forecasting and planning coefficients within the educational system. Such data were not included in the proposed tabulation scheme except where: *a)* they were seen to be of overwhelming importance for making educational forecasts, *e.g.* data by age on the population of school age; *b)* the statistics in the form required were unlikely to be collected for purposes other than educational planning, *e.g.* tabulations of occupation by educational characteristics and branch of activity which were unlikely to be produced except to meet the demands of educational planners. Within both of these categories of data, and in response to the growing interest in international comparisons, the Handbook made an attempt to provide a basis for a set of indicators of educational effort which could be of help to individual countries to evaluate the magnitude and orientation of their educational achievements in relation to those of other countries at various stages of economic development.

The preparation of the Handbook involved a complex process of Secretariat consultations with leading experts in the field and statisticians in Ministries of Education so as to ensure that the end-product was scientifically sound and at the same time practically useful to Member countries. The draft was finalised at a special conference of national educational statisticians, held in Bandol (France) in February 1966. The final version was endorsed by a Recommendation of the OECD Council itself "as a suitable framework for the compilation of educational statistics", which also urged Member countries "to develop their programmes of educational statistics along the lines indicated in the handbook, insofar as it is possible in the conditions prevailing in each country". Thus, the recommendations in the Handbook were not binding on Governments and the Organisation never took the step of installing a unified "Educational Accounting" system of the kind that had been set up for economic accounting. Nonetheless, the Handbook remained a basic source of reference and inspiration in the development of national systems of educational data collection and classification, even though in certain areas, such as the development of individualised data systems of pupils, teachers and institutions, its recommendations were far ahead of where governments were prepared or able to go.

Within OECD itself, country progress in implementing the Handbook's recommendations, and technical problems which arose in the harmonisation of educational statistics, were closely monitored through regular meetings of a special *Working Party on Educational Statistics,* composed of the chief statisticians in national ministries of education. A first major task was to operationalise the conclusions of the Handbook on international comparisons. Such comparisons could not be meaningfully undertaken without first developing a classification system and set of definitions applicable to all Member countries, and by which published national data could be readily converted on the basis of the standardised systems set out in the Handbook. Work, therefore, was undertaken leading to the preparation of a "conversion key" by which each type of education or institution in the various Member countries was reclassified under the OECD system, both from the standpoint of standardised designation and in terms of its position on the educational ladder by year of study.[38] On the basis of this standardised clarification, and drawing on published national data, it was thus possible to prepare a first compendium of comparable basic educational statistics in OECD countries, in essence the precursor of subsequent work on International Educational Indicators.[39] A similar compendium was produced a few years later.[40]

In the meantime, the international educational statistics scene had changed, following the adoption by all the UNESCO Member States in 1978 of the *International Standard Classification of Education Systems* (commonly referred to as ISCED), itself largely inspired by the recommendations of the Handbook. At the request of its own Member countries, in order to avoid duplication of workload and to harmonise the data published by these two Organisations, the OECD adapted the ISCED system. This meant that in its work on international comparisons the OECD depended henceforth on the replies to the three questionnaires that UNESCO sent annually to *all* its Member States, one dealing with school education, the second with educational expenditure and financing, and the third with higher education. It soon became clear, however, that the policy concerns of OECD countries could not be adequately covered by the kind of data that were geared to the concerns of the UNESCO membership. This eventually led to detailed negotiations between the two Organisations, resulting in an agreement on special versions of joint UNESCO/OECD questionnaires, with which the Statistical Office of the European Communities (SOEC) was also associated. It is on the basis of replies by OECD countries to these special versions of the questionnaires that subsequent issues of the OECD *Educational Statistics Compendium* have been prepared on an annual basis beginning with the school-year 1983-84.[41]

Training for human resource planning: the Fellowship Programme

It was recognised from the start that one of the main obstacles to the development of educational planning was the extreme shortage of specialists in human resource development, an as yet non-existing discipline. The most effective way of creating such personnel was by training on the job, *i.e.* by a solid apprenticeship with a team working on these problems within the practical framework of a national policy for economic development. The MRP provided an ideal setting for this purpose. An imaginative, and very successful, initiative was thus set afoot at an early stage of the project, by which young economists, sociologists, statisticians and educationalists could undergo their apprenticeship and at the same time become useful members of the national teams. Subsequently they would be able to provide assistance in human resource planning to their own or to other developing countries.[42]

The scheme combined an intensive training course with a fellowship programme. The training course, usually lasting four weeks, consisted of a combination of lectures, seminars and group discussions intended to provide both the theoretical bases and practical approaches to the planning of education in relation to economic growth. Such courses were held annually between 1962 and 1965, and the course material was subsequently published.[43] These training courses were self-contained and some of the participants went no further. For a number of them, however, who were fellowship-holders, this was only the first stage, the next being a twelve-month apprenticeship with one of the national teams. Twenty such fellowships, out of a total of 500 applicants, were awarded in 1962, 18 in 1963 and 19 in 1964. During the first year the fellowship programme operated exclusively in conjunction with the MRP. With the establishment of the EIP in 1962, additional training opportunities became available to which fellowship holders were attached. With the support of funds from the Ford Foundation, a limited number of awards was also made to qualified applicants from non-OECD countries, while OECD fellowship-holders were equally attached to the national teams in Latin America. In all cases, fellowship-holders played a vital role in the work of the teams, often producing original contributions of high professional quality.[44]

The fellowship scheme proved highly successful. Through it, young university graduates were turned into educational planning specialists, thus generating a pool of people who later on acquired important positions within their own national administrations or achieved high academic positions. Not a few of them were recruited into the OECD Secretariat and provided the backbone to the further development of its educational activities. The scheme was interrupted in 1965, together with so many other of the operational activities of the Organisation.

Postscript

This chapter has intentionally concentrated on presenting a coherent picture of the role of OECD in legitimising the growth of education in the sixties and in establishing the concepts, techniques and mechanisms by which this growth could be planned and, at the same time, be articulated into the broader polity. It has not dealt with the substantive aspects relating to the size, nature and directions of this growth, nor with its consequences, intended or otherwise. It has also omitted detailed references to the significant changes which took place during this period within the OECD structures themselves and their repercussion on the ways in which the Organisation's role in education evolved. These matters will be taken up in the next chapter.

Notes and references

1. I. *Summary Report and Conclusions and Keynote Speeches.*
    II. *Targets for Education in Europe in 1970.*
    III. *The Challenge of Aid to Newly Developing Countries.*
    IV. *The Planning of Education in Relation to Economic Growth.*
    V. *International Flow of Students*, OECD, 1961.

2. *Policy Conference on Economic Growth and Investment in Education*, OECD, 1965.

3. For a discussion of the methodology used in the paper see *Educational Planning: An Historical Overview of OECD Work*, OECD, 1980.

4. Full text of the Resolution in MED-15-2 (Council of Europe), pp. 29-30.

5. *Economic Aspects of Higher Education*, OECD, 1964.

6. Eide, *op. cit.,* p. 13. Kjell Eide was at the time the staff member in the Secretariat servicing the Study Group.

7. OECD, 1966.

8. OECD, 1966.

9. OECD, 1967.

10. For a succinct description of the whole project see: *The Mediterranean Regional Project: An Experiment in Planning by Six Countries*, OECD, 1965.

11. *The Mediterranean Regional Project: Country Reports: Greece, Italy, Portugal, Spain, Turkey, Yugoslavia*, OECD, 1965.

12. *Education in OECD Developing Countries: Trends and Perspectives*, OECD, 1974.

13. For a brief summary of the orders of magnitude in the future requirements of these countries, see: *An Experiment in Planning by Six Countries*, pp. 17-19.

14. This is best exemplified in H. Parnes: *Forecasting Educational Needs for Economic and Social Development,* OECD, 1962; and in: *idem: Planning Education for Economic and Social Development*,OECD, 1963.

15. For a summary discussion of them see: *Educational Planning: An Historical Overview of OECD Work*, OECD, 1980. A detailed critical analysis of the methodology was undertaken within the MRP project itself: R. Hollister, *A Technical Evaluation of the First Stage of the Mediterranean Regional Project*, OECD, 1967.

16. See: *Human Resources, Education and Economic Development in Peru*, OECD, 1967; *Education, Human Resources and Development in Argentina*, OECD, 1967; *Problems of Human Resources Planning in Latin America and in the Mediterranean Regional Project Countries*, OECD, 1967.

17. The proceedings were published in *Problems of Educational and Manpower Planning in the Arab Countries and Mediterranean Regional Project Countries*, OECD, 1967. It is the totality of this experience which is critically analysed in the *Technical Evaluation of the MRP*.

18. *Manpower Forecasting in Educational Planning: Report of the Joint MRP/EIP Meeting*, OECD, 1965.

19. Eide, *op. cit.*, pp. 16-17; see also *Educational Planning: An Historical Overview of OECD Work*, pp. 8-9.

20. *Ireland: Investment in Education*, OECD, 1966.

21. *Reviews of National Policies for Education; France, OECD, 1973*. It is true that much of the work for the preparation of the Background Report for this review – *Educational Policy and Planning in France*, OECD, 1973 – was done within the Secretariat, but working closely with the French Ministry of Education.

22. *Educational Policy and Planning: Germany, OECD, 1972; Reviews of National Policies for Education: Germany,* OECD, 1973.

23. OECD, 1971, including the Background Report.

24. It is indicative of the substantive interest which the Department maintained in the programme that relations with OECD were kept under the Planning Branch whereas those with other Organisations were brought together within a new International Relations Section set up around this time.

25. *Educational Policy Review of England and Wales*, OECD, 1975.

26. *Educational Policy Review of Norway* OECD, 1976, including the Background Report.

27. See: *Educational Planning: A Reappraisal,* OECD, 1983.

28. For a brief overview see: *An Historical Overview of OECD Work op. cit.* A detailed review is available in : M. Webster: *Policy Planning for Education in OECD Member Countries: Changing Perceptions and Emerging Concerns, Syracuse University, New York*, 1970. The relationship of planning to the evolution of educational policies is analysed in M. Kogan: *op. cit.,* which also contains an account of the aftermath of the England and Wales Review.

29. – *Econometric Models of Education: Some Applications*, 1965;
    – *Mathematical Models in Educational Planning,* 1967;
    – *Efficiency in Resource Utilisation in Education*, 1969;
    – *Budgeting, Programme Analysis and Cost-Effectiveness in Educational Planning*, 1968.

30. See P. Levasseur: "A Study of Inter-Relationships between Education, Manpower and the Economy" in *Socio-Econ. Plan. Sci.*, Vol. 2, 1969, pp. 269-295.

31. *SOM*: *A Simulation Model of the Education System*, OECD, 1970.

32. See, in particular: *Systems Analysis for Educational Planning: Selected Annotated Bibliography*, OECD, 1969.

33. *Decision-Making in Educational Systems: The Experience in Three OECD Countries – Vol. I: Synthesis and Evaluation; Vol. II: Country reports*, OECD, 1976 and 1977.

34. *Demographic Accounting and Model-Building*, OECD, 1971.

35. *Mathematical Models for the Education Sector: A Survey*, OECD, 1974.

36. *Ibid.,* p. 244.

37. *Methods and Statistical Needs for Educational Planning*, OECD, 1967. For a useful summary, see Gareth Williams, "New Horizons for Educational Planning statistics" in the

OECD Observer, No. 27, April 1967. Gareth Williams was the staff member who masterminded the whole statistics operation within the Secretariat. He had come into the OECD staff through the Human Resource Development Fellowship Programme.

38. *Classification of Educational Systems*, series of country reports, OECD, 1972-73.

39. *Educational Statistics Yearbook: Vol. I – International Tables; Vol. II – Country Tables*, OECD, 1974 and 1975.

40. *Educational Statistics in OECD Countries*, OECD, 1981.

41. See, in particular, *Education in OECD Countries*, 1986-87, which also contains a brief account of the educational statistics story recounted here as well as a discussion of the main outstanding problems in the international comparability of educational statistics.

42. For a brief description of the scheme see: *An Experiment in Planning by Six Countries, op. cit.*, pp. 10-11.

43. See, for example, *Lectures and Methodological Essays in Educational Planning*, OECD, 1966.

44. See, for example, *Manpower and Education: Fellows' Reports*, OECD, 1964.

Chapter IV

EDUCATIONAL GROWTH AND ITS LEGACIES
(mid-sixties – early seventies)

The advent of mass education, which is the hallmark of the sixties, had a profound effect on the orientation of educational policies in OECD countries. Confronted with the onslaught of demand and caught up in the runaway process of educational expansion – with educational systems bursting at their seams in trying to cope with this by-and-large autonomous phenomenon – public authorities were forced to shift their attention to how, beyond coping with numbers, their educational offerings could be made meaningful to the diversified needs of their vastly expanded and variegated clienteles. The quest for relevance and equality came to replace the primacy of the earlier concern about meeting the manpower needs of the economy. At least, there was need to demonstrate that these two objectives were not in contradiction with each other. This shift in the directions of policy, with its diverse ramifications, is the central theme of this chapter. It is also reflected in the changes which occurred in the Organisation's approach to its educational activities, beginning at around the mid-sixties. It would be convenient to deal with these changes first.

Changes within OECD: CERI and the Education Committee

In its report on the setting up of OECD, the Preparatory Committee had made specific provision for the reconstituted Organisation to conduct "operational" activities to support its programmes in a number of fields, including that of Scientific and Technical Personnel. Much of the early work of the Organisation in this area, as described in the previous two chapters, was in fact sustained by this provision and the considerable financial resources which were made available under it. Over the next three years operational activities across the OECD as a whole proliferated to such an extent that they began to be seen as distorting the central purposes of the Organisation and making too heavy a demand on its budgetary and staff resources. This was all the more serious as the costs of these activities, which in many cases (such as in STP) were formerly borne by special contributions by the US Government, were now a charge on the ordinary budget of the Organisation. These financial considerations, coupled with the felt need of streamlining the work of the Organisation along its essential policy functions and objectives, led the Council to institute a detailed *"Review of the Operational activities of the Organisation"*, which was completed in May 1964, under the leadership of Michael Harris, Deputy Secretary-General of OECD.[1]

The entire STP programme came within the remit of the review and each activity was subjected to in-depth scrutiny, for its usefulness to Member countries and its relevance to the OECD role and objectives. The general conclusion was that "probably the most significant action of the Organisation has been to initiate and encourage comprehensive long-term planning of educational investment in general and in special sectors. This should remain the principal theme of the Programme", concentrating on problems of major policy importance to Member countries. It recognised that "he role of the Organisation in this field is in part that of an innovator", and that it was important that it be in a position to point the way to corrective action; but it should do this "without becoming involved in too many experimental projects where the degree of comparability between Member states is low, or assuming the actual responsibility for measures of implementation. The latter should normally be handled by individual Member countries".

In practical terms, the net outcome of the review was three-fold:

a) a number of activities were entirely discontinued. This applied, in particular, to all the work relating to science teaching and curriculum development in science and mathematics, the "OECD having successfully accomplished its promotional objective";

b) a group of activities directly related to the training and employment of scientific and technical personnel were either to be phased out or be given a stronger policy orientation by focusing on the identification of major problems and the collection and exchange of policy relevant data. A good example of this was the work on technicians, which led to the preparation of a series of country surveys, each prepared on the basis of a standard pattern and then used for inter-country comparisons and discussion at special review meetings between two or three countries;[2]

c) for all activities, direct financial support by the Organisation for country participation was discontinued. This applied equally to country-based programmes or activities and to the financing of country participants attending OECD meetings. It contributed, in particular, to the demise of the MRP and related activities in MRP countries. The EIP group, however, was able to continue, even though henceforth financed by the respective governments.

Drastic as these changes were, it is paradoxical that they helped to strengthen rather than weaken the programme. The resulting budgetary and staff reductions were compensated by greater concentration on policy analytical work within the Secretariat, on the one hand, and, on the other, the influx of new resources from the countries themselves in financing their own participation in the programme activities. The main losers were, of course, the Mediterranean countries.[3] Even more paradoxical was the fact that out of the most negative of the conclusions of the review exercise – the discontinuation of the work on school curricula and teaching methods – was to be born the germ which eventually led to the setting up of CERI.

The genesis of CERI would make an interesting story in its own right which unfortunately cannot be recounted here in any detail. It is a story of the interplay between individual personalities and institutional circumstances, against the background of a new wave of educational aspirations and sharper new perceptions about the role of education in social progress. The chief architect of the enterprise was Michael Harris himself. His previous experience at the Ford Foundation had made him sensitive to the importance of education in social and economic development and the value of inter-country co-operation in this field if properly organised and adequately financed. In carrying out the Operational Activities Review, he paid particular attention to each one of the items under the STP programme, often drawing on the advice of independent experts. He was particularly impressed by the innovative approach which the OECD applied to its work, and by the strength of country interest in and support for these activities. Even though he had to come to the conclusion that such activities could not, in their existing form, be handled by the Organisation on a continuing basis, he saw clearly the potential which this experience held for a broader approach to educational development policies, an approach which would bring the ''qualitative'' and ''quantitative'' aspects of education together as an integrated function of educational policy planning. He encouraged the Secretariat and the Committee to begin to think along these lines.

The STP Committee itself, under the shock of the review, and now under a new Chairman, had already taken steps in this direction. Based on its own comprehensive review of its past activities in science education,[4] it set up a special group of three of its Members to draw on the broader implications of this work, by examining, in particular, the relationship between curriculum improvement and educational planning and development. The group's report was completed in 1965 and was widely disseminated. It appeared in published form the following year and was soon out of print.[5] The popularity of the report is explained partly by its brevity and the terseness of its recommendations and partly by the fact that this was the first authoritative statement by the OECD, based on a review of recent trends in research and in the actual practice of Member countries, to place curriculum issues squarely within the ambit of educational policy and planning. It also came at the right time, marked by an upsurge of interest in the relevance and quality of education to match its quantitative expansion.

Interest in the curriculum was of course already widespread among educational researchers and practitioners, but much less so among policy-makers and planners. It was to this latter group that the recommendations of the report were addressed, in an effort to bring home to them the urgent need for a new approach to curriculum construction and change, the main principles of which could be summed up as follows:

- curriculum development must be seen as an integral and continuing part of educational development policies and planning;
- a piece-meal approach to the several disciplines within the curriculum was no longer adequate; what was needed was an overall approach to the constant renewal of the contents and methods of teaching, in which the humanities and sciences are reconceived as part of a common educational goal, and which effectively caters to the different needs and interest represented in the expanded school population now drawn from all parts of the community;

– in consequence, Member countries should regard curriculum development as a continuing function which required appropriate national permanent mechanisms to deal with it; in this, co-operation with the teaching profession was essential as was the need of ensuring an adequate level of research in learning.

Thus, a central theme running through the entire report was a sense of urgency concerning the measures and attitudes to be adopted if educational systems were to be endowed with the necessary capacity for change and innovation so that they could adequately respond to the legitimate pressures and demands of modern society.

CERI was set up as a direct response to this need. Using his Ford Foundation connections, Michael Harris secured from them the offer of a grant to the Organisation of one million dollars in support of a two-year experimental programme of co-operation in educational research and innovation. In making this offer, the Foundation made it clear that the purpose was to contribute to the development of *lasting* co-operation between Member countries in this field. An essential condition of the offer, therefore, was agreement by the Organisation to examine, at the end of the experimental period, "the establishment of a continuing effort by an appreciable number of Member countries". A prerequisite to this was the drawing up of a viable initial programme of work, backed by clear evidence of country interest and willingness to actively participate in it. This was achieved through a series of meetings between the Secretariat, with Michael Harris taking the lead, Ford foundation officials and a select group of senior educational policy advisers from Member countries, particularly France, Germany, Sweden and the United Kingdom. They culminated in a final session held at Ditchley Park (UK) which was hosted by Anthony Crosland himself (the Education Minister for England and Wales). A strong advocate of a new social contract for education, Crosland had been initiated into the CERI project by one of its chief protagonists, the Oxford sociologist A. H. Halsey, whom he had appointed as a part-time adviser on research policy at the Department of Education. Halsey was later to be appointed as the first Chairman of the Governing Board of CERI.

By early 1967, a detailed proposal on the substantive and operational aspects of work under a new Centre for Educational Research and Innovation was ready to go to the OECD Council. There still remained a few organisational problems to be resolved, which need not concern us here. They mostly had to do with internal OECD and Ford Foundation politics, the Foundation showing a clear preference for the new Centre to operate at some distance from the Organisation while benefiting from its inter-governmental structures and auspices. In the end it was recognised that, for its successful launching, the new programme had to lean heavily on existing OECD work and professional and managerial capacity, even though it was essential that it be given an identity of its own in terms of its governance and objectives. The solution was to set it up within OECD, under Part II of the budget, with its own staff, Governing Board and Statutes, marginally adjusted to give it greater flexibility than those applying to Part I activities. Its objectives would focus on research, development and innovation in education, including support for pilot experimentation in these fields, and would thus be complementary to the policy-oriented character of the activities of the CSTP. It was, however, judged essential that the two programmes should work closely together and this called for their being put under the same leadership at the top. On these bases, in July 1967 the Council approved the setting up of CERI for an initial two-year period, beginning on 1 January, 1968. Ron Gass, already in charge of the work of the CSTP as Deputy Director for Scientific Affairs, and who had, in this capacity, played a leading part in the preparatory stages leading to the Council Decision, was appointed Director of the Centre, with myself as his Deputy for both CSTP and CERI, thus ensuring the joint management of all the educational activities of the Organisation which has prevailed ever since, as explained in Chapter I.

The organisational saga of CERI was not to be fully played out until 1971, when the financing of the Centre was taken over by the Member countries. The initial Ford Foundation grant, supplemented a year later by a similar grant from Royal Dutch Shell, enabled an extensive and vigorous programme to be launched, drawing on the momentum of the already established pattern of co-operation. The activities, which featured strong country components, attracted considerable interest among Member countries during this innovation-thirsty period. A wide network of supportive interest groups was created across the OECD membership, which in turn put pressure on Governments to maintain their participation in CERI. On their side, Governments found in CERI a useful instrument by which to channel their own meagre R & D resources into purposeful innovative policies and at the same time profit from the experience of others, with richer resources. They were also anxious to exert more direct influence on the programme of the Centre, through their nominees on the Governing Board, which had so far been made up of a small group of independent researchers. When the future of CERI came up for review in 1970, all the Member countries, except one, were ready to pay their share for its financing on the basis of the normal scale of country contributions to the OECD budget.

The exception was the United States. Partly for internal reasons – which involved differences of opinion between the Department of Education and the State Department – and partly for reasons of general policy with regard to the criteria governing the rate of US contributions to international organisations, the US Government did not see its way to becoming a full member of CERI at this time. That this was not a question of lack of interest or of money was made clear by the willingness of the Administration to make voluntary contributions to individual CERI projects. These contributions amounted in effect to one quarter of the total CERI budget, which corresponded to the norm of the US contribution to OECD. This arrangement was pragmatically maintained for a couple of years, after which the US became a full member under the norms and conditions applicable throughout the Organisation. Full membership by all OECD countries has been maintained even since.

The integration of CERI into the OECD structures was part of a package deal which included the transformation of the CSTP into the Education Committee. Taken together, these changes represented a deliberate act to give formal legitimisation to the educational role of the Organisation. As early as the mid-sixties, it had become clear that neither the name nor the mandate of the Committee for Scientific and Technical Personnel corresponded with the work it was doing or the problems it was tackling. In 1964 the Secretary-General had actually proposed that this be recognised by transforming it into an Education Committee, with a broader mandate; but this was not acceptable to some Member countries, particularly Germany and mainly on formal grounds to do with the delicate relationships between the Lander and the Federal Government in educational matters. (It should be noted, in this connection, that when the decision was finally taken in 1970, representation by Germany on the Education Committee invariably included both sides and similar provision was formally made for German representation on the Governing Board of CERI.)

In the years that followed, these formal objections became increasingly difficult to sustain, under the logic of the development of the programme itself, reinforced by the setting up of the purely educational body that CERI was, and changes in the perception of economic growth with emphasis on the qualitative aspects and broader objectives of such growth. This was best exemplified in the declaration of the 1970 OECD Ministerial Council which stressed that economic growth was not an end in itself, but rather an instrument for creating better conditions of life, *i.e.* economic growth being looked upon as a means to a variety of economic and social objectives. Given the reality that education serves many objectives which lie beyond the field of education, the conclusion could not be avoided that the full range of objectives of education had to be taken into account if the educational activities of the Organisation were to make their rightful contribution to economic policy; and that is was only on this basis that criteria could be established for the choices involved in the allocation of growing resources both to and within the educational sector. This line of reasoning was powerfully reinforced by the discussion at the June 1970 Conference on Policies for Education Growth (see below). It led to the inevitable conclusion that the Organisation could not properly discharge its obligation to deal with such matters unless it disposed of a body able to discuss effectively at a high level of policy responsibility and to co-operate with other bodies of the Organisation dealing with the qualitative and quantitative aspects of the growth process. The outcome was the setting up of the Education Committee, with a broader mandate than that of its predecessor, to deal with the evaluation of ''prospects and policies for educational growth and development to meet social and economic objectives, both in relation to the general problems of allocating resources and for the efficient management of resources in education as such''. The new Committee held its first meeting in Autumn, 1970.

Educational growth: patterns and problems

The changes within OECD described above illustrate the ways in which the Organisation's approach to education deliberately endeavoured to mirror the shift in educational policy realities in Member countries, at least its own interpretation of these movements, set against broader social and economic movements. Throughout the sixties, educational expansion, by its sheer size, remained the dominant feature of this shifting landscape. By the end of the decade, the ambitious targets set at the Washington Conference were fully met, and in certain cases surpassed; so much so that by 1970 education represented the biggest, and still growing rapidly, organised activity in OECD countries. About a quarter of the OECD population, *i.e.* about 180 million people, were pupils in some kind of formal education. Many others were engaged in part-time training or evening classes – perhaps the equivalent of 15-20 million when adjusted to a full-time basis. Nine million teachers – roughly 3 per cent of the population – provided educational services, not including figures on non-teaching personnel. During the decade, the number of people seeking education rose by approximately a quarter. The biggest expansion in absolute terms was in secondary education, followed by primary, though the highest *rate* of growth was in higher education. Corresponding increases occurred in the supply of teachers, with teacher input per pupil year rising about 20 per cent on average in OECD countries and at most levels of education. Educational growth resulted in an annual growth rate for educational expenditure which was considerably larger than that for national income, with the costs of education increasing by about 15 per cent a year on average in OECD countries, compared to a growth in national product of about 9-10 per cent a year.[6] If these trends were extrapolated to 1980, 10 per cent of national income would be devoted to education in eight OECD countries, 5-10 per cent in seven countries and around 5 per cent in others.

These figures are indicative of the magnitude of the educational achievements of the sixties, and of the pressures to which educational systems were subjected. With the exception of the Mediterranean countries, universal enrolment for the age-group 6-15 had been practically achieved, leading to an extension of compulsory schooling and resulting in the gradual merging of primary with lower secondary education. Voluntary enrolment in full-time upper secondary education rose sharply, ranging from one-half to two-thirds of the 16-18 age-group, according to the country. Extended facilities were also made available for part-time education and training linked with the introduction into employment. This raised new questions about the purposes and structures of upper secondary schooling and how to reconcile its terminal versus its continuing education functions in a situation in which about half of the pupils were in schools or streams which led to higher education. The generalisation of secondary education led to massive demand for higher education, enrolments here increasing by 8 per cent a year from 1960-1970, forcing governments to provide significant additional facilities and resources, as well as to create a wide range of new options and types of higher education institutions, to accommodate this demand. To all this must be added the sharp rise in the demand for early childhood education, which expanded at an annual rate of about 4-5 per cent during the decade, and the consequent need for a rethinking of its purposes, as between its custodial and educational functions.

Thus, this euphoric growth picture must be tempered with some of the harsh realities behind it. It is clear that the driving force behind growth was social demand and democratisation, sustained by the demographic boom, on the one hand, and the accelerated growth in real incomes (4 per cent a year during the period 1950-1970), on the other. No doubt, the increased output of qualified people had been adequate in global economic terms, but it also led to growing structural problems arising from a mismatch between the labour market and the educational profiles of school leavers and graduates. More significantly, massive educational expansion only very partially succeeded in increasing equality of educational opportunity or equality of income distribution. If anything, the gap between aspirations and realities became much more sharply perceptible, and this is not unrelated to the causes behind the 1968 student revolt, as we shall see below.

Moreover, the growth of education helped to dramatise the main bottlenecks that stood in the way of making it more effective in terms of its economic, social and individual goals. These bottlenecks were of three kinds: limitations on resources – financial, teachers and buildings; the difficulty in bringing about necessary structural and qualitative, including pedagogical, changes in educational systems not known for their propensity to change; and related new problems in the management and efficiency of complex and expanded educational systems. Taken together, these consequences of educational growth presented a formidable set of new challenges for educational policy and planning which were to be taken up within the Education Committee and CERI programmes. The urgency of dealing with these problems was highlighted by the student unrest movement.

The student revolt

The setting up of CERI coincided with the onset of student unrest, culminating in France in May 1968. This was of course a broader political phenomenon, reflecting the transformed relationship between the individual and society brought about by rapid economic growth, technological advance and social change and the tearing down of the national, class, professional, ideological and religious supports which bound the individual to the prevailing social structures. The spread of education contributed significantly to this process; but it remains paradoxical that educational systems in full expansion should be so drastically contested by their very clients. The process followed a more-or-less common pattern in a large number of Member countries:

- students attempt to lay grievances before university and/or government authorities;
- dissatisfaction with response to their demands lead to a determined student group taking up the issues, winning much sympathy and publicity;
- a hardening of position on the part of the authorities;
- police intervention, followed by riots;
- conversion of the student protests into a radical political movement, involving larger sections of the educational establishment and, in certain cases, of the working population.

Among official circles, and the international establishment, the topic remained taboo, generally considered as a passing aberration. Within OECD, the educational staff felt differently and, with the personal encouragement of the Secretary-General, Thorkil Kristensen, undertook a collective analysis of the phenomenon and its underlying causes. A summary of this was published in the *OECD Observer*.[7] The multifarious streams which fed student unrest were grouped under three headings:

- uncertainty as to the permanent aims of society beyond material satisfaction, and student desire to participate as adults in shaping the destiny of the university and of a new society;
- student preoccupation with professional and career prospects after graduation, particularly in the professionally unanchored disciplines;
- dissatisfaction with, and on many cases utter rejection of, the existing internal structure, organisation, contents and methods of the educational system.

One general conclusion from this analysis was that the fundamental problem which student unrest had raised – demands for participation – had come to stay and that there was need therefore to ensure a constructive outlet for it and absorb it into the framework of educational and other relevant structures. A further conclusion related to the need for universities to rethink their purposes and functions and, more particularly, how to transform the frustrated intellectual and professional potential of the social sciences and the humanities into a force in society of equal weight to science and engineering. Both of these were to influence the future directions of OECD activities. As an immediate step, a series of open and often heated discussions were organised between the Secretariat and student leaders from a number of countries, in one of which the Secretary-General himself took part. There was no immediate follow-up as such, the student movement in its radical manifestation having gradually fizzled out. But the way was paved for a more sustained analysis of the participatory movement in higher education, with the help of a small number of newly recruited staff with a student activist background.

Education and the economy: the elusive relationship

A decade of rapid economic growth, and of even more rapid educational expansion, demonstrated how outdated was the initial controversy between those favouring an economic analysis of the need for growth and those holding that policies for educational growth should respond to individual and social demand. The economic argument had, of course, provided strong support for the expansion of education in order to meet shortages in highly qualified manpower, and the production of graduates in Member countries increased more rapidly than ever before in the 1960s. In France and Japan, for instance, the stock of graduates increased by about three-quarters from 1960 to 1969, and in the United States by more than half.[8] So much so, that by the end of the decade new questions began to be raised, mostly by economists, about fears of an "over supply" of graduates, reinforced by an apparent increasing imbalance between the structure of skills and qualifications resulting from individual and social educational choices and the "needs" of the economy. That abundant supply was changing the labour market for graduates, leading to graduates experiencing difficulties in finding jobs or taking jobs below their expectations, was quite natural. But this was more the result of levels of economic activity in individual countries rather than of the nature of educational output as such. And attempts to explain the phenomenon through an analysis of costs and benefits proved as futile for long-term planning purposes as had the earlier narrow manpower approach to planning.[9]

The limitations, and outdatedness, of *global* analyses of the relationship between education and economic development were conclusively demonstrated in the classic OECD study on *"Occupational and Educational Structures of the Labour Force and Levels of Economic Development"*.[10] The report stands as a methodological monument to the study of international comparisons of the links between education, labour force and economic variables, based on the most comprehensive data available at the time to which it applied sophisticated regression analysis techniques. Its permanent interest lies as much in its methodology, representing as it does the most advanced exposition of the economics of education, as in its conclusions.

It is the latter that is of direct relevance to the discussion here and it can be simply stated: of all the efforts made to show the relationship between economic indicators and the educational profile of occupational categories the only one which proved useful was to take account of the educational stock embodied in the labour force, *i.e.*, the actual supply of qualified personnel for each category. In other words, the availability of different kinds of educational qualifications plays an important role in determining the educational profiles of different professional categories, and it is the cumulative production of the educational system which is embodied in the educational structure of the labour force as a whole. In practice, this means that manpower forecasts by levels of education should *always* be accompanied by forecasts of the education system's supply of graduates.[11]

One implication of the above conclusion – the "substitution" factor in the development of the stock of trained people – was already evident in the last stages of the work of the Organisation on scientific and technical personnel. The original concern with shortages of specific categories of such personnel had, by the mid-sixties, given way to new concerns about the utilisation of the increased number of scientists and engineers coming out of the educational systems and the consequent need of closer co-operation between education and labour market policies, on the one hand, and between educational institutions and enterprises, on the other. In this, the emphasis was put on the labour market aspects of the problem, *i.e.* quantitative adjustments to demand and supply. Discussion of these problems at two successive conferences, in 1966 and 1971,[12] showed clearly that the issue could no longer be restricted to scientific and technical personnel, but had to include the whole range of qualified manpower needed for economic and social progress.

Inevitably, this brought to the foreground the underlying *educational* problems of maintaining a vast supply of such manpower: the kind of specialised education that was needed under modern conditions of rapid social, economic and technological change; the framework of *general* education within which specialisation should be developed so as to avoid highly qualified "morons", as the student activists would call them; what were the needs for life-long learning to combat the obsolescence of high-level skills, and what were the respective roles of industry and the educational systems in these matters. It was to these issues that the future work of the Organisation in this area was addressed, marking the winding up of specific work on scientific and technical personnel with which the whole educational enterprise of OECD had begun.

The sixties in retrospect: the Educational Growth Review

Ten years after its 1961 Washington Conference on Economic Growth and Investment in Education, the OECD brought its full analytical panoply to bear on a detailed review of the educational record of the sixties. This "Educational Growth Review", as it came to be known, took the form of a series of studies on the different aspects of the development of education – in terms of numbers, structures, resources, social and economic impacts and the evolution of educational planning – which together constitute the best available comprehensive analysis of the nature and consequences of a decade of massive educational expansion. They provided the background material for a discussion of the main problems confronting education policies in the OECD countries in the years ahead, which took place at the *1970 Paris Conference on Policies for Educational Growth.*[13]

The salient features of the Educational Growth Review have been anticipated in the preceding paragraphs; others will be taken up in the next chapter. For the rest, the individual studies themselves provide an invaluable mine of information for the student of the history of education during this period. But perhaps four important conclusions can be usefully restated. Firstly, the magnitude of the quantitative task achieved. Education systems were able to increase their capacity to absorb both the post-war demographic explosion (in France, which experienced the largest increase of all the OECD countries, the number of births rose from 626 000 in 1945 to 844 000 the following year and stayed above 800 000 up to 1967) and the constant rise in the average level of education as an increasingly large fraction of each age group stayed in the education system longer and longer. Secondly, such vastly expanded educational systems raised new and urgent questions about their planning, management and administration which policy could not longer ignore. Thirdly, the fact that this expansion, though it affected all levels of societies, did not alter materially the relative chances of different socio-economic categories. "The typical history of educational expansion in the 1950s and 1960s for the OECD countries can be represented by a graph of inequality of attainment between the [various] social categories which has shifted markedly upwards without changing its slope".[14] Fourthly, and related to the above, was the demonstrated inadequacy of the traditional concepts of "effectiveness" and "efficiency" in education, derived from industrial models based on a mere quantitative relationship between inputs and outputs for a given, predetermined objective. The total equation now needed to be redefined, to include consideration of relevance and quality, change, and indeed uncertainty. The "quality" debate of the late 80s was thus prefigured in the 60s.

Looking to the seventies

Of much more immediate importance were the formal conclusions of the Conference. In their different context, they were no less significant than those of Washington ten years earlier, and the difference between the two marks the political, even more than the chronological, distance which separates the two events. They were still couched in terms of continuing educational growth against a background of equally continuing economic growth. Two weeks earlier the OECD Ministerial Council had set a collective growth objective for the decade 1970-80 an increase in the real national product in the OECD area as a whole of the order of 65 per cent. It was not to be known, of course, then that the first oil crisis would seriously upset this objective, as it was not to be foreseen that sharp demographic decline would lead to a drop in school enrolments. But what was new was the emphasis on the qualitative aspects and the social dimension of economic growth, with consequences for the allocation of resources. This new flavour was captured in the conclusions of the Paris Conference and it is what distinguishes them from those of Washington.

Insofar as these conclusions provided a broad framework for educational policy thinking in Member countries, and even more so for the development of the educational work of the Organisation during the seventies, the general guidelines for policy which they put forward are worth quoting:

"In approaching the problems of educational growth and change in the next decade, the Conference agreed to the following guidelines for policy:

  i) In the coming decade, the objectives of educational growth should be examined in their inter-relationship with the more general goals of society and the economy.
  ii) Goals for educational growth in the 1970s should be made more explicit, and where possible indicators which would measure the performance of the educational system, both in relation to educational goals as such and the contribution of education to the wider social and economic objectives, should be established.
  iii) The establishment of such goals and indicators will assist the effective allocation of resources both to and within the educational sector, and assist Member countries to make the choices between the alternative paths now open for the continued growth and change of the educational systems.
  iv) It will also assist the more effective use and management of the real and financial resources which are now becoming an over-riding necessity in the educational sector, because of the large proportion of total national resources now enjoyed in the educational sector of the OECD Member countries.
  v) It will also provide an indispensable starting point for the development of necessary qualitative changes, which must be a priority in the coming decade, leading to more effective learning processes in schools and universities, and for the establishment of priorities in research and development work to improve such processes.
  vi) Such qualitative changes can be greatly facilitated by the efficient organisation of the planning and innovation process, for which governments much accept a clear responsibility, according to their national circumstances, but which must also involve the full participation of all parties concerned".[15]

The presence at the Conference of a considerable number of Ministers of Education and other senior policy makers gave these conclusions added weight. We shall see, in the chapters that follow, the extent to which they were followed up in the actual policies of Member countries and within the OECD itself.

Notes and references

1. CES/64/22.

2. See *The Education, Training and Functions of Technicians*, series of Country Reports, OECD, 1964-1966.

3. This was part of the price they had to pay for the evolution of their OECD status – from their original categorisation as "less-developed" to "developing", then to "countries with special problems of development", before they got finally assimilated into the general OECD vocabulary.

4. STP (64)8.

5. *Modernising our Schools: Curriculum Improvement and Educational Development*, OECD, 1966.

6. Based on figures presented in *The Educational Situation in OECD Countries*, OECD, 1974.

7. G.S. Papadopoulos: "Student U Impact on Educational Systems, the Economy and Society in G", *OECD Observer*, No. 37, December 1968.

8. *The Educational Situation in OECD Countries*, *op. cit.*, p. 36.

9. See, in particular, G. Psacharopoulos: *Earnings and Education in OECD Countries*, OECD, 1975.

10. OECD, 1970. The data on which this study was based were published separately: *Statistics of the Occupational and Educational Structure of the Labour Force in 53 Countries*, OECD, 1969, together with an accompanying volume: *Further Analyses and Statistical Data*, OECD, 1971.

11. *Occupational and Educational Structures of the Labour Force,* p. 248. See also Jean-Pierre Jallade: *L'Économie des Ressources Humaines*, Paris, 1988. Jallade was the principal author of the OECD study, under the supervision of Louis Emmerij, both of them on the educational staff of the Organisation at the time, having begun their careers as OECD Human Resource Development Fellows. A useful summary of the "Economic Objectives of Education: Reflections on the OECD Experience" by Louis Emmerij can be found in the *OECD Observer*, No. 27, April 1967.

12. *Policy Conference on Highly Qualified Manpower*, OECD, 1967; *The Utilisation of Highly Qualified Personnel*, OECD, 1973.

13. The General Report of the Conference was published under the title: *Educational Policies for the 1970s*, OECD, 1971. It was accompanied by the following series of supporting studies, also published at the same time:

    – *Educational Expansion in OECD Countries since 1950;*
    – *Trends in Educational Expenditure in OECD Countries since 1950;*

– Group Disparities in Educational Participation and Achievement;
– Teaching Resources and Structural Change;
– The Development of Educational Planning;
– Education and Distribution of Income;
– Alternative Educational Futures in the United States and E : Methods, Issues and Policy Relevance.

14. *Educational Policies for the 1970s*, p. 14.

15. *Ibid.,* pp. 136-7.

Chapter V

EXPERIMENTING WITH CHANGE: PROBLEMS OF EDUCATIONAL DEVELOPMENT

(early and mid-seventies)

The Paris Conference ushered a new era in the educational work of the Organisation. Its central message was that in the 1970s policies should seek to combine quantitative growth with the fundamental qualitative changes necessary for the achievement of educational goals and the better use of resources in relation to such goals. There was thus a shift of attention from growth as such to the developmental aspects of growth, from policies for educational growth to policies for educational development. In practice, this meant closer attention to specific micro educational problems, directed at enhancing the effectiveness of educational systems, as against the more global approaches of the past. Key areas calling for such attention were identified in fair detail at the Conference and the way in which the OECD programmes responded to them is dealt with in the present Chapter and the one that follows.

Context

Compared to the sixties, these programmes give the impression of a much more diffused, though educationally more exciting, activity. This was necessarily so, in view of the range and diversity of the problems that needed to be tackled. A number of contextual considerations are necessary here to help explain the pattern underlying these diverse activities.

In the first place, in its reconstituted Education Committee and CERI, the OECD now disposed of well-established mechanisms which legitimated its role in dealing with educational issues as such. In this, the socio-economic context remained imperative, though the ''social'' came to dominate over the ''economic'', with education being increasingly seen as a *social service,* relevant to a wider range of policy objectives than in the past. These broadened objectives were evident, for example, in the increasing role assigned to education in the care of young children in their very early years of life; in the provision of services to the family in the context of a new social role for women; in the effective adjustment of young people to working life; in improving the flexibility of the labour force; in community action to influence the rapidly changing social and natural environment; and in the adjustment of individuals to new roles as their pattern of life changed. All this called for a judicious approach in the work programmes balancing problems internal to education with those of its socio-economic context.

Secondly, educational expansion provided a propitious environment for change and innovation, and for experimentation with forward-looking approaches to overall educational strategies and structures as well as the actual operation of educational systems and pedagogical applications. Here, again, a nice balance had to be maintained between continuity and change, between the realities of actual policies and longer-term alternatives.

Finally, strategic areas of educational change could not be considered in isolation of one another. "It is an iron law of educational development that no change can be self-contained".[1] Nor could they all be handled simultaneously, because resources were limited. Priorities, therefore, needed to be established; and this could not be done except within a *strategy for development,* which, reflecting the historical circumstances and needs of each country, could define a pattern for the allocation of resources. The need for such strategies, which also provided the link between the micro and macro approaches to educational development policies, was in fact strongly urged by the OECD following the Paris Conference. It was one of the principal recommendations of a report on the state of education in Member countries and on priority areas in educational policy which had been prepared at the request of the European Ministers of Education and was submitted to them at their 1973 meeting, in Berne. The recommendations of the report were generally endorsed by Ministers.[2]

With the above considerations in mind, we can now deal with the extensive activities which were undertaken in the wake of the Paris Conference, recognising, of course, that a number of them had their antecedents in earlier OECD work. The activities dealt with below cover questions of resource bottlenecks, particularly educational building and teachers; and educational innovation; its content, strategies and management. The story will continue in the next chapter which will deal with changes in educational structures; education and equality; and second generation educational policy/planning. For the sake of convenience they are treated separately, but their inter-relationships should be constantly kept in mind.

Educational Building

The origins of the OECD interest in educational building go back to the Washington Conference which took up the issue as a central component of the planning of education. As stated in the conclusions of the Conference, "it was considered of the first importance for sound educational planning and for the development of educational programmes that, ... in order to reduce building costs, research should be undertaken into methods of school building. Here the example of certain countries, such as the United Kingdom, was mentioned".[3] This recommendation was motivated by rough estimates presented to the

Conference, indicating that capital expenditure over the next decade would continue to amount to some 20 per cent of total educational expenditure.[4]

The problem was particularly acute for the less developed Member countries where it was evident from the national MRP reports that the targets set for educational expansion would impose a major effort in school building which was likely to strain resources to the limit. It was important, therefore, to explore how several new approaches to educational building problems, which were being discussed internationally at the time, might best be applied in enabling MRP countries to save on costs. Drawing on the MRP model, agreements were made in 1963/64 with the Governments of Greece, Portugal, Spain, Turkey and Yugoslavia for a joint project on Development and Economy in Educational Building (DEEB), by which national teams were set up ''to identify the measures necessary for securing the most efficient use of school building resources in the light of national targets for educational expansion and national economic circumstances''. The teams were financed jointly by the Governments concerned and the OECD Technical Assistance Programme. They worked closely with the Secretariat, under the leadership of Guy Oddie, seconded for this purpose to the Organisation from the UK Department of Education and Science (*pace* the hint given at Washington). Their reports were completed by early 1967 and were submitted to their respective governments.[5]

The work under the DEEB project was truly pioneering. In relating costs to the scale of accommodation and standards of physical performance appropriate to each type of educational establishment, it demonstrated that levels of capital expenditure could not be established without reference to educational aims, teaching methods and techniques; in other words, that decisions about school building resources could not be dissociated from the institutional structure within which broader educational policy decisions were made. School building was thus shown to be an integral part of educational development policies, and for the first time, the issues and concepts involved were brought together in a comprehensive attempt to inter-relate them. They were spelled out in analytical detail in a seminal report,[6] which drew heavily on the DEEB experience, supplemented by examples from more advanced countries, particularly the United Kingdom and the Netherlands. For many years, this report remained the standard reference for those concerned with the development of school building policies and their practical applications.

The wider applicability of the lessons learned from DEEB was formally recognised by the European Ministers of Education, who, at their Fifth Conference (Vienna, 1965), invited OECD to make available a report on the project and at the same time prepare a survey of activities in the field of school building in Member countries. This would be followed by a meeting of senior officials responsible for school building programmes to consider practical measures for institutionalising systematic international exchange of information and experience in this area. The OECD itself was not innocent of these initiatives: it recognised the pressure from Member countries for extending the scope and geographical coverage of its work, but realised that it could not sustain continuing activity on school building under its normal programme and budget, already overburdened by other priorities. Alternative management structures and special financing arrangements were necessary.

The Survey was, therefore, rapidly completed[7] and its results, together with the two OECD reports already mentioned, were considered at a series of meetings of Senior Officials, convened by the OECD in close liaison with the Council of Europe. The concluding meeting, in February 1969, recommended the setting up of "an appropriate mechanism by which this work could be carried out on a continuing basis at the international level". After considering various alternatives for the location of such a "mechanism", including an offer by the Netherlands Government to set it up and finance it within the Information Centre for School Building (I.C.S.) in Rotterdam, and having ruled out the feasibility of a separate international agency, they concluded "that the proposed mechanism should come within the framework of an existing international organisation, and for this reason recommended, as the most appropriate solution, that the OECD be invited to take the necessary measures for setting up a Special Programme under Part II of its Budget."[8] It took a few more months to negotiate the contents, management structures and financing arrangements of the new programme before it was finally accepted by the OECD Council, CERI serving as a precedent. The OECD Programme on Educational Building (PEB) became effective as from the beginning of 1972, with 18 Member countries participating. Membership, which does not include Canada, Germany, Japan or the US, has remained more or less constant ever since (with Italy absconding in the early eighties), each participating country paying its share according to the OECD norms.[9]

The central functions of the Programme – focused on "the collection and dissemination of information on aspects of school building research and development judged to be important by the participating countries" – have not changed over time. The substantive areas of concern, however, have witnessed the same evolution as those in other areas of educational policy. The initial preoccupation with quantity and speed to meet enrolment pressures has given way to more qualitatively oriented concerns, in response to changes in pedagogy, classroom organisation and educational structures, and the social and community role of the school.

Teachers

We need to be reminded of a double truism: that teacher costs represent a very high proportion of total educational expenditure – between 80 and 85 per cent in some countries – and that teachers hold the key to the effectiveness of educational systems. It is not surprising, therefore, that teacher problems have been a constant preoccupation of the OECD programmes. What *is* surprising is the fact that, though the emphasis in the approach to these problems has changed over time, according to changes in the educational, economic and political context, the problems themselves have remained essentially the same, and largely unresolved. They revolve around questions of supply and demand, of initial and in-service training, of roles and tasks and, hanging over all these, of status and remuneration. The most recent OECD report on this subject[10] shows how these various facets are inextricably intertwined and that they cannot be handled outside a holistic approach to teacher policies. The evolution towards such policies was already evident in the Organisation's work on teachers during the decade spanning the mid-sixties to the mid-seventies. In this, as in so many other areas, the 1970 Paris Conference marks a turning point.

Under the pressure of numbers, questions of supply and demand remained the dominant preoccupation throughout the sixties. The situation varied from country to country and from one level of education to another, and the STP Committee launched an extensive fact-finding survey designed to identify the size of the problem and how individual countries were coping with the situation.[11] The Survey dealt with primary and secondary school teachers. It was supplemented by a separate global analysis of the situation in higher education.[12] Preliminary results of the Survey were made available to the Paris Conference on Educational Policies for the 1970s,[13] and were subsequently elaborated in greater detail, together with their broader policy implications, in a general report.[14] Documented by actual country experience and national data, the report provides a comprehensive picture of the state of teacher policies at the end of the sixties. Only a few of the salient features of this picture can be given here.

Among these, perhaps the most striking was the evidence from the Survey that despite the sharp increase in teacher demand over the previous two decades, countries managed in almost all cases to find the necessary number of teachers, and even, in certain cases, to improve teacher/pupil ratios. But this was essentially a quantitative solution achieved mostly through palliative emergency measures. Intended as provisional, many of these measures remained in force well into the seventies exerting a negative influence on both the qualitative improvement of education and the development of coherent teacher policies. They were of two kinds: *a)* more intensive use of existing teaching staff, *e.g.* by increasing overtime and extending the retirement age of teachers; *b)* lowering of recruitment standards, including the use of uncertificated teachers, assigning subject teachers to teach subjects outside their specialities, and lowering the duration and level of courses in teacher training institutions. By the mid-sixties, in spite of some improvement, there were still, in many countries, 10-15 per cent uncertificated teachers in primary education; in secondary education the figure varied between a quarter and a fifth in general subjects and almost a third in technical subjects. Up to a third of the teaching in some subjects, particularly in science, mathematics and technology, was in the hands of improperly qualified teachers.[15]

By the end of the sixties, in spite of some persisting imbalances between supply and demand, particularly in the scientific and technical subjects, the quantitative aspects of teacher recruitment began to ease up. Available forecasts of teacher requirements in the next two decades indicated even greater improvements, facilitated by a slowing down of population growth and the increased number of graduates flowing out of higher education. Attention, therefore, began to shift to more integrated approaches to teacher policies, linking recruitment to improved standards of training, and these two together to the changing roles and tasks of teachers in a context of broader changes directed at improving the effectiveness of mass education. In this, the heritage of the sixties weighed heavily in three specific respects.

Firstly, the absence of adequate research and planning machinery for defining future requirements in an area that lies at the crossroads of quantity and quality in education. This was reflected in and aggravated by the notorious difficulties in establishing viable statistics of teacher stocks and flows, difficulties which have yet to be overcome.[16] Secondly, the hurried and vastly increased rate of recruitment had indeed rejuvenated the teaching force in all Member countries, and these new teachers were due to spend a long time in service. But their qualifications were not always up to the desired standards, and without programmes for systematic continuing training little progress could be expected in improving their performance. In-service training for these teachers, as well as for the whole of the teaching body in response to rapid educational change, emerged as an absolute priority for the future. Finally, the underlying economic structure within which the teaching profession operated was unveiled. Compared to other similar professions, it was one which was characterised by relatively low training costs, resulting in a relatively low professional status with difficult working conditions and low salary which in turn led to a very high leaving rate from the profession, certainly the highest for professions demanding a similar level of education. The feminisation of the teaching profession is largely explained by these characteristics. An upgrading of teacher training and of the status of teachers was thus seen as an essential prerequisite to attracting and retaining high quality recruits in the face of competition from other branches of economic activity.

In the light of the above, a second phase of the work was inaugurated in 1970, concentrating over the following four years on investigations into the transformation of the teacher's role under the impact of educational change, in this way situating teacher policies in the centre of the innovation process. Questions of teacher education and teacher tasks were seen to be at the heart of such policies, and it is on these two sets of issues that a number of detailed analytical studies were carried out, bringing together the latest findings from research and the actual experience of innovative approaches in Member countries. The scope and coverage of this very extensive work, whose sum total represents a first systematic attempt at integrating the quantitative and qualitative aspects of teacher policies, is reflected in the series of ensuing publications.[17]

The work aroused considerable interest in the Member countries, at a time when teacher shortages were in many cases beginning to give way to teacher surpluses and when interest in innovation was spreading rapidly, fanned by political pressures and even more so by the sudden eruption of a new breed of social researchers cashing in on this bonanza. To extract the practical implications for policy, the Education Committee set up a special Working Party on Teachers, with the immediate task of preparing an Intergovernmental Conference on Teacher Policies. The Conference was held in Paris, in November 1974. It was a prestigious event, particularly notable for the quality of the analytical material at its disposal and the policy structure which was derived from it to guide the discussions, built around four sets of issues: the changing context of the professional activity of teaching; changes in working conditions and needs for teachers; new standards for teacher education; the consequences for costs and planning. These were issues normally dealt with by different governmental agencies, and not the least value of the Conference was in demonstrating the need for a co-ordinated approach to them.[18] In addition, for the first time teacher organisations, through TUAC, were strongly represented at an intergovernmental discussion of issues vital to their profession. They were thus able to put their views to governments, calmly, but none-the-less forcefully, in the relaxed atmosphere of an international debate, in contrast to the more polemical confrontations which are a feature of discussions of this topic at national levels.

No prescriptive recommendations emerged from the Conference, but a reading of its proceedings and conclusions[19] brings out its value as an educative exercise. It definitely helped to set the agenda for teacher policies and to identify priorities, for both governmental action and for research, over the next decade. Of these, three stand out most clearly: the upgrading of initial teacher education; the imperative need for sustained continuing education for teachers; and the redefinition of teacher tasks in the general context of the renovation of educational systems and also essential to the development of more realistic approaches to calculating future teacher requirements. Innovation became the dominant consideration, and provided the leitmotif for further OECD work on teachers, both in the Education Committee and, more particularly, CERI, over the next few years.[20] By the time the results of this further work were put together in a general report[21] the whole political context of education had significantly changed, as we shall see in another chapter.

Innovation: strategies, management and process

The educational scene at the turn of the sixties was marked by a veritable innovation fever, generated by the widely felt need for change, particularly at secondary and higher education levels which bore the brunt of the educational explosion. Change advocacy emanated from a variety of sources and motivations, ranging from the search for greater efficiency in resource utilisation to the quest of improved educational effectiveness in terms of individual development, the quality of life and equality of opportunity. Three general strands in the innovation movement stand out:

a) there was a marked tendency to assimilate educational change into the broader process of social change. This led to corresponding attempts to develop a coherent theory of educational innovation as a process which could and should be properly organised and managed. Piecemeal reform was ineffectual;

b) however, there was also recognition that the research/development/ application model which applies to science and technology could not be the basis for explaining the complexities of social change, and could not therefore be used for organising the change process in education; hence the importance of giving priority not to research as such, but rather to developmental work and experimentation, widespread throughout the educational system, decentralised in control and based in the school and the university system itself;

c) this was accompanied by similar recognition of the need to arrive at a better understanding of how the innovation process works and to create the roles, skills and professional training needed for an effective process of educational change. This implied a different role for central government from the traditional one which saw legislative action as the principal instigator or instrument of such change.

All three strands are represented in the extensive work on educational change on which the Organisation embarked as from the end of the sixties, through its newly set up centre for Educational Research and Innovation.

It should be remembered that the year in which CERI was set up, 1968, was dominated by the educational effervescence caused by the student revolt and the feeling to which it gave rise that there was a sort of crisis in the relations between education and society. It is not possible, here, to cover in any detail the wide variety of activities, necessarily often of an ad hoc nature during the early life of CERI, that were launched in response to this situation.[22] Only a synoptic account can be given, concentrating on those activities which were directly concerned with innovation policies, practices and processes, and the substantive areas of their application. Others will be dealt with later, according to their thematic relevance.

A first task was to get to grips with the plethora of innovations that educational systems were witnessing at the time. There was a general feeling, shared widely among educationists and politicians, that many of these innovations were ill-prepared, with no clear definition of aims and objectives, little appreciation of possible side-effects and an almost total absence of any attempt at a systematic appraisal of their progress and coherence. What seemed to be needed, therefore, was the development of a *policy framework* within which educational innovations could be articulated, informed by better understanding of the innovation process itself. A seminal step in this direction was taken at a CERI ''Workshop on the Management of Innovation in Education'', held at St. John's College, Cambridge, in July 1969, officially sponsored by the Governments of the Netherlands, Norway, Sweden and the United Kingdom. Preparatory work for the workshop had resulted in a series of commissioned papers dealing with various aspects of the theory and practice of innovation as well as an analytical framework of the main stages in the process of innovation covering: planning/utilisation/creation; construction/design/production; trial/experimentation; evaluation/revision; dissemination/diffusion. The report which resulted from the workshop[23] provided a skeleton framework for the elaboration of guiding principles for the development of educational innovation policies and their practical applications. It also charted out the principal substantive areas in education which called for urgent attention, and on which future CERI work was to concentrate.

At the policy level, the Cambridge Workshop provided an authoritative stimulus to the building up of national capacity to sustain the necessary rate of educational change and innovation. In this, it was fully recognised that a wide range of policies and instruments would need to come into play; but as a first practical step the CERI Governing Board proposed that ''all OECD countries should draw up an Educational Development Programme and establish an educational Innovation Agency to co-ordinate and promote the development and experimental work necessary for its implementation''.[24] Such agencies – in the form of 'National Councils'' or ''Boards of Education'', ''Schools Councils'', ''Curriculum Development Centres'', etc., – were already operative in a number of countries. The recommendation, thus, fell on fertile ground and helped reinforce the position of educational innovation groups and institutions and their integration into the policy-making structures. One is reminded of the effect of similar OECD recommendations ten years earlier on the setting up or strengthening of national educational planning mechanisms.

At the operational level, the most direct follow-up to the Cambridge Workshop was a massive attempt, through a series of case-studies, to arrive at a better understanding of the change process in education in relation to its political, administrative, organisational and educational dimensions. Seventeen such case-studies were carried out, representing notable innovation examples at the central, regional and school levels. This wide coverage was felt essential in recognition of the fact that the influence of various forces in the innovation process operate at one or more of these levels. For analytical purposes, the case-studies were grouped under four categories of innovation concerns: objectives and functions of the school; the organisation and administration of the educational system; role definitions and role relationships; the teaching/learning process, its aims, content, evaluation and the internal organisation of instruction. As a basis for the analysis, a process-oriented model of innovation was used, developed in North America and usually referred to as the "planning-research-development-diffusion model".[25]

It was a monumental enterprise, involving the professional and organisational efforts of a considerable number of people. The marshalling of some twenty-four among the leading researchers in the field to work together within a coherent framework for the analysis of the change process in education was in itself quite a remarkable achievement. As a record of the state of educational innovation and the identification of the broad features of an innovation system that could respond to the needs of the time, it remains unique. What perhaps is more controversial was the underlying assumption of innovation as a "manageable" process, implying a voluntarist concept of educational change, with technocratic undertones of social engineering. It does not, therefore, come as a surprise that the next step in this work focused on the management of educational change and, more particularly on the development and dissemination of the knowledge and skills necessary to sustain the innovation process. This took the form of a special, and quite substantial, programme on *International Training for the Management of Education Change* (IMTEC), under which a series of international training courses were held annually in different Member countries, well attended by middle-level educational leaders. The programme developed a life of its own and in 1973 it was established as a decentralised project, with its own finance and Steering Committee. Subsequently, it was relocated to Oslo, with the Norwegian Government providing financing and logistical support. It was discontinued as an OECD activity in 1976, but IMTEC has continued to operate ever since as an independent organisation, under the same acronym although with a more diversified mandate.

It had fulfilled a useful function, meeting a much felt need at the time in propagating a certain perception of educational change and in helping create a wide network of "innovation managers" in Member countries. It was particularly useful to those countries which, because of their relative paucity in innovation paradigms, did not themselves have an indigenous capacity to sustain the training of their personnel in this field. This was especially so for the non-English speaking countries, as the bulk of the material for the training courses derived from Anglo-Saxon, particularly North-American, and Nordic experience.[26] In a very real sense, IMTEC had served as a mechanism for the transfer to Latin culture countries of the rich experience of educational innovation available in the Anglo-Saxon world.

Higher education management

The management of educational change described above dealt exclusively with schools. Similar concerns, but of a different order, existed at the level of higher education and these were dealt with in a separate set of activities, resulting eventually in the setting up of the *Programme on Institutional Management in Higher Education* (IMHE).

From the beginning, the distinctive feature of this work was its dedication to improving the management functions within higher education establishments, *i.e.* a concentration on problems of *institutional* management as against the management of overall change in higher education policies. As in so many other areas, the initial stimulus was provided by the rapid development of systematic analytical approaches to these problems in North America, much of which was already evident in the Organisation's work on quantitative analysis techniques and mathematical models described in an earlier chapter. For most European universities, the study of such techniques, let alone their application, was quite a novel aspect; and the information base for them was critically lacking, at a time when institutional objectives were changing under the pressure of student numbers, governmental reforms of higher education systems and evident resource limitations. A first important step in sensitising Europeans to these problems was taken in 1969 at an OECD Conference on *University Planning and Management Techniques,* widely attended by university rectors and administrators, as well as by governmental representatives. The presence of the latter was indicative of a growing interest by governments to encourage institutional leaders to become more management conscious – recognising that, under the autonomy which universities traditionally enjoyed, and defended, opportunities for direct intervention were limited. This remained a feature which marked the whole subsequent history of the IMHE programme and partly explains the continued support which it has received from both governments and institutions. (It is worthy of note that in a number of cases, *e.g.*, Germany and Sweden, membership fees for institutions participating in the programme were, at least initially, paid by governments.)

The report of the Conference[27] brings out the wide range of management issues which called for further research and empirical analysis. CERI provided an ideal setting for such work and over the next two years (1969-71) a vigorous programme was mounted, with individual universities in various European Member countries undertaking pilot studies in selected specific topics covering finance, information systems, physical plant and equipment, academic planning, student flows, participation in decision-making. The reports which resulted from these studies,[28] complemented by centrally organised data collection and analysis of a comparative nature, were brought together at a major Evaluation Conference organised in November, 1971.[29] It was this Conference that formally recognised the need for continued co-operation among institutions of higher education in this field and proposed the setting up of a special Programme to ensure this. Out of this proposal IMHE eventually emerged as a decentralised, self-financing project, supervised by its own Directing Group, in the form in which it has continued ever since.[30]

That IMHE has been a success story is in no doubt: the most tangible evidence for this is the continuous growth in its membership over the years, in spite of mounting costs – about 50 when it started to over 150 now. Many factors account for this success: the specificity of its objectives; its uniqueness, particularly within the European setting which contributes the bulk of its membership; its relative freedom from the control of governments, but which does not prevent it from relating to governmental concerns through its OECD affiliation; the vested interest of its direct clientele – university planning, administrative and budget personnel – who find in the Programme a useful forum for discussing their own roles and how they should respond to their enlarged responsibilities consequent on the growing devolution of decision-making to the institutional level. Above all, there is the proven capacity of the Programme to adjust its methods and activities to shifts in priorities and changes in the general climate of higher education. Thus, the initial emphasis on institutional research and self-study gave way to co-operative research and training and then to dialogue and exchange. In a similar way, in terms of substance, there has been a shift from the early concern with management techniques, resource allocation models,[31] and information systems[32] to problems of assessing institutional performance, maintaining institutional vitality in a changing economic climate and managerial responses to changing functions, to quote only a few examples. In all this, it has established itself as a recognised international forum for the dissemination of the most up-to-date management experience, as attested by the popularity of its biennial General Conference and the kudos of its *International Journal of Institutional Management in Higher Education* (recently renamed *Higher Education Management*) through which the results of its activities are regularly reported.

Focus on the school

In many respects, the "management movement" in educational change, exemplified by the IMTEC and IMHE programmes described above, represented a particular view of innovation, as something which could be normatively promoted through organisational processes and structures. That *training* came to be the dominant component of both programmes is indicative of their underlying philosophies. Yet it was recognised that such management training could not operate in a vacuum. It had to build on the multiform changes which educational systems were experiencing at the time as they struggled to adjust their structures, objectives and practices to new perceptions of their role in societies marked by rapid technological advance, increasing affluence and growing demands for equality.

Many of these changes were generated by creative forces within the educational system; others were propelled by outside factors. But in all cases the focus of attention was the *school* itself; and this at a time when the very notion of the school as an institution was dramatically – even though without lasting effect – contested by the so-called de-schooling movement. (Ivan Illich's *De-Schooling Society* appeared in 1970). Traditionally the corner-stones of social stability and continuity, schools saw their educational role increasingly merged with their new functions as instruments of social change and service to the community. The two were not always compatible, their relative weight reflecting broader political stances prevailing in individual countries, including attitudes to the role of governments in the management and control of educational systems.

Thus, if one is looking for a central theme around which the innovation debate during that time can be articulated it could be this: how these two roles of the schools can be reconciled and the extent to which the changes necessary to bring this about can be achieved through an organised process of innovation, but one which does not stifle the creativeness of the individual teacher and school. This, at least, is the thread that runs through the wide range of OECD activities undertaken in response to these dilemmas. With the school as their primary focus, these activities dealt with each of the main factors that affect the quality of the teaching/learning process, its contents, methods and evaluation, and contribute to the creative capacity of the individual school to generate sustainable change and respond to its social environment. A theme common to all these activities was the advocacy of more active participatory roles by all the actors involved – the school as an entity, the individual teachers and their pupils, parents and the community – as a prerequisite to successful innovation. A constant objective underlying all this work was to facilitate the international transfer of innovative teaching and learning programmes and materials developed nationally and, more generally, to strengthen the arrangements for international exchange on educational innovation. (To this end, in addition to its general programme, CERI devised a series of specific projects under its "Innovation Exchange" rubrique, designed to facilitate co-operation among groups of countries on topics of particular interest to them. Representative examples of such regional co-operation were the Mediterranean Educational Innovation Programme, German-Speaking Seminars, US/Europe Seminars on the management of large school systems, and the "Pacific Circle"[32a], many of which have continued to the present day, largely financed by the countries directly involved.)

We have already seen how the work on *Teachers* came to focus on the central role which they occupied in the innovation process and how teacher policies needed to be redesigned to take this into account, with extended and renovated systems of in-service training as a top priority. It was only logical that the next area to be tackled was that of the *Curriculum,* picking up the thread of the work in the sixties, but placing it in a broader context of "teaching-learning systems", *i.e.* all the learning experiences provided by schools, and drawing on the large body of knowledge on curriculum development issues which had emerged in the meantime. In a matter as culturally sensitive as the curriculum, the initial approach had necessarily to be cautious, concentrating on general principles and common problems, on the one hand, and on technical methods to changing the curriculum, on the other. Two early reports illustrate this approach.[33] In addition to their intrinsic value as records of the state-of-the-art, they demonstrated the advantages of the exchange of experience between Members countries in an area which so far had been regarded as pertaining to domestic issues and thus paved the way for the habit of co-operation in curriculum development which developed rapidly under the CERI programme. Moreover, in placing the curriculum at the centre of the educational change process; in laying the myth of a conflict between content and pedagogy in this process; and in demonstrating that curriculum development "is not a cold, objective, scientific exercise with right and wrong answers which can be derived from research, but an expression of a whole range of social, political and pedagogical goals, like the rest of the educational process",[34] they pointed to the main substantive directions which such co-operation should take.

It was in direct response to this initial work that, at the request of a number of countries concerned with establishing policies for curriculum development, CERI was invited to carry out a more systematic analysis and appraisal of the experience of different countries in this field. Over the next three years, an international team of leading curriculum development leaders and researchers worked on this, resulting in the preparation of a *Handbook on Curriculum Development*.[35] Despite its title, the Handbook was not a simplified manual for practitioners. Drawing on multinational examples, including a series of nationally organised seminars for curriculum developers, it was rather a critical analysis of contemporary curriculum thinking and practice, consolidating information on some of the crucial curriculum changes planned within national systems which could contribute towards the formulation of new policies and strategies. Two such strategies were particularly explored: those based on curriculum project teams; and those in which planned curriculum change was integrated with broader policies for educational and social change. But it was also recognised that there existed a wide variety of change processes in curriculum reform for which the term strategy was not applicable, but which were nevertheless important and might indeed be the most appropriate form of progress in certain situations; for example, the revision of textbooks and teaching materials.[36]

One lesson that could be clearly drawn from this study was that changes in the curriculum are a long-term process, calling for careful preparation, experimentation, gradual application supported by teacher training and most importantly, *the active involvement of the schools themselves,* including teachers and pupils. It was this last aspect – the call for more active and direct school participation in educational innovation – that led to the development of the concept of ''School-Based Curriculum Development'' (SBCD) and on which the next phase of the work was to concentrate, merging it with the parallel work on teachers and school creativity. The inspiration came from a double source: the general political trend of growing demands for increased autonomy and participation in the management of all sectors of public life – for which the schools were clamouring just as loudly as the others;[37] and accumulating evidence that centrally-geared curriculum development programmes had been by and large less successful than expected, either because they were too far removed from the realities, needs and specific characteristics of each school affected and/or they failed to motivate the teaching staff called into action. In contrast, SCBD focused on the full range of organisational changes within the educational network rather than the production of new curriculum materials as such. Increased participation was seen as leading to better implementation. Many countries were experimenting with SBCD as an alternative strategy to centrally developed curricula, and this led to a series of case-studies, on the results of which a general report was prepared,[38] marking the end of an important phase of curriculum work in CERI. It was not to be taken up again until the late eighties, in quite a different educational and political context.[39] The most far-reaching conclusion of the SBCD report was that curriculum development based on the school required devolution of real authority by the central administration, giving the schools and their teachers sufficient autonomy and reasonable freedom to enable them to respond creatively, rather than adjust uncritically, to changing demands made upon them.

The preoccupation with innovation strategies, with the school as their focus, persisted throughout the seventies. It found its most elaborate and comprehensive expression in the CERI project on the *Creativity of the School.* Recognising that little practical information was available on the factors which enhance or constrain the innovative capacity of the school, the project took the form of a vast programme of investigation designed to identify the principal factors involved and analyse their potential for activating forces within the school itself to bring about change, *i.e.* to make schools more creative. Four clusters of such factors were studied: incentive systems for teachers; the internal organisation of the school; the role of the inspectorate and other external support systems; the allocation and control of financial resources. Each of these areas was explored in detail, as was the concept of "creativity" itself, drawing on actual country experience and research findings.[40]

It was this process of investigation, and the inter-country exchange among policy makers and researchers, that proved particularly useful, reflected in the strong interest which was shown throughout the duration of the project (1972-1976) by Member countries. On the substantive side of the investigation, it would be fair to say that the dominant influence was that of researchers interested in the analysis of creativity as a *process,* a feature widely shared among scholars of educational innovation at the time. And this coloured the formulation of the final findings of the project, which were embodied in the concluding report.[41] By the time these conclusions were put together, "creativity", and educational innovation more generally, had become more precarious values, getting submerged into the changed context of restricted budgets and increasing demands for accountability. This was in striking contrast to one of the main conclusions of the study, namely that "in order to be innovative the school needs adequate resources and control over their use" – where "adequate" was understood as "uncommitted resources over and above basic operational costs".

The teaching/learning process

The systematic approach to school innovation – which was the central concern of the activities described in the previous sections – could not ignore the need of developing more creative teaching and learning situations and corresponding pedagogical infrastructures. Indeed, a recurring lamentation among "innovation strategists" was the immobility of traditional, teacher-based learning systems, with the instructional process remaining essentially unchanged in its passivity and closed organisation; and this, in spite of the emergence of a new climate of more permissive pedagogies, generated by such concepts as "mastery learning", and reflected in new approaches to the structure and organisation of teaching, such as team-teaching and individualised learning, enriched by more imaginative teaching materials and teaching aids. Prominent examples of these applications had been brought out in the *Case Studies of Educational Innovation,* particularly those at *School Level,* already mentioned.[42] But these studies had also demonstrated the limited extent and impact of such reforms. They were seen as representing for the most part isolated achievements based on the work of outstanding individuals or locally inspired initiatives, failing to be generalised or even institutionalised and leaving the essentials of class teaching unaltered, thus adding fodder to the strictures fired at the school as a socially relevant educational institution by the de-schooling movement. The renovation of learning systems became a common battle cry for both the schooling and the de-schooling camps.

The main features of the OECD contribution to this debate can be briefly recounted. The initial point of entry was through *educational technology,* and the promises which the new communication methods, visual aids and the computer held for improving the teaching and learning process. It was realised from the start, that in spite of its magic appeal, there could be no technological miracle in education – that neither the television camera, nor the computer or programmed learning could provide ''instant'' education. Educational technology could not be seen as a bag of mechanical tricks, but as part of a persistent and complex endeavour of bringing pupils, teachers and technical means together in an effective way, *i.e.* the organised design and implementation of learning systems taking advantage of modern communication methods, visual aids, classroom organisation and teaching methods. This was the principal message of an early report on this subject,[43] which concluded with a set of specific guidelines on how such integrated learning systems could be designed and implemented as part of overall innovation policies – conclusions which were not dissimilar to those emerging from parallel activities on curriculum development and the creativity of the school. But at least one new feature was specifically stressed: the large-scale production and distribution of learning systems required new forms of co-operation between developers of such systems, producers, publishers, users (*i.e.* teachers and students) and educational authorities. In other words, effective arrangements had to be made to ensure that the educational system as a whole could respond to the rapid growth of educational products developed by private firms for sale in the educational market and to do this in ways which did not allow commercial interests to dictate educational objectives and practices.

In these new industrial products, the *computer* was of course of special fascination and it is not surprising that its potential, both as a scientific subject in its own right (based on the algorithmic logic used in computer programming) and as an aid to teaching and learning, came under detailed investigation from the late sixties onwards. As an educational tool for general use its costs were still prohibitive and initial attention concentrated on the use of the computer in higher education where its cost was considered reasonable in relation to the level of expenditure. The hope, in fact, was that the advent of the computer would help relieve some of the logistics of mass higher education, in addition to improving the instructional process itself. In actual practice, it was the latter dimension which dominated this early work, with the accent on developing the programming languages and other techniques, still in their infancy, for computer-based and computer-assisted instruction with which a number of universities were already experimenting and were eager to share their experience. In this, the CERI programme provided a useful and much needed forum of catalytic support and critical analysis, not the least value of which was to relate university initiatives and interests to governmental policies in this area.[44] Out of this work arose an extensive programme of inter-country co-operation on ''Computer-Based Learning Systems for Universities'', leading to the creation, in 1972, of a special unit at the University of Louvain, Belgium, initially as a decentralised project of CERI, to co-ordinate research in, and exchange of information on, all aspects of the use of the computers in higher education, in both teaching and research.

At the school level, the initial concern focused on what should be taught about computers to secondary school pupils, and in particular the place of "computer science" in the curriculum. The computer was rapidly becoming an important part of the technological environment which children had to understand if as adults they were to escape from either undue wonder or exaggerated fear. In addition, the whole system of information concepts, in which "software" was more important than the computer itself, was leading to the development of a budding science based on algorithmic constructs which opened up new forms of logical reasoning and problem solving, a "language" which many claimed was as fundamental as mathematics or natural language itself. As such, it had to find a place in the school curriculum, a by no means easy matter considering all the other pressures on the schools to change teaching content and methods. The fact that computer science was still at an early stage of development added to the complexity of the issues involved, at technical as well as policy levels. These complex issues were aired in detail at an international conference in 1970 hosted by the French authorities, whose discussions and conclusions were put together in a widely disseminated report.[45]

The Conference helped to sensitise educationalists to the value of computer science in schools, although opinion was divided as between those who favoured its introduction as a separate course and those, the majority, who argued in favour of integrating it with normal school subjects – but both stressing the value of the algorithmic approach and the imperative need for teacher training. In the follow-up to the Conference, over the next three years, both sides received satisfaction. A specialist working group was charged with the design of an actual computer science syllabus for all secondary school pupils,[46] drawing on the experience of Member countries; while a series of panels of experts examined the impact of computer science on the teaching of specific subjects – physics, biology and chemistry, human and social sciences, and mathematics. The concluding report,[47] rather paradoxically, took a more sceptical view of the educational possibilities of this new technology from the one originally held out. In stressing the criterion that "the computer should be used within the teaching/learning system only for tasks that either it alone can fulfil *or* that it can carry out markedly better than any other resource, all within the limitations of economic possibilities", it ruled out the original emphasis on Computer Assisted Instruction and on drill and practice as at the moment inappropriate at school level, mainly because of costs. Concentration should rather be on "simulation and modelling" and on limited aspects of Computer Managed Instruction, with which the Japanese were experimenting. This dampening of enthusiasm marked the end of this phase of CERI work. It was to be taken up again in the changed circumstances of the eighties, with the spread of new information technologies. (It is to be noted that, as part of this early phase of CERI work, an International Centre for the collection and dissemination of information on computer research and experimentation relevant to schools at secondary level was set up at Edinburgh, with the active support of virtually all Member countries. Financial stringency caused most contributors to retire in 1976 and the work of the Centre was discontinued.)

If no pedagogical breakthroughs could be expected from the computer sciences, and from educational technology more broadly defined,[48] what contribution could the "*learning sciences*" make to guide innovation policies and practice? This question was squarely faced from the very early years of CERI with a project on "Science and Pedagogy", the first result of which was the preparation of an annotated survey of the work of the Geneva School, published subsequently under the title: *Piagetian Inventories: The Experiments of Jean Piaget.*[49] It was an encouraging beginning which led to the establishment of a more ambitious activity – the "International Learning Sciences Programme" (PISA) – designed to foster the development of research on factors affecting formal and informal learning, taking into account the full range of relevant research in the social and biological sciences. A number of interesting research papers by leading researchers were produced.[50] Yet the programme took no roots in the intergovernmental setting within which CERI operates; in fact it became highly controversial, in terms of both its outcomes and relevance, and was discontinued in 1977, never to be revived. One is tempted to ask why?

The central aim of the activity was to tap relevant scientific findings for their applied use in education. That this was perfectly appropriate to the CERI role and mandate is not in doubt. However, in the absence of a "science of education", there was the problem of deciding what was "relevant", of making choices among the wide-ranging fields of science relevant to education, without becoming hostage to any one particular school of professional researchers. And this was not simply a question of methodologies, but rather of the values and motivations underlying scientific activity – with the concomitant danger that an uncritical application of such scientific findings to education could amount to a caricature of the scientific process.[51] It was to this fundamental and politically sensitive objection that the project failed to produce convincing arguments, and on which it finally foundered. At stake was the issue of who has authority over the knowledge base and who regulates the value structures in education.

Policies for educational R & D and innovation

The experience with the "learning sciences" described above provided clear demonstration of the tensions which still prevailed between the goals of academic and of developmental research; and this in spite of an evident trend during the previous decade to bring the two closer together as countries began to grope with the establishment of more coherent policies for educational innovation; R & D was seen to be an essential part of such policies, as the Educational Policy Reviews of Norway and Sweden had shown. An even more striking example was provided by the United States Review, which, as we have seen, was exclusively concerned with the role of the Federal Government in educational R & D, with the accent on the financial, institutional and political aspects of the relationship between government and science in this field, contrasting sharply with the weak position of R & D which prevailed in the majority of other OECD, particularly European, countries.

These differences in the role, volume and purpose of R & D between the two shores of the Atlantic were dramatically demonstrated in a state-of-the-art report which was prepared under the Education Committee programme in the early seventies.[52] The paucity of the information and data sources on which the Survey drew was itself indicative of the uncertain status of R & D on the European side. Whereas the functions of knowledge production and development were well established – in institutions of higher learning, in research centres and in developmental agencies – functions directed at supporting research, and the dissemination and application of its findings, enjoyed a much less-established status. There was no shortage of bodies contributing to the definition of research policies, but this was seldom the outcome of deliberate policy favouring the overlapping of responsibilities, as was the case in Norway with its research model based on the provision of "informative" as opposed to "prescriptive", criticism.[53] It consisted rather in the juxtaposition of different agencies created at different times and with different purposes, with little care for their functional relationships or their links to planning and policy-making. Particularly striking was the low level of R & D financing and personnel. With the exception of Sweden and the United States, in no country did the proportion of the educational budget devoted to R & D exceed 0.5 per cent; in the majority of countries it was less – sometimes much less – than 0.1 per cent.

Yet the picture was not entirely dismal. Country forecasts pointed to considerably increased financial investments over the next few years, with similar expansion foreseen in relation to personnel, leading to expectations of a decisive take-off by the mid-seventies. There were also clear signs of increasing concern for co-ordination and planning which had already taken root in the Northern European countries and was spreading to the southern countries as well. Ad hoc initiatives and laissez-faire policies were steadily giving way to different forms of integration and more structured organisation, according to country circumstances. Policies for R & D were beginning to come of age and in this the conclusions of the OECD Survey provided a useful impetus.[54]

The next requirement was to drive home the point that it was essential that such policies should be viewed together with policies for educational innovation and that both had to be related to the broader process of social change in which educational change is embedded. To propagate this, the Education Committee, with the approval of the OECD Council, took the unprecedented step of issuing a formal and carefully worded *Statement* on the general concepts which should guide the formulation and development of policies for innovation, research and development in education, thus bringing together, in succinct form, the analysis and findings emerging from the totality of OECD work in these areas.[55] That such a *Statement* on such complex issues could be put together and get the agreement of all Member countries was an indication of the level of political interest which surrounded educational change at the time.

Recognising that policies for R & D and Innovation and the machinery for implementing them were bound to be pluralistic and idiosyncratic to take account of the political and administrative structures of individual countries, the *Statement* was articulated around three principal axes:
- creating an environment within which the school can innovate, as the first essential prerequisite;
- the need for formulating an indicative strategy for the future development of the educational system;
- the possibilities and limitations of direct intervention by the public authorities in the process of educational innovation.

Under each of these themes the principal requirements of policy-making were clearly identified and their implications spelled out in terms which were applicable across the different politico-administrative systems of the OECD membership. A re-reading of the *Statement* today shows that its basic precepts and recommendations have stood the test of time.

Notes and references

1. Kogan, *op. cit.,* p. 49.

2. See *The Educational Situation in OECD Countries*, OECD, 1974.

3. *Policy Conference on Economic Growth and Investment in Education*, p. 13.

4. *Ibid.,* pp. 44-45.

5. For a detailed description of the DEEB project and its results see: *Development and Economy in Educational Building*, OECD, 1968.

6. *School Building Resources and their Effective Use*, Guy Oddie, OECD, 1966.

7. *Survey of Planning, Research and Development in the Field of School Building in OECD Member Countries*, OECD, 1968-69.

8. The discussions and conclusions of the Senior Officials are reported in document DAS/ EID/69.10, OECD, March 1969.

9. This arrangement has continued to apply even after a final change in the status of the Programme in the early eighties when, for overall budgetary reasons, PEB, together with IMHE, was removed altogether from the Organisation's Programme Budget, but allowed to operate, under a special status within the normal OECD administrative, financial and management procedures. This special status was conceived as a practical solution to the expressed interest of participating countries in maintaining their co-operation in this field, but without burdening the budget of the Organisation as such.

10. *The Teacher To-day*, OECD, 1990.

11. See *Study on Teachers*, series of Country reports and Statistical Data, OECD, 1968-69.

12. *Quantitative Trends in Teaching Staff in Higher Education,* OECD, 1971.

13. *Vol. V: Teaching Resources and Structual Change*, OECD, 1971.

14. *Training, Recruitment and Utilisation of Teachers in Primary and Secondary Education.* OECD, 1971.

15. *Ibid.,* pp. 21-16.

16. For a discussion of this problem see: *Statistics on Teaching Personnel: Needs and Methods*, OECD, 1983.

17. The Teacher and Educational Change: A New Role.
   Vol. I – General Report, OECD, 1974.
   Vol. II – Recent Trends in Teacher Recruitment, OECD, 1974.
   New Patterns of Teacher Education and Tasks: General Analyses, OECD, 1974.

The Development of Student-Teachers: A Comprehensive Study of Professional Socialisation, OECD, 1974.
Country Experiences:
  Belgium, France, United Kingdom, OECD, 1974.
  Sweden, OECD, 1974.
  United States, OECD, 1974.
  Canada and Japan, OECD, 1976.
Teachers as Innovators, OECD, 1976.
Institutions Responsible for Teacher Training: Issues and New Trends in Some Europe an Countries and in North America, OECD, 1975.

18. It is interesting to note that, in the case of the US, which sent a very large delegation to the Conference, the members of this delegation constituted themselves into the **US OECD Forum of Education Organisation Leader**s which met on at least three subsequent occasions to discuss the co-ordination of teacher policies across the country on the basis of the recommendations of the Conference.

19. *Teacher Policies: General Report of the Conference*, OECD, 1976.

20. See, in particular, *Teacher Tasks in Innovative Schools*, Vols. I, II and III, OECD, 1977; and *Innovation in In-Service Education and Training of Teachers: Practice and Theory*, OECD/CERI, 1978, together with accompanying *Country Reports*.

21. *Teacher Policies in a New Context*, OECD, 1979.

22. For a useful summary see: *CERI: The First Ten Years*, OECD, 1978.

23. *The Management of Innovation in Education*, OECD/CERI, 1971.

24. *Ibid.*, pp. 5-6.

25. The case-studies were published in three volumes, *Case-Studies of Educational Innovation: Vol. I – At the Central Level*; *Vol. II – At the Regional Level; Vol. III – At the School Level*, OECD/CERI, 1973, accompanied by a final synthesis *Case-Studies of Educational Innovation: – Vol. IV – Strategies for Innovation in Education*, OECD/CERI, 1973.

26. For an example of the material produced see: *IMTEC Bibliography*, Issue No. 3, Oslo, 1975.

27. Geoffrey Lockwood: *University Planning and Management Techniques*, OECD, 1972.

28. See: *Studies in Institutional Management in Higher Education, series of reports*, OECD/CERI, 1971-1972.

29. *Institutional Management in Higher Education: Report of a Conference in Paris*, OECD/CERI, 1972.

30. For a brief summary of the origins and early years of the Programme see the IMHE brochure: *Ten Years of Service to Universities*.

31. *Institutional Resource Allocation Models in Higher Education*, OECD/IMHE, 1970.

32. *Management Information Systems in Higher Education*, OECD/IMHE, 1977.

32a. H. M. Cornell "Establishing an International Educational Consortium: The Pacific Circle Experience", *Pacific Education*, Vol. 1 (2), pp. 1-167, 1988.

33. *The Nature of the Curriculum for the Eighties and Onwards*, OECD/CERI, 1972; and *Styles of Curriculum Development*, OECD/CERI, 1972.

34. *Styles*, *op. cit.*, p. 49.

35. OECD/CERI, 1975.

36. In addition to the national curriculum seminars, a number of pilot projects were undertaken for the transfer of curriculum development projects and learning systems, by adapting specific examples from one country to the circumstances of other countries. See, for example, *The International Transfer of Micro-teaching Programmes for Teacher Education*, OECD/CERI, 1974.

37. See *Participatory Planning in Education*, OECD, 1974.

38. *School-Based Curriculum Development*, OECD/CERI, 1979.

39. Malcolm Skilbeck: *Curriculum Reform: An Overview of Trends*, OECD/CERI, 1990.

40. The progress of the work can be followed in the three preliminary reports of the project: *Creativity of the School: Report on a Workshop held at Estoril, Portugal*, OECD/CERI, 1973; *Creativity of the School: Position Papers by Member Countries*, OECD/CERI, 1975; *Creativity of the School: A Survey of Research in 12 Countries*, OECD/CERI, 1974.

41. *Creativity of the School: Conclusions of a Programme of Enquiry*, OECD/CERI, 1978.

42. *Op. cit.*, Vol. III.

43. *Educational Technology: The design and Implementation of Learning Systems*, OECD/CERI, 1971.

44. See, in particular. *The Use of Computers in Higher Education: Perspectives and Policies*, OECD/CERI, 1971.

45. *Computer Sciences in Secondary Education*, OECD/CERI, 1971.

46. *Guidelines for an Appreciation Course*, OECD/CERI, 1973.

47. *The Use of the Computer in Teaching Secondary School Subjects*, OECD/CERI, 1976.

48. A balanced statement of the possibilities and limitations of educational technology at the time was presented to the 1970 Paris Conference: "Educational Technology: Practical Issues and Implications", in *Teaching Resources and Structural Change, op. cit.*, p. 149 ff.

49. OECD/CERI, 1977.

50. See, for example: H. Nathan, *Stable Rules: Science and Social Transmission*, 1973; B. Bernstein, *Class and Pedagogies: Visible and Invisible*, 1975; J.C. Chambredon, *Infancy as an Occupation: Towards a Sociology of Spontaneous Behaviour*, 1975; T.G.R. Bower, *Pathways in Development*, 1977; Judith Blake, *The Shadow-Price of Children*, 1978.

51. This was the essence of European criticism of the *"What Works"* publication issued by the US Department of Education in the late eighties as a guide to high quality school performance.

52. *Research and Development in Education: A Survey*, OECD, 1974.

53. See Kjell Eide: *Educational Research Policy*, OECD/CERI, 1971.

54. See, in particular, the concluding Chapter of the *Survey: "Current Strategies for Educational Research"*.

55. *Policies for Innovation and Research – and – Development in Education: A Statement of Issues and Conclusions by the OECD Education Committee*, OECD, 1974.

Chapter VI

EXPERIMENTING WITH CHANGE *(continued)*: EDUCATIONAL STRUCTURES AND STRATEGIES FOR EQUALITY

Educational change of the kind described in the previous chapter, with the accent on content, pedagogy and school organisation, proved to be a slow and often frustrating process and its results not readily visible. It was not something which could be brought about without significant new resources – which were not forthcoming – or by mere legislative fiat. This was not the case with the other side of the educational change coin, viz., reforms affecting the organisational structures of the educational system and the relationships between its various levels, branches and institutions. Ideally, the two should have gone hand-in-hand, propelled by the advent of mass education and in pursuit of the dominant objective of its effective democratisation. In practice, the two developed asymmetrically, with structural reforms advancing very rapidly without being accompanied by corresponding pedagogical adjustments. This was perhaps inevitable, given the political motivations behind many of the structural reforms, on the one side, and the traditional inertia of instructional systems, on the other. A consequence of this discrepancy was growing disillusionment in many quarters with the capability of established educational systems to further the equality of opportunity and other objectives of education. In turn, this led to the search for alternative educational strategies, among which *recurrent education* attracted the most attention. The OECD response and contribution to this, more visible, side of educational change during the sixties and early seventies will be dealt with in the present chapter.

Changes in educational structures

Organisational change in the structure of educational systems represents the most visible, and enduring, outcome of the educational reforms instituted in the wake of educational growth. It was the chosen instrument by which governments sought to influence the volume and direction of growth, and to achieve the new policy objectives and priorities set for the educational system, with their twin focus on the global expansion of educational opportunity and its social and economic relevance. This redirection of purposes and values had its most profound effects in the reorganisation of the provision of secondary and higher education, *i.e.* the two levels at which, as explained earlier, the impact of growth had been most effectively felt – highest overall increase in the case of secondary and highest rate of growth in the case of higher education. It is significant that preschool education, in spite of having witnessed a growth rate similar to that of higher education, did not begin to receive serious attention on the part of policy-makers, and of the OECD programmes, until well into the seventies. Even then, it continued in most countries to remain outside the ambit of the statutory provision of education and to be looked upon as part of broader policies for early childhood rather than for its educational role *per se*. We shall come back to this in the next chapter.

Secondary education

The development of secondary schooling, and its crucial role in a country's overall policy for educational development, occupied a prominent place in both the M.R.P. and E.I.P. programmes as well as in the series of Country Educational Policy Reviews throughout the sixties. In 1965, the European Ministers of education, at their Fifth Conference (Vienna), invited the OECD to undertake a general review of secondary education, resulting in the first international comprehensive survey of this sector, published four years later.[1] In spite of country differences, depending on their stage of development, two salient features were common to the secondary education scene as it emerged from this analysis: the extension of compulsory schooling and the emergence of the comprehensive school. The raising of the compulsory school attendance age – from 12 to 14, 15 and then to 16, depending on the country – was a policy measure based on social and political reasons, even though in practice it often merely consecrated the *de facto* situation created by increased voluntary enrolment. Its basic rationale – that the higher the proportion of the population with extended education, the better for the individuals concerned and for the well-being of society – was not contested, apart from the de-schoolers. And as late as 1969, the European Ministers of Education, at their Sixth Conference (Versailles), when they considered the results of the OECD secondary education report, could state it as their formal view "that the period of education should be extended to 11 or 12 years for all and that education be based on a broad common curriculum".[2]

The extension of compulsory schooling, resulting in the merging of primary and lower secondary education, was not unrelated to the spread of the *comprehensive school,* with its basic philosophy of providing all children with a common educational experience. Starting on an experimental basis in Norway and Sweden during the early fifties, over the next ten years or so the comprehensive school, or variations of it, took root in the majority of European countries, though still not matching the fully comprehensive high schools which had developed in Canada, Japan and the United States. As noted in the Canadian Educational Policy Review, "the most important development in the educational system of Canada in the last two decades has been the systematic build up of a public comprehensive school system, in all ten Provinces and in the two Territories administered by the Federal Government".[3] In Europe, reorganisation on comprehensive lines applied essentially to the lower secondary cycle, *e.g.*, the nine-year common school in Norway and Sweden, the *Scola Media* in Italy[4] and the *Collèges d'Enseignement Secondaire* in France. A prominent convert to the new system was the United Kingdom, where in 1965 the Department of Education and Science instructed local authorities in England and Wales to submit plans for the reorganisation of secondary schooling into a comprehensive system.[5] In Holland, where streaming at the age of twelve persisted right through the sixties, the position was radically altered, at least in intent, by the 1975 Contours Plan which moved towards a comprehensive school for 12-16 year-olds – a move which was explicitly supported by the OECD team of examiners.[6]

In a few countries, however, with strongly entrenched selective patterns of education, comprehensive schooling never took root; on the contrary, it was strongly resisted. This was particularly the case in Austria, the majority of the Lander in Germany and Switzerland, who saw the comprehensive school as a threat to the very foundations of their well-established and highly successful "dual systems". The ensuing controversy had, in fact, clear political undertones. The protagonists of comprehensive schooling were seen by the other side as being primarily inspired by social-democratic ideology, of the Scandinavian type, in support of which they amassed an impressive corpus of pedagogical arguments backed by the findings of specially commissioned research. Conversely, the defenders of selective systems were seen by their opponents as merely reflecting conservative values and mainly interested in maintaining the existing social structure. At a time when questions of social justice and equality of opportunity were at the top of the political agenda, in an economic environment as yet unclouded by stagnation, inflation or unemployment, it was only natural that the educational "conservatives" should be on the defensive. It was the precociously early and irreversible selection arrangements of these systems that came under the most severe criticism and that were the most difficult to defend. And this came out most clearly on the occasion of the Austrian Educational Policy Review – as late as 1978 – with the Austrian delegation itself admitting, during the review meeting, their concern about these constitutionally enshrined arrangements.[7] Similar concerns had been voiced during the earlier Review of Germany (1972). In this case, the situation was more complicated because of differences among the Länder: some, in particular Baden-Wurtenberg, Berlin, Bremen, Hamburg, Hessen and Nordrhein-Westfalen, were experimenting with comprehensive schooling, clearly favoured by the social-democrat Federal Government of the time, while others, headed by Bavaria, remained staunchly opposed to the idea.[8]

In its own analysis of the problems of compulsory schooling,[9] the Secretariat, while recognising the general trend towards the extended common school, underlined that the crucial issue still remained of how such schools could best operate; and this was essentially a problem calling for pedagogical, side by side with organisational and structural, reforms, directed towards greater individualisation of school instruction – with all that this implied for changes in the content and methods of teaching, in the "class" concept and in the traditional role of the teacher. Such changes were particularly relevant to improving the educational chances of socially disadvantaged children. These were, and still are, the children who constitute the bulk of the "low ability group", who leave education at the end of compulsory schooling, often "over-aged" because of repeating and consequently without having obtained any formal qualification – having, in effect, benefited little from a prolonged, but irrelevant general education and badly prepared for active life. What was needed, a subsequent OECD report argued, was nothing short of a fundamental re-examination of the total lower secondary stage, of its aims and objectives, its curricula and teaching processes and practice, and of the means, including new resources, needed to implement the necessary changes.[10] The report underlined that the starting point in any such re-examination had to be better understanding of the nature of the *adolescent* pupils from all social contexts and of the experience they underwent during this crucial stage of their development within rapidly evolving societies – noting that "the problems of the adolescent will not be solved in the schools alone; in fact, much of what should be achieved in schools may only be possible if the problems are tackled in their whole social context ... This is particularly true in relation to the disadvantaged and the steadily increasing number of delinquent adolescents".[11]

This emphasis on the psychological and social contexts of pedagogical change illustrates the complexity – and enormity – of the problems with which the comprehensive school had to grapple. They were only aggravated with time, as shown by a retrospective review of the experience with comprehensive schooling in four countries (France, Denmark, Scotland and the USA) which was carried out some ten years later.[12] Its status and desirability were not questioned; nor was its relative success in extending educational opportunity and in laying the common foundations for the subsequent social and educational progress of entire new generations. But the problem of socially biased school failure remained unresolved and many problems characteristic of earlier elitist systems were merely transferred to the various forms which comprehensive schools have taken in different countries. Above all, the alchemy has yet to be discovered of how to apply educational differentiation in ways which do not replicate, and often reinforce, differences deriving from socio-economic background. Lost educational opportunities at this early stage cannot easily be retrieved and eliminating school failure and underachievement continues to be the biggest challenge which confronts compulsory schooling, whether of the comprehensive or the selective type.

The problems posed by the selection function of educational systems comes into sharper relief when we move to the *upper secondary level.* The consolidation of generalised lower secondary education resulted in rapid enrolment increases at the post-compulsory secondary level. They more than doubled in most European countries between 1960 and 1970, amounting to some 50 per cent of the 15-18 age group, and were estimated to grow to two-thirds of the age-group by 1980. While still well below the enrolment rates in Canada, Japan and the United States, this enormous increase in numbers was bound to raise in a very compelling way the same need for structural transformation of upper secondary education as had occurred in the past with the level below. In fact, if the redefinition of the objectives and structure of compulsory schooling was the main structural issue of the sixties, the reorganisation of upper secondary education became the crucial issue from the seventies onwards.

The dilemma here was all the sharper because of the difficulty – more acute at this level than the one below – of integrating the academic (*i.e.* university entry preparation) functions served by this level of education to its technical/vocational (*i.e.* labour market entry preparation) functions. This was particularly the case in European countries, where the distinctions between general and vocational education were much sharper than those which prevailed in the non-European Member countries – with vocational education being held in lower esteem, meeted out to the poor and less gifted, reflected in the social composition of the student body and illustrating the socially biased selection which operates most dramatically at this level. In other words, the policy issue here was how to meet the rising social demand for further study without depriving the economy of needed middle-level manpower. Modifications in the relationship between general and vocational education were thus at the heart of many of the reform plans for upper secondary education which were actively pursued during the seventies. The problem is still with us today.

The approach to reform varied considerably from country to country, even if they all agreed on the need for closer links between school and real life. Two, apparently conflicting, principles were at play – differentiation and integration; and these were often used to justify quite different concepts, depending on whether the newly-proposed structures advocated extending the comprehensive model to the second cycles – as was the case with the Swedish reform of 1971 – or maintaining the differences between courses – as was the case in the majority of other countries. How these principles were translated into practice within different systems was the subject of a special OECD study,[13] undertaken as a sequel to the earlier survey of secondary schooling. Five distinct themes were identified as the focal points of attention of the different country reform plans and their operational approaches:
- the unification of the institutional framework;
- the diversification of the structure of studies;
- the integration of general education with technical and vocational education;
- the reorganisation of vocational education;
- the alternation between education and employment.

In spite of the differences, in all cases the basic aims of the reforms appeared to be the same: to introduce into specialised upper secondary education a variety of options and courses, greater flexibility and more common curricula. By analysing the content of the different reforms in terms of these common objectives, the study at least helped clarify the issues at stake and thereby lower the tone of controversy that raged around them.

With incipient youth unemployment, it was a sign of things to come that the study placed its analysis of upper secondary education in the broader context of the changed social situation of young people. In its conclusions, it emphasised that the re-organisation of study structures was an essential, but not in itself sufficient condition to bring about change meaningful to the needs and interests of the young people concerned. "The problems with which secondary schools are confronted do not boil down to simple institutional dysfunctions, but need to be analysed in relation to young people's social situation, the other possibilities open to them, and the changes that have taken place in their behaviour and expectations ... Changes in second-cycle secondary education should form one of the main aspects of a policy defined to make it easier for young people to take their place in society".[14]

Higher education: patterns of growth and diversification

Quantitative growth and structural reforms in secondary education had direct repercussions on higher education, leading to changes which were even more marked here than those at the levels below. Dominating these changes was the enormous expansion in access, of which the biggest direct cause was the increase in the numbers of secondary school graduates. So much so, that by the end of the sixties higher education was no longer for an elite, but for significantly larger sections of the population. This transformation was particularly felt in European countries, which found themselves moving towards systems of mass higher education, even though of more modest dimensions than those which prevailed across the Atlantic and in Japan. Resource constraints, among other things, forced governments to adopt more interventionist positions in attempting to shape the volume and directions of this growth and in reconciling pressures arising from spontaneous demand to social and economic requirements. More than in any other educational sector, explicit *policies* for higher education emerged as a serious and constant concern of governments.

The same is true of the OECD educational programmes. No other sector received similar continuous systematic attention over the years as that given to higher education and in no other sector was the influence of OECD work more directly felt. That the influence of OECD in the field of higher education has been considerable has been attested by outside opinion. It has in fact been suggested that "it was some sort of informal OECD network that made the expansion of higher education, and the resulting changes, thinkable".[15]

The thrust of the work varied from time to time, depending on the nature of the evolving policy concerns and priorities in the Member countries. For the period under consideration, in the aftermath of the student revolt, the accent was on getting a grip on the sources and consequences of the runaway process of growth, on management and participation in decision-making in higher education institutions (as we have already seen under IMHE above), the organisation of their courses and structure of studies, and above all on charting the future shape of the overall structure of the system so as to enable countries to adapt to the transition to mass higher education. Extensive studies were carried out in all these areas, both in the Education Committee and CERI, and their policy implications were subsequently brought together for intergovernmental discussion at a Conference on "Future Structures of Post-Secondary education", held in Paris in June 1973.

Along with technological and scientific progress and the process of urbanisation, the rapid expansion of higher education was probably one of the most visible and far-reaching aspects of social development during the two post-war decades or so. While the phenomenon was well-known, no comparative documented analysis of it as yet existed; and it is to this task that the Secretariat's initial efforts were addressed. The results, published in two volumes,[16] provided the indispensable basis for the discussion at that time of future policies in this field, as they do now for the student of the contemporary history of higher education in advanced industrialised societies. Based on country statistics on new entrants, enrolments and degrees awarded, broken down by sex, field of study and type of institution, the study and its accompanying analysis covered almost exclusively those aspects of the development of higher education which could be directly related to the evolution of student numbers. Presentation of the country data within the standardised OECD classification of educational systems (elaborated in the *Statistics Handbook*) ensured the necessary inter-country comparability.

Only a few of the more significant findings of the study can be mentioned here. They contain the germs of the predicaments which would confront higher education systems and policies in the years to come.[17] Over a period of ten to fifteen years, higher education systems across all OECD countries had to double or treble their intake capacity to cope with the growth in numbers. The rate of this expansion was roughly parallel in the university and non-university sectors, though universities were still the principal points of expansion, having received about 80 per cent of total enrolments. Though all branches of study benefited from this expansion, the biggest increases were in law, medicine, the social sciences and the humanities. In terms of socio-economic background, the increase was much more rapid for the middle and upper classes, which meant that in absolute terms the disparities in the participation rates of the different social classes had increased rather than diminished. There was steady and substantive increase in female enrolment, which in general had doubled in fifteen years, representing 15 per cent on average of the total rise in enrolments. However, the opportunities for admission of women were still only half of those of men in 1965-1966 – leaving considerable growth potential for the future.

But the most striking finding of the study was the independent nature of higher education expansion. It was affected neither by the ways in which higher education was organised and controlled, nor by the extent of aid to students or the amount of registration fees. Similarly, the rate of increase in enrolments appeared to be quite independent of admission systems, and other similar policy measures. The influence of economic variables also appeared to be minor or very indirect, so that the expansion of higher education in no way depended on levels of economic or technological development or on fluctuations in the growth rate of the National Product. The same absence of correlation was evident between the rate of increase in enrolments and the rate of increase in expenditure on higher education: the fact that such expenditure was much greater in all countries merely indicated that the expansion in enrolments had been accompanied by a general increase in unit costs. Finally, in respect of the distribution of students by field of study, the systems showed a similar degree of resistance to policy incentives, *e.g.* those designed to encourage science and technology, as in the case of other policy measures. More surprising was the limited role which the demographic factor played in the overall expansion of higher education, thus leaving the primary role for this expansion to the increase in the numbers of secondary school graduates, as already mentioned.

These were all findings deriving directly from an analysis of the quantitative and statistical aspects of the development of higher education. They show OECD analytical work at its best. Important as they were, it must not be assumed that these findings provided an adequate explanation to all the problems of higher education. They needed to be supplemented by similar analyses of qualitative and structural changes with which higher education policies, systems and institutions were confronted at the time. Innovation was as much in demand in this sector as at other levels of the educational system, even though problems were posed differently because of the relative autonomy which higher education institutions traditionally enjoyed. The expansion of higher education, and the new demands made on the system by its more variegated student body, on the one hand, and the economy and society more generally, on the other, provided countries with an opportunity to introduce and test such innovations in a variety of domains. In most cases, the two basic approaches used to implement innovation were through major overall reforms of higher education and in newly created universities and similar institutions. A representative sample of national experience at these two levels was, therefore, chosen for in-depth investigations, leading to a series of case-studies on innovation in higher education.[18]

It is extremely difficult to attempt a summary of the findings from this extensive work, dealing as it did with the idiosyncratic systems in a variety of different countries. But at least the case-studies brought out clearly an agreed set of problems, a checklist against which the effects of innovation could be assessed, thereby establishing a common language for further international exchange and discussion. These problems can be briefly enumerated: Coping with increased numbers; advancing equality of opportunity; re-organisation of the content and structure of studies, with particular reference to an interdisciplinary approach; the desired degree of specialisation of individual institutions of higher education; reform of the organisational structures, administration and management of institutions and its implications for institutional autonomy; the recruitment and status of teachers; the links between teaching and research; organisation and methods of teaching and new approaches to teacher-student relations; the role and status of students in the academic community, their participation in decision-making and in matters concerning their living conditions and material welfare; strengthening the links between higher education and the outside world and coping with the new expectations of society; improvement in evaluation, planning and accountability; and a whole set of new questions about containing costs and seeking alternative sources of financing. These are all problems which have retained their prominence in the continuing debate on higher education and which in turn would come up for re-examination in subsequent OECD work.

Among these, one specific, and particularly complex, problem came up for separate attention at this time. This was the problem of *interdisciplinarity*. It was part of the more general question of reforming the content and structure of studies, widely discussed in Member countries and representing perhaps the most striking feature of new institutions of higher learning, *i.e.* the most apparent deviation from the traditional pattern of maps of learning. It took a variety of forms: creation of pluri-disciplinary programmes; combined degrees; obligation or possibility for students to take courses belonging to different disciplines; and for teachers to belong to two or more constituent units of the university. Interdisciplinarity as such, however, remained a controversial issue, reflecting a conflict between the scientists and the pedagogues, between the interests of the individual disciplines as the basis for the organisation of knowledge, including its teaching purposes, and the multi-problem oriented needs of society, of the individual student, other than those who were destined to become scholars or researchers. This, in turn, was reflected in different attitudes as to the role and functions of the university and its organisation. What was needed at the time was careful analysis of what interdisiplinarity really was, and its real impact on teaching and research adapted to changes in both knowledge and society. This was precisely the purpose of a special CERI study, based on an analysis of the limited experience with interdisciplinary approaches across the OECD area and on discussions at an "inter-disciplinary" seminar held in Nice in September 1970.

The report which resulted from these endeavours[19] shows how well this purpose was achieved. In its clarification of the *concepts* underlying interdisciplinarity, of its epistemological and pedagogical implications and of the conflicts which they generate, the report broke new ground. It is still highly regarded to-day. Not its least merit was the demonstration it provided of the enormous difficulties that stood in the way of practical applications of interdisciplinarity, raising as they did "a whole battery of questions about the goals and functions of the university, and about the status of knowledge rather than about how it is divided up".[20] It paved the way for the more cautious, empirical realism with which interdisciplinarity was approached over the next 10-15 years, focusing on university responses to new social multidimensional problems, of which the environment, health and technology were the examples, and to which discipline-based university structures could not adequately respond, as we shall see in the next chapter. When, some fifteen years later, overall developments in interdisciplinarity were reviewed at a joint OECD/Swedish seminar, progress was shown to be still very limited. Inter-departmental co-operation had indeed grown, and new concepts such as "study areas" had evolved, particularly within the new universities. But the dominant position of the traditional structure of disciplines as the arbiters of academic respectability remained unshaken. Institutional strategies for interdisciplinarity came up against the lurking fear of intellectual marginalisation which haunted many of those committed to the concept. "The quest for academic respectability leads inevitably to a regression back to individual disciplines... Interdisciplinarity, even when it succeeds in unscrambling existing curricula, remains a hostage to the disciplines."[21]

Towards new structures of post-secondary education

The problems dealt with above were peculiar to the universities, still the preponderant sector of higher education. They were not directly the concern of governments. But the broader question on which they touched – the organisation and structure of studies – was crucial to the very objectives and functioning of the nascent, but rapidly developing non-university sector which in most countries was subject to greater public control and direction. The origins of this sector lie, in fact, in explicit strategies adopted by governments to diversify their higher education provision in response to the increasing numbers and diversity of students. For the majority of countries this meant setting up, or further developing, institutions or courses offering post-secondary education of shorter duration and with a strong vocational component, usually known as "short-cycle higher education institutions" (SCIs). Over time, this non-university sector was to establish itself as a dynamic partner within the higher education systems of many countries and come to be seen as probably the most far-reaching reform of higher education of the post-war period.

OECD work contributed to this process, some would argue significantly, through its detailed analyses of the objectives and motivations behind this reform, of the characteristics of the different institutional models which were developing in the Member countries and of the substantive issues and dilemmas which had to be tackled and resolved; and by bringing the policy implications of all this to the attention of governments in relation to both the development of the non-university sector itself and its consequences for the overall higher education system. This was done during the crucial formative years when the short-cycle sector was still searching to establish its identity. The two main reports which incorporated the results of this work had wide appeal in the Member countries.[22] Their findings can be briefly summarised.

Four main objectives and motivations were seen as lying behind the origins and rapid development of the non-university sector: to cope with the pressure of numbers; to contribute towards greater equality of opportunity; to respond to growing needs for a wide and diversified range of qualified manpower; and to generate change in the post-secondary systems as a whole by assuming a number of functions in relation to the above objectives which traditional universities could not perform, or were often reluctant to accept. The immobility of the universities made it necessary to by-pass them. But it may well be that, in some cases, this was also seen as a convenient way of protecting the universities from the armageddon of social demand for post-secondary study.

In terms of their functions and general characteristics, three broad models were identified within which existing types of SCIs could be classified:

i) *The multi-purpose model,* of which the prototype was the American Junior or Community College which had developed as a direct consequence of general-ised comprehensive secondary education, as was also the case in some of the Provinces in Canada (particularly the CEGEPs in Quebec) and, with some differences, in Japan. SCIs in this category were multi-functional institutions with highly diversified curricula ranging from purely academic programmes which prepared for continuation of studies at university to various types of general and vocational training of a terminal nature, geared to local or regional needs. The *Vise Skole* in Yugoslavia and the *District Colleges* in Norway had some of the characteristics of this model.

ii) *The specialised model,* which prevailed in the majority of European countries until the early sixties, represented by institutions designed to provide vocational post-secondary education to students from the non-academic streams of secondary schools and who, therefore, were not admissible to universities. During the late sixties, however, many European countries began introducing far-reaching reforms which brought these institutions closer to the multipurpose model, *e.g.* the creation of the *IUTs* in France and the reorganisation of the *Fachhochschulen* in Germany.

iii) *The binary model,* exemplified by the United Kingdom's further education sector developing independently of the university or autonomous sector and comprising highly diversified institutions, not only in the type and level of studies provided, but also in their patterns of study, *e.g.* sandwich courses, part-time day and evening courses, etc. Some of these institutions, mainly the *Polytechnics,* offered, independently of universities, degree-level and post-grad-uate courses while retaining their specialised and vocationally oriented raison-d'être.

Over-simplified as this classification no doubt was, it did provide a useful analytical framework within which the substantive problems facing the different types of institutions could be identified and discussed and the rapidly changing position of the whole SCI sector be kept under review.[23] Clearly, this position was dominated by the dichotomy which characterised the overall higher education sector, between its "noble" – the universities – and its "less noble" – SCIs – parts, generating the phenomenon of "academic drift", *i.e.* a trend towards institutional upgrading, an escape from the "less noble" status. Thus, many SCIs, which had originated from an upgrading of secondary schools, strove to gain university status, and often succeeded. However, in doing so they no longer fulfilled some of the main functions for which they had been created, as for example was the case with the British Colleges of Advanced Technology (CATS), and some American Junior Colleges. A similar trend was observable in some of the European SCIs which, when unable to acquire full university status, were tempted to add one or two years to the duration of their study courses so that they could be considered of university level. The dilemma between separate development or integration with the university sector was to dominate the choice of options available to SCIs in their search for identity over the next ten years or so. How this dilemma was eventually resolved was documented in a subsequent OECD study,[24] as we shall see in another chapter.

That this question lay at the heart of the wider debate in the period under consideration about policies for the overall development of higher education, was evident in the discussions at the OECD *Conference on Future Structures of Post-Secondary Education* (Paris, June 1973). "The central concern of the Conference was to examine the advent of mass higher education in its main patterns and characteristics and to identify alternative policy measures for facilitating the overall structural transformation of the system towards meeting its new objectives in the context of social and economic development."[25] Attended by Ministers, senior officials, academics and representatives of professional organisations, the Conference had at its disposal an impressive corpus of descriptive and analytical material by which, in the words of an independent observer, "the Organisation has performed for countries outside the United States many of the functions in the field of higher education that within the United States have been undertaken [over a period of six years, resulting in the issue of over one hundred titles] by the Carnegie Commission".[26] In fact, the US experience, amply presented at the Conference, served as a point of constant reference to the European countries, not so much as a model for emulation, but for the lessons it provided about the problems that arise in the transition from elitist to mass systems of higher education – brilliantly analysed in a keynote address by Martin Trow.[27]

In every advanced society, Trow argued, the problems of higher education are problems associated with growth. They arise in every part of higher education – in its finance, its government and administration; in its recruitment and selection of students; in its curriculum and forms of instruction; in its recruitment, training and socialisation of staff; in the setting and maintenance of standards; in the forms of examinations and the nature of qualifications awarded; in student housing and job placement; in motivation and morale; in the relation of research to teaching; in the relation of higher education to the secondary school system on the one hand, and to adult education on the other. Growth, in brief, has its impact on every form of activity and manifestation of higher education and these problems have to be treated together and not in isolation. It is these problems, and the need for a coherent approach to them, that provided the agenda for the detailed discussions at the Conference, by direct reference to the major reform plans in different countries. The report *Higher Education* of the Swedish U68 Commission and the United Kingdom's White Paper, *Education: A Framework for Expansion,* were but two representative examples of the different approaches used in Member countries, the former based on the idea of a comprehensive higher education system, the latter reflecting the binary model – with the German co-operative model of the *Gesamthoschscule* in between the two.

We cannot, in the space available here, do justice to the extensive coverage these problems received at the Conference, nor to its detailed conclusions. But the flavour of the preoccupations of the Conference is perhaps best caught in a single question, as summarised by the General Rapporteur:

> In planning new structures and responding to pressures and proposals emerging from within existing systems, how can societies reconcile, on the one hand, the need for institutional diversity and differentiation of programmes occasioned by widened access and new relationships between post-secondary education and employment, with, on the other, the need to maintain and enhance the values of scholarship and science, all within a politically sensitive context of limited resources, demands for greater public accountability and a process towards greater democratisation?

At the time, these questions were still discussed in a context of mounting confidence and expected continuing growth in higher education. But as growth gradually levelled out and, in many cases, began to give way to contraction, and as public confidence began to wane, these questions, though still valid, took on an increasingly sinister character which, at a similar OECD Conference ten years later, was to be translated into the notion of higher education being in crisis.[28]

The quest for equality

Central to the motivation behind the reforms of educational structures described above, and the most explicit objective promulgated in these reforms, was to bring about a fairer distribution of educational opportunities and of the social benefits deriving thereof. This was the declared intention of the spate of major national reports on education which saw the light during the sixties – such as the *Robbins, Newsom and Crowther* reports in the UK and the *U68* report in Sweden alongside the series of national reports prepared under the OECD EIP and Country Review programmes – and which lay at the origin of many of these reforms. At the same time, however, the gap between intentions and expectations, on the one hand, and actual achievements on the other, was highlighted in a series of research studies, of which the *Coleman* report in the United States was the most thoroughly documented and striking example, followed a few years later by the work of Jencks on *Inequality* (1972) and, on the European side, by Boudon's analysis in *Education, Opportunity and Social Inequality* (1974). The clear message from these studies was that more educational investment does not necessarily lead to greater equality of educational opportunity, and that more equal educational opportunity does not necessarily lead to greater social mobility or social equality.[29] This was also the central message which the OECD, in an analytical report on *Educational Opportunity for All,* summing up its ten-year work in this area, conveyed to the European Ministers of Education at their Sixth Conference, held in Versailles in May 1969.[30]

It will be recalled that the beginning of OECD efforts to delve into the issues of educational opportunity, at the 1961 Kungalv Conference, stemmed from a recognition that considerable reserves of intellectual resources among the population were going underdeveloped and that this large waste of human talent was historically inappropriate and technically unnecessary. Extending educational provision was thus a central concern of social policy, the minimal starting point for which was acceptance of the principle of providing formal equality of educational opportunity.[31] But it was also recognised, even at this early stage, that educational opportunity, beyond this formal minimum, should comprise the opportunity to overcome social, economic and cultural obstacles which limit the development of ability itself and which, therefore, limit effective educational participation. Inherent in this position was an abandonment of the concept of a fixed pool of ability in the population in favour of the idea that the development of ability can be the object of deliberate public policy. ''The intellectual potential of a nation is not a fixed quantity, it is a variable. The nation itself, through its social and educational policy, can increase or decrease its intellectual resources.''[32]

The relevance of the Kungalv message was not lost on the countries. It was reflected in the data collection and analytical investigations which were undertaken over the next few years within the new planning programmes in the Member countries and by the Study Group in the Economics of Education, whose final meeting, as we have already seen, was devoted to the ''Social Objectives in Educational Planning''. It was at this meeting that a refinement of the content of the objective of equal educational opportunities, based on a three-level hierarchy of definition, emerged, viz:

  i) equal *access* to non-compulsory education for all youngsters of equivalent measured ability – regardlenss of sex, race, place of residence, social class or other irrelevant criteria;
  ii) equal *rates of participation* in non-compulsory education by members of all social classes;
  iii) equal opportunity to acquire academic ability for youngsters of all social classes, *i.e.* effective participation by all *social classes* – the most stringent definition of all.[33]

These definitions represented ideal positions to which few, if any, countries could aspire. But at least they facilitated analysis of the further data presented on educational inequalities. And in shifting attention from ''opportunity'' to ''participation'' in education, they brought out the range of policy measures that were necessary for progress along this scale – in terms of structural changes in educational systems; new educational strategies, both in the schools and in the communities that support them; the development of new forms of organisation, curriculum and technologies in education; a compensatory redistribution of resources and the flow of new resources for the relevant research and innovational developments aimed at solving the problems of social and cultural gaps in educational participation.[34] The question of resources was, of course, crucial. Equality could not be achieved on the cheap and few countries had shown the political will to commit resources at a level which was necessary to influence the redistribution of educational opportunities. These were all areas which were already receiving attention within the OECD programmes, an attention which was to be accentuated in the light of the discussions and conclusions of the 1970 Conference on Policies for Educational Growth.

Equality of educational opportunity was, in fact, a theme central to all the discussions at the Conference. For the first time, countries had before them a fully documented analysis, based on massive statistical evidence, of the extent to which group disparities in educational participation had changed during the past period of rapid educational growth. The evidence showed dramatically that these disparities – among geographical or regional groups, between urban and rural segments of the population, between the sexes, and among social and economic groups – had not changed significantly during the previous twenty years.[35] A parallel analysis found no conclusive evidence that the observed increase in educational opportunities had had a marked impact on income distribution.[36] Everyone was getting more, but the differences between groups remained substantially the same.

Disappointing as these conclusions were, at least they made it plain that the problem of achieving greater equality of educational opportunity – which by now was interpreted to include equality of *achievement* – was more difficult than had been usually supposed and needed, in fact, to be posed in new terms. For one thing, too much had been claimed for the power of educational systems as instruments for the wholesale reform of societies, characteristically hierarchical in their distribution of life chances. The schools were not agencies which in themselves could redress deep social and cultural disadvantage, since they do not, in fact, control the well-springs of this disadvantage. Moreover, as many Conference participants observed, there had been a tendency to treat education as the "waste-paper basket" in dealing with social problems: "when no one knows the solution to a problem, or when there is a disinclination to wrestle with it seriously, it is dubbed an 'educational' problem and turned over to the schools to solve. But it is now increasingly plain that the schools cannot accomplish social reforms such as the democratisation of opportunity unless social reforms accompany the educational effort."[37] The implication of this, at least for some of the academic analysts, was that the goal of equality of educational achievement may have been somewhat unreflectively accepted by governments and public opinion, and that there were obstacles on the path even to approximating it that may be impossible and, at the least, would be costly to overcome. "Improvements in teaching methods capable of raising the level of achievement of children from disadvantaged groups will also be available, for example, in teaching the children from more fortunate groups; moreover, it is likely that these groups will adopt these methods sooner and apply them more effectively. In consequence, the differences in level of achievement between the more and the less advantaged may well increase or, at best, remain constant."[38]

In spite of this disillusionment over the extent to which more education led to more equity, the Conference conclusions were couched on a more sanguin note. For one thing, there was ample empirical evidence around the Conference table itself that, whatever the indications that could be derived from statistical aggregates, education did make a difference to the social upgrading of individuals. Moreover, no government could decently renounce the goal of equality of educational opportunity in the face of their commitment to democracy, of the growing demand for education at all levels and the need for larger numbers of highly educated people required by increasingly sophisticated economies. Admittedly difficult as were the tasks which this goal imposed, it was agreed that it nevertheless *set a direction in which national policies should try to move*. In the years that followed, the OECD programmes endeavoured to maintain the momentum already generated and preoccupation with the problems of educating the socially and culturally disadvantaged became a high priority in the programme of work of CERI.

Programmes for the disadvantaged

The work was pursued at two levels: an analytical one, concerned with the whole school population and with alternative strategies for bringing about equality of educational opportunity; and an experimental one, concerned with concrete programmes carried out in various Member countries for socially disadvantaged populations. Under the former, a "Strategy Group" of policy-makers and research workers – with strong Swedish participation at both levels – was set up to examine the implications of the most recent research evidence in this area. Beginning with an initial statement of the overall problem as it emerged from the evidence gathered at the 1970 Conference,[39] the group concentrated its attention on an analysis of research findings on the social factors affecting educational achievement. The results were embodied in two reports by Torsten Husén, which in many respects did for Europe what the Coleman report had done for the USA[40] Both reports led to the same conclusion: education remains relatively powerless to overcome the disadvantages of parental and social background so long as the destiny of all individuals is settled decisively by their examination results at the end of compulsory schooling. Educational opportunities, therefore, have to be provided on a recurring basis, in new combinations with work and leisure so as to enable individuals to pursue their development, in terms of both income and social status, over much of their working life. This was the central concept behind the advocacy of the recurrent education strategy, which we shall discuss in the next section.

At the experimental level, the work focused heavily on drawing lessons from the rich American experience with compensatory programmes for the socially disadvantaged as a guide to policies, research and experimentation in other Member countries. Historical examples of "positive discrimination" and special educational provision for the poor were, of course, to be found in many of these countries, but these in no way matched the massive and purposeful programmes which had been in operation on the other side of the Atlantic for several years, such as the Head Start programme set up under the Economic Opportunity Act of 1964 or those under the various headings of the Elementary and Secondary Education Act of 1965, particularly Title I. The lessons to be learnt from these programmes derived not so much from their specific content and operation as from the ongoing debate about methods and strategies of educational change and their underlying objectives and assumptions, that accompanied the setting up of new projects. In this way, the US experience was analysed under the following headings:

- the social and economic problems that many compensatory programmes attempted to alleviate, and a discussion of their objectives and of the concepts employed;
- educational programmes that introduced change into the "learning situation", principally within the school or classroom;
- projects designed to alter the relationship between schools and other social institutions, by new methods of organisation or new personnel;
- the problems of evaluation and research connected with such programmes.

The results of the study were embodied in a general report[41] which, in addition to its value for other countries, proved useful to the US constituency itself as an objective outside evaluation of what was as yet an amorphous range of experimental approaches to, rather than a doctrine of, compensatory education. So much so, that the US authorities were encouraged to submit to a subsequent and more generalised scrutiny of "Federal Policies for Education for the Disadvantaged" through the Country Review procedure.[42] Taken together, these two exercises remain a useful historical record of the inventiveness and financial resources, and of their impact and limitations, which the United States devoted to their belief in the role of education in eliminating social inequalities, stemming from the "Great Society" legislation of the mid-sixties. That one of the conclusions was that education could not do this alone does not diminish either the value of this work or the considerable impact which compensatory programmes had actually made.

"During this review", the OECD Examiners stated in their Conclusions of the US Review, "we have become increasingly convinced that the education system cannot bear the whole burden of being an instrument of social change. Educational reforms, if they are to have an impact, cannot be conducted in a social vacuum. In order to succeed they have to be part of wider social and economic reforms".[43] This was simply restating the by now generally accepted view, the reality of which had been made abundantly clear, in all its complexities, at an interdisciplinary conference of leading sociologists, economists, educationalists and policy-makers, held at the OECD in 1974. On the basis of considerable analytical work done in the Secretariat and in various Member countries, the conference represented an attempt to bring together the income distribution, social mobility and educational aspects of equality and thus provide the launching pad for an integrated attack on these problems within the Organisation and in Member countries. The two-volume report of the conference[44] bears testimony to the wealth of academic research that had been generated around these issues, much of which had been encouraged by governments themselves in the rather naive hope for better information to guide their decisions involving distributive justice in many fields of policy. No amount of academic research, and the controversies around it, could of course resolve problems which were essentially political, having to do with what kind of society one would like to see develop. This was clearly illustrated by the debate around the concept of *meritocracy* which was a recurring theme throughout the conference. While no-one disputed seriously society's needs for the recruitment of individuals into leadership roles on the basis of merit, the operative question which arose was how "merit" could be redefined in ways which did not favour existing elites.

Selection and certification

In essence, this was a question about the social selection role of educational systems and how such systems could be used to develop a wider range of talents, abilities and attitudes in children and young people which were needed in modern societies, thereby extending the notion of merit beyond that which was predetermined by existing social structures and hierarchies. This brought into prominence the *credentialling and certification* functions of educational systems and the dominant role which educational credentials had come to occupy in the functioning of these systems and, by extrapolation, as instruments for occupational placement and social selection. These matters had already been aired at the 1970 Paris Conference, with ample illustrations of how credentialling practices reinforced the dominantly selective function of existing educational systems, with a corresponding general adjustment of the occupational structure such that entry to it was in the process of upward redefinition of educational qualifications, leaving the traditional social pattern of selection remarkably stable.[45] What was now needed was a more detailed investigation into how credentialling and certification actually operated at the various levels of the educational system, of their intended and unintended consequences, and of the uses of credentials in the labour market, particularly as evidenced by the recruitment and promotion practices of employers. A special Secretariat study was devoted to these issues, resulting in a report which remains basic reading in the continuing debate on this subject.[46]

In discussing certification, the report fully recognised its important social and educational function, as a means of regulating the quality of education and training provided, thus serving to inform and protect the public both as consumers of education and as clients and/or employers of graduates. As attainment in formal education had come to be one of the best single predictors of success for attractive positions in society, it was inevitable that educational credentials had also become central to the social selection process. But it was stressed that this new social role of educational certification had been used historically to replace dubious social criteria such as inheritance, family connection, ability to pay, etc., and "that it is doubtful whether at present any agents other the formal educational system could fulfil this role in a more equitable and efficient way".[47] But the report also discussed, by reference to each level of education, the detrimental effects of having, in a situation of mass education, a selection process based on a rather narrow definition of achievement which responded primarily to the norms and standards of the top levels of the system where academic requirements and values prevailed.

Problems of a different order arose in relation to the use of credentials in employment. Three distinct features of the situation stood out. Firstly, it was clear that some depreciation in the value of most educational qualifications had occurred in OECD countries, and that for many occupations the basic educational qualifications needed had been rising steadily, resulting in unrealised expectations of many school and college leavers at all levels. It remained an open question whether this was due primarily to the slower economic growth, and consequent lower levels of employment, of recent years or to a structural imbalance between the level of educational attainment of the population and the nature of jobs that the economy was able to provide. Secondly, and rather paradoxically, it was equally certain that educational qualifications were increasingly being used by large firms and by the public sector as a basic *screening device* when new employees were recruited to all but the most unskilled jobs. This made the position of youngsters with low levels of qualification increasingly difficult and of those without qualifications quite disastrous. Finally, there was a clearly discernible trend towards raising the professional standards of many occupations, reinforcing in this way the influence which the different occupational groups, in their efforts to maintain their bargaining power, exercise on the training and certification required for admission to such occupations. To the extent that such training and certification were in the hands of institutions, such institutions remained in practice hostages to those who controlled entry into the profession.

The Recurrent Education venture

The dominantly selective function of educational systems, and the difficulties of getting round it, was a constant source of frustration to the egalitarians. Neither strategies for compensation at the preschool and primary levels nor the comprehensive school at the secondary level and the diversification of post-secondary structures had proven capable of overcoming socially-determined educational inequalities. Similarly, Illich's deschooling strategy, the extreme manifestation of this frustration, did not present an operable valid alternative: liberating individuals from the constraints of institutionalised schools would not necessarily improve the educational chances of the weak in unequal socio-economic systems and might indeed make them worse. At the other end of the spectrum, attempts to explore *alternative educational futures* proved equally unproductive, posited as they were on unverifiable assumptions about alternative future states of the society and of its goals and value structures.[48] It was in these circumstances that the concept of recurrent education emerged as a possible way out of this stalemate.

Recurrent education occupied the centre of the stage in the OECD, particularly CERI, activities for the major part of the seventies. It represents the nearest OECD ever came to advocating an explicit strategy of its own for the long-term development of educational systems in advanced, industrialised societies. The concept was of Scandinavian origin, with its roots in the long tradition in these countries of adult and continuing education and their egalitarian policies not only as between social and regional groups, but also between the older and younger generations in the population. Already in 1967, the Ottosen Committee in Norway put forward a full-fledged programme of "post-work education" with the emphasis on the updating of knowledge and counteracting obsolete qualifications, with implications for the organisation and institutional responsibility for education. As a distinct concept, however, recurrent education was actually first launched in 1969 by the Swedish U68 Educational Commission as part of its work on the functions and structure of higher education.[49] But behind the thinking of the Commission lay the influence of Olöf Palme, the then Minister of Education. It was Olöf Palme himself who first promulgated the concept internationally, at the 1969 Versailles Conference of the European Ministers of Education, on the occasio of the discussion of the report submitted by the OECD on "Educational Opportunities for All", for which he made the introductory statement – and for which he received the "warm thanks" of his fellow ministers for the broad avenues which it opened. (The term "recurrent education" was actually invented outside the Conference room, the Hall of Mirrors, at Versailles, in conversation between Palme, Sandgren, Ron Gass and myself, just before Palme made his statement.)

In making his statement, Palme's intention was to launch a debate on this new idea rather than to lay down a policy. The basic principle of the new strategy was clear: post-school education should be provided on a recurring basis, involving alternation between work and study, and opportunities for this should be *effectively* available to all individuals throughout their active life. It was this feature of a *right* to education, to be taken at any time during the individual's working life, that distinguished recurrent education from "life-long learning" and "permanent education" expounded in reports by UNESCO and the Council of Europe, respectively. It was a principle which in practice aimed at redressing the balance between youth and adult education, in favour of the latter, making at the same time for a more equitable and more efficient distribution of educational opportunities across the population as a whole. The application of such a principle, however, was open to different interpretations, according to national circumstances, and this partly explains the alacrity with which the concept was so readily and widely espoused across the OECD countries. It was left to the OECD, in the years that followed the Versailles Conference, to clarify the concept and work out its policy ramifications and organisational implications – a task which was greatly facilitated by the willingness which Member countries showed in contributing on the basis of their respective experience and viewpoints. For many of them, in fact, as well as for the Organisation, this new strategy came to fill a vacuum in educational policy thinking at a time when the optimism of the sixties was giving way to the uncertainties of the seventies.

Further political impetus was given by the 1970 Paris Conference on Policies for Educational Growth which, in its conclusions recognised the need to bring about changes in educational structures "that will make it easier for those students who wish to do so to obtain the education they want in recurrent periods throughout life rather than following immediately after completion of their secondary education".[50] In the meantime CERI had already embarked on the process of clarification, with an initial analysis of the relevance of recurrent education to policies for equality of educational opportunity,[51] leading eventually to the preparation of a "Clarifying Report" which became the blue-print for all subsequent discussions and the analysis of policy developments in different Member countries in this area.[52] The report drew on an initial series of monographs describing policy developments with regard to recurrent education in a select number of Member countries, subsequently extended to cover all the major OECD countries.[53] A significant contribution to the ongoing debate, bringing together US and European experience, was made at an international conference at Georgetown University in June 1973, organised jointly by the National Institute of Education of the US Department of Health, Education and Welfare and CERI.[54]

Preliminary results from all this developmental work were presented to the 1973 Conference of European Ministers of Education, held in Berne, Switzerland. Not all

Ministers were as yet ready to endorse the concept and vigorous opposition to it was expressed by the UK representative, Margaret Thatcher. As a compromise, it was agreed that recurrent education would be the major topic of discussion at their following meeting to be held in Stockholm in 1975. For this purpose, the OECD was invited to put together a summary of its findings so far and lay out the policy issues which arose for Ministerial consideration. This was done in a brief report,[55] on the basis of which the Stockholm Conference adopted a statement endorsing recurrent education as "a strategy for the long-term planning of education, primarily for the post-compulsory sector, but with repercussions on other areas of educational provision. Its objectives, however, entail the progressive implementation of short and medium-term measures. It forms an indispensable part of broader socio-economic and cultural policies for translating the concept of permanent education into practice... It has implications for the organisation of work and leisure, and requires a close co-ordination between education, social, cultural and economic policies. It also means co-ordinating the various sectors of educational provision – formal and informal, vocational and non-vocational – which are often today insufficiently inter-related". While recognising that recurrent education would necessarily develop differently in different countries, they nevertheless agreed on a number of common objectives to which recurrent education policies should be directed, such as ensuring a greater measure of educational and social equity, co-ordinating policies for education, social welfare and employment, and re-deploying educational opportunities and resources as part of the responsibility of public authorities in securing the effective exercise of the right of the individual to resume education in later life.[56]

This Resolution marks the political apogee of the recurrent education venture. It came at the end of a long process of analysis and advocacy, the main features of which have been sketched above. What we have not done is to spell out the detailed considerations and justifications behind the strategy, but these can be followed in the OECD reports. They will show why, in spite of all the rhetoric and genuflections that policy makers made in their support of the concepts behind recurrent education, the strategy was never translated into policy. This was partly due to fears on the part of the establishment that the application of recurrent education would result in a radical transformation of existing educational systems. But it was also due to the fact that recurrent education was much more than a purely educational policy issue. Its effective implementation would involve co-ordinated approaches with other sectors of policy, implying extensive changes in labour markets, enterprise practices, social insurance and income transfer policies, in short, much of the fabric of social and economic organisation – changes which were made even more difficult with the slowdown of the economy and the rise of unemployment that set in around the mid-seventies.

The magnitude of the problem had been squarely put to Ministers:

It is suggested that the coherent contribution of a policy of recurrent education must be made along two axes: a vertical axis along which the integration of adult education opportunities with initial schooling might be affected, breaking the current lockstep by encouraging individuals to defer the exercise of their educational rights; and a horizontal axis, along which educational and training provision is co-ordinated with other policies such as employment and manpower policies which affect the work and leisure of the population.[57]

Few governments, even if they were willing to accept this double challenge, had the machinery to confront it effectively. Yet it must not be assumed that the effort had been wasted. Many of the elements of the recurrent education strategy in fact gradually found their way into national educational policies and practices. This was particularly true in the development of more flexible post-compulsory education structures, the growth of modular courses and new admission procedures in higher education, new combinations of work and study programmes, including the educational recognition of work experience, and the recognition which also came to be given to the education of adults as of at least equal priority to that given to youth education. Above all, the long debate around recurrent education helped to bring about greater awareness among educationists as well as other stakeholders of the inter-relatedness of their concerns and the need for concerted action for their solution.

These lessons were not lost on the OECD itself, and its subsequent work moved away from the conceptual approach to recurrent education to more empirical analysis of concrete problems and bottlenecks that had to be overcome. Particular attention was given to how the working force, in the dramatic changes which were taking place in the employment situation, could have access to continuing education and training, a move which was encouraged by the prominence given to paid educational leave in the 1974 ILO Convention. A review of the actual practices in Member countries regarding this problem[58] was followed by a more empirical analysis of how educational leave of absence operated at the enterprise level, giving rise to a discussion of the more general problem of alternation between education and work.[59] Parallel analyses were undertaken of the level and modes of participation by different groups in continuing education, the specific problems encountered by individuals themselves, by the trade unions and by industrial management as part of the general move towards industrial democracy, and by the educational and other authorities concerned, with particular reference to costs and financing.[60]

When, in March 1977, governmental representatives and experts from the Member countries met to review developments, they were able to note that such progress as had been achieved was still of a piece-meal nature, unevenly spread across the countries. The biggest obstacle to the development of a coherent policy for recurrent education remained the intractable problem of the co-ordination of policies. Such co-ordination as had been achieved operated at local rather than at national level; and this was also true for the educational sector itself, as exemplified by the inability, or unwillingness, of national authorities to integrate their traditional, and expanding, systems of *Adult Education* into a coherent set of recurrent education opportunities. This was true even for countries like Sweden with its strong addiction to the concept of recurrent education alongside its long tradition of municipal and other forms of adult education.

The extent to which adult education, in spite of considerable growth since 1960 and repeated formal declarations of its importance, remained the pariah of public educational provision, functioning as a discrete, but structurally and financially weak sector, was fully documented in a special OECD study in the mid-seventies.[61] In a sense, the study was a plea that the time was ripe for adult education to change its peripheral position in relation to the formal education system and that its development could no longer be left, as in the past, to enterpreneurial efforts by groups of professional adult educators who had set themselves up in many countries as lobbies to advance its cause. It was also a plea to adult educators themselves to broaden their own perspectives in the light of the new social, economic and cultural needs of the community, and present to public authorities concrete evidence of an explicit social demand for adult education and its relevance to general policy concerns; in other words, to move away from a view of adult education in such stereotyped forms as literacy classes for the urban poor, needlework for housewives, rehabilitation training for the unemployed or liberal studies for the cultivated.

It is difficult to assess what effect this twin plea has had. Government preoccupations were primarily with boosting up occupational preparation for the work force, and this they supported, but not necessarily within the adult education ambit. In many respects, adult education continued to be a community based and financed activity rather than a vital sector of public policy.

Notes and references

1. *Development of Secondary Education: Trends and Implications*, OECD, 1969.

2. Resolution No. 4, on ''Educational Opportunity for All''.

3. *Reviews of National Policies for Education: Canada*, OECD, 1976, p. 30. Quoted in Kogan, *op. cit.*, p. 47.

4. See: *New Approaches to Secondary Education: Italian Problems and Projects*, OECD/ CERI, 1971.

5. On this, as well as trends in other European countries, see: *Development of Secondary Education*, *op. cit.*, p. 144.

6. *Reviews of National Policies for Education: Netherlands (Contours of a Future Educational System)*, OECD, 1976.

7. *Review of National Policies for Education: Austria, School Policy*, OECD, 1979, p. 19.

8. *Reviews of National Policies for Education: Germany*, OECD, 1973. The divide in Germany was clearly along party political lines, complicated by suspicions among the Länder of a bid by the Federal Government to reinforce its role in educational matters, and that it was using the OECD Review for this purpose.

9. In addition to *Development of Secondary Education*, *op. cit.*, see ''Issues in Educational Structures'', in *Educational Policies for the 1970s*, *op. cit.*, pp. 91-98, and ''Changes in Secondary and Higher Education'', in *Teaching Resources and Structural Change*, *op. cit.*, pp. 105-147 – both papers prepared for the 1970 Conference on Policies for Educational Growth.

10. Tim McMullen, *Innovative Practices in Secondary Education: The Lower Secondary Stage: Problems and Possibilities*, OECD/CERI, 1978.

11. *Ibid.*, p. 97.

12. *Adolescents and Comprehensive Schooling*, OECD, 1987.

13. *Beyond Compulsory Schooling: Options and Changes in Upper Secondary Education*, OECD, 1976.

14. *Ibid.*, p. 73.

15. Kogan, *op. cit.*, p. 53, and the same author's *Educational Policy-Making,* Allen and Unwin, 1975, Chapter 10; see also W. Taylor in *Policies for Higher Education*, OECD, 1974, p. 138.

16. *Development of Higher Education, 1950-1967: Statistical Survey*, OECD, 1970; and *Development of Higher Education, 1950-1967: Analytical Report*, OECD, 1971.

17. For a fuller development of this argument see : G.S. Papadopoulos, "Higher Education Predicaments: What Can be Said about them that is New?", in *Higher Education Management*, OECD/IMHE, 1991, Vol. 3, No. 2, pp. 184-190.

18. *Innovation in Higher Education:*

    – *New Universities in the United Kingdom*, OECD, 1969;
    – *French Experience Before 1968*, OECD, 1970;
    – *Reforms in Yugoslavia*, OECD, 1970;
    – *Three German Universities*, OECD, 1970;
    – *Technical Education in the United Kingdom*, OECD, 1971.

19. *Interdisciplinarity: Problems of Teaching and Research in Universities*, OECD/CERI, 1972.

20. *Ibid.*, p. 74.

21. *Interdisciplinary Revisited: Reassessing the Concept in the light of Institutional Experience*, OECD/CERI, Swedish National Board of Universities and Colleges, Linköping University, 1985. This meeting was one of a series of nationally organised seminars, with international participation, on various aspects of innovation in higher education, in an attempt, under the CERI Innovation Exchange Activities, to maintain a minimum of momentum in innovative thinking at a time (mid-eighties) when innovation was no longer the central pre-occupation of either governments or higher education institutions. Countries hosting such seminars were Austria, Japan, Germany, the United Kingdom and the United States. Resulting reports were circulated to all Member countries. See, for example, *Innovation in Higher Education* and *The Changing Functions of Higher Education: Implications for Innovation*, Research Institute for Higher Education, Hiroshima University, 1981 and 1984; *Higher Education and the Community: Relations and Exchanges between University and Industry*, University of Karlsruhe, Germany, 1983; *Expectations of Higher Education: An OECD Conference at Hatfield Polytechnic*, DES, London, 1983; and the proceedings of an international conference at Klagenfurt, Austria, published in *Studiente mit Berufserfahrung: Eine Herausforderung fur die Universitaten*, Herman Bohlau, Vienna, 1986.

22. *Towards New Structures of Post-Secondary Education: A Preliminary Statement of Issues*, OECD, 1971, (Part two of this report deals exclusively with short-cycle higher education); and *Short-Cycle Higher Education: A Search for Identity*, OECD, 1973.

23. A detailed analysis of these problems and of their application to specific national systems and models is contained in *A Search for Identity, op. cit.*

24. *Alternatives to Universities*, OECD, 1991.

25. *Policies for Higher Education: General Report*, OECD, 1974.

26. *Ibid.*, p. 138 – comment by W. Taylor, General Rapporteur of the Conference. In addition to the *General Report*, already cited, the Conference material was published in two volumes: *Structure of Studies and Place of Research in Mass Higher Education*, OECD, 1974 and *Towards Mass Higher Education: Issues and Dilemmas*, OECD, 1974. A number of supporting reports were also available, in addition to those on *Short-Cycle* already mentioned. See, in particular: Anderson and Bowman: *Mass Higher Education: Some Perspectives from Experience in the United States*; Gardner and Zelan: *A Strategy for Change in Higher Education: The Extended University of California*; John Lowe, *New Approaches in Post-Secondary Education; Post-Graduate Education: Structures and Policies*, OECD, 1972; *New College Systems in Canada*, OECD, 1974; *Students in Short-Cycle Higher Education: France, Great Britain* and *Yugoslavia*, OECD, 1976. Comparison with developments in the

Soviet Union was facilitated by a separate Secretariat report: *Higher Education in the Soviet Union*, OECD 1973.

27. *General Report*, pp. 51 ff.

28. *Policies for Higher Education in the 1980s*, OECD, 1983.

29. Kogan, *op. cit.*, pp. 27-28.

30. *Educational Opportunity for All: Background Report on OECD Work and its Policy Implications*, CME/VI (69)4.

31. *Ability and Educational Opportunity*, *op. cit.*, pp. 17-18.

32. *Ibid.*, p. 65.

33. *Social Objectives in Educational Planning*, *op. cit.*, p. 15.

34. *Educational Opportunity for All*, *op. cit.*, p. 4.

35. *Group Disparities in Educational Participation and Achievement*, OECD, 1971.

36. *Education and Distribution of Income*, OECD, 1971.

37. *Educational Policies for the 1970s*, p. 14.

38. *Ibid.*, p. 15.

39. *Equal Educational Opportunity*, OECD/CERI, 1971.

40. *Social Background and Educational Career*, OECD/CERI, 1972; and *Social Influences on Educational Attainment*, OECD/CERI, 1975.

41. Alan Little and George Smith, *Strategies of Compensation: A Review of Educational Projects for the Disadvantaged in the United States*, OECD/CERI, 1971. See also M.A. Brimer, *Evaluation and Action Programmes Amongst the Educationally and Socially Disadvantaged*, OECD/CERI, 1971.

42. *Reviews of National Policies for Education: United States*, OECD, 1981, and accompanying background report by the US authorities: *Compensatory Education Programmes in the United States*, OECD, 1981.

43. *US Educational Policy Review*, *op. cit.*, p. 12.

44. *Education, Inequality and Life Chances*, Vols. I and II, OECD, 1975.

45. *Educational Policies for the 1970s*, *loc. cit.*

46. *Selection and Certification in Education and Employment*, OECD, 1977.

47. *Ibid.*, p. 9.

48. See for a full discussion of the state-of-the-art in these futuristic visions: *Alternative Educational Futures in the United States and in Europe: Methods, Issues and Policy Relevance*, OECD/CERI, 1972.

49. Jarl Bengtsson, *The Swedish View of Recurrent Education*, OECD/CERI, 1972.

50. *Educational Policies for the 1970s*, p. 142.

51. *Equal Educational Opportunity: A Statement of the Problems with Special Reference to Recurrent Education*, OECD/CERI, 1971.

52. *Recurrent Education: A Strategy for Lifelong Learning*, OECD/CERI, 1973.

53. *Recurrent education: Policy and Development in OECD Countries*, OECD/CERI, Series of 13 Country reports, 1972-77.

54. *Recurrent Education*, National Institute of Education, Washington, 1974.

55. *Recurrent Education: Trends and Issues*, OECD/CERI, 1975.

56. For the full text of this Resolution see Council of Europe, M/ED/15.2.

57. *Trends and Issues*, *op. cit.*, p. 5.

58. *Developments in Educational Leave of Absence*, OECD/CERI, 1976.

59. *Alternation Between Work and Education: A Study of Educational Leave of Absence at Enterprise Level*, OECD/CERI, 1978.

60. The results of these studies were grouped together in an omnibus report: *Recurrent Education Revisited: Modes of Participation and Financing*, OECD/CERI and Almqvist and Wiksell International, Stockholm, 1987. This report also contains a realistic assessment of policy developments in recurrent education during the previous fifteen years.

61. *Learning Opportunities for Adults*:

    Vol. 1 – General Report, OECD, 1977.

    Vol. 2 – New Structures, Programmes and Methods, OECD, 1977.

    Vol. 3 – The Non-Participation Issue, OECD, 1979.

    Vol. 4 – Participation in Adult Education, OECD, 1972.

    Vol. 5 – Widening Access for the Disadvantaged, OECD, 1981.

Chapter VII

EDUCATION AND SOCIETY: THE SEARCH FOR NEW LINKS
(the seventies)

We have seen, in the preceding two chapters, the extent to which the legacy of growth was translated into changes at the strategic and operational levels which, taken together, amounted to a not so quiet revolution in the educational landscape of OECD countries. A prime motivation behind these changes, and a principal objective to which they were directed, was the search for a new social relevance for education, one that could reconcile the needs of individuals to those of society interpreted much more broadly than what could be derived from the economic functions of education. This was the principal message of the 1970 Policy Conference, as already explained. Forging closer and more direct links between education and its social context emerged as a major priority for the seventies, and this was fully reflected in the OECD programmes. The various activities undertaken within these programmes to explore new policy approaches to and concrete examples of such education/society links, before this priority was eclipsed by the onset of harsher economic realities from the middle of the seventies onwards, constitute the central theme of the present chapter.

Education relocated within OECD

The decision taken in 1974 to detach Education from the Science Directorate – which in exchange got Industry and Technology – and amalgamate it into a new Directorate for Social Affairs, Manpower and Education under Ron Gass, was not entirely fortuitous. True, the change was facilitated by the almost simultaneous retirement of Alex King and Gösta Rehn, Directors for Scientific Affairs and for Manpower and Social Affairs respectively, both of whom, in their fields of responsibility, had pioneered work which left its permanent mark on the Organisation and contributed to its image as a body endowed with intellectual vivacity and capacity for innovative policy-thinking. More than anyone else, they were instrumental in leading OECD to giving explicit and serious concern to the social effects of economic policies and in building up a ''social arm'' for the Organisation, with education as an important component of it.

It had become clear for some time that the links which had tied education to science were becoming increasingly tenuous as science policy interests moved away from the original concern with scientific and technical personnel to problems of technological innovation and industrial revitalisation. The main common interest which remained was fundamental research and the role of universities therein, with post-graduate education lying athwart science policies and policies for higher education. Problems in this area were actually handled separately by the science and higher education sectors, with different emphases reflecting their respective, and at times conflicting, viewpoints and interests.[1]

At the same time, with incipient unemployment, education and training were increasingly drawn into the mainstream of the Organisation's approach to manpower and employment policies: they were in fact an integral part of the package of measures advocated in the "Active Manpower Policies" framework adopted by OECD in 1964.[2] One immediate consequence of the 1974 reorganisation was the transfer of responsibility for training from the Manpower to the Education sector, in a conscious attempt to rationalise all relevant Secretariat work in this area to serve the joint interests of the two Committees. How this worked out we shall see in the next chapter. Another consequence was a reinforcement of the "Social Affairs" remit of the new Directorate which, under the previous regime, had received less attention than its "Manpower" partner. This move towards a more aggressive approach to social policies, strongly pushed by Ron Gass, was not without its repercussions for the educational sector itself, as the episode of the abortive attempt to set up a "Social Innovation Centre" shows.

A Social Innovation Centre?

In reality, there never was a precise proposal to turn CERI into a Social Innovation Centre. The idea was mooted as one of the possible options of dealing with the broader problems of social innovation, drawing on the experience of what had been done, through CERI, in the field of educational innovation. It originated with the Secretariat in the context of the discussion in 1975 about the renewal of the mandates of the educational activities of the Organisation. In a sense, it was a bid – premature as it turned out – to cash in on the growing importance which Member countries attached to social problems in order to launch an inter-governmental R & D mechanism to promote more co-ordinated national policies and action in relation to these problems.

That the attempt failed in its immediate objective was due to two main reasons. Firstly, although it was clear that the several domains of social policy interacted more closely than in the past, both at the level of general policy formulation and in operational programmes, and that the social sector could no longer be treated as a residual factor in relation to economic activity, neither the concepts of social policy nor the administrative structures to implement them were yet sufficiently clear to launch a unified approach to these problems. In other words, there were as yet no established national interest groups on which such an international endeavour could lean for support. Secondly – and this became evident during the long and often heated discussions which took place within the CERI Governing Board, the Education Committee and the Council of the Organisation – the educational establishment saw the proposal as an intrusion into their own preserved territory and as diverting CERI from its essential function of serving the direct interests of its educational clientele. There were, of course, dissenting views in much sympathy with the idea, but these did not prevail against the determined stand of the ''opposition'', one of its arguments being that CERI would thereby forfeit its well established education-based support in the countries without any guarantee of a viable alternative within national administrations.

In the end, the solution was a compromise. The feasibility of a Social Innovation Centre was discarded, even though the need was accepted of exploring alternative arrangements for co-operation in the field of social innovation, involving in particular education, manpower, social and science policies and relevant research and development. Nothing concrete emerged from this exploration, which in effect never took place. It was, in fact, deemed wiser to assume that each administrative sector should promote its own developmental concepts and programmes, with carefully designed interactions between them which did not put too high a strain on the capacity to implement. In this spirit, it was specifically agreed ''that, to the fullest extent possible, relevant CERI projects should be developed so as to meet the need for educational innovations to be related to other sectors of social policy''. This was seriously taken up within the 1976 and subsequent CERI programmes, leading to a series of socially-oriented developmental projects, as we shall see below.

Thus, the debate on social innovation had not been wasted. It helped raise the level of consciousness within the Organisation about the relation between social problems and the objectives of traditional economic growth and provided an impetus to the important work on aspects of social policy which was subsequently undertaken within the new Directorate. It demonstrated the leadership role which the educational sector could play in innovative policy approaches and in providing concrete examples of how this could be put into action. Above all, it led to CERI, and the educational sector more broadly, being given an explicitly more enlarged social remit which marked its programmes of work in the years that followed.

Education and social concerns: the policy/planning dimension

The immersion of education into the new interest in social concerns had significant consequences for educational policy and planning. It was seen by many as providing a fresh platform for securing continued political support for education, similar to the role which the economics platform had played during most of the previous decade. Making a convincing case for it, however, was another matter: the analytical base was fragile and the argument had essentially to be couched in politically normative terms. That education should make a contribution to social progress was readily accepted. But what ''social progress'' meant, and how this contribution could be measured or evaluated, depended on what goals society set for itself. How these goals were defined and the impact which, in turn, they had on the definition of educational goals, were *par excellence* political questions peculiar to each country, hardly amenable to analytical treatment of the kind that had been applied to the economics of education.

These questions, and the challenge which they posed to educational policy and planning, were debated at length at the 1970 Policy Conference.[3] In its conclusions, the Conference stressed the need for educational planning to be more closely related to the complex processes of educational policy formulation. It should, in particular, provide analyses of alterative policies for education based on explicit goal-formulation, with short- and long-term consequences for the individual, the educational system, the economy and society as a whole. "In this respect it should provide for and facilitate the widest possible participation and discussion among interested groups in the community." It should be increasingly long-term, comprehensive and inter-sectoral and also take account of the need for educational policies to become more responsive to individual demand as well as the cultural needs of society. It should also endeavour to develop social indicators which monitor the performance of the school system, the evaluation of the costs, effectiveness and results of courses, the outcomes of learning, student and teacher behaviour, etc.[4]

Second generation educational planning

These recommendations provided the broad framework within which the OECD educational planning programme developed in the seventies.[5] In contrast to the previous phase with its focus on planning mechanisms and techniques, as recounted in a previous chapter, this so-called "second generation" educational planning dealt with a series of specific planning issues which became fashionable in educational and broader social planning during the upsurge of social concerns in the seventies. Less technocratic and more speculative in its approach, it broadened its coverage to encompass longer-term perspectives, the links to other sectors of policy and a larger variety of social variables, including the role of value systems on policy decisions. Planning was perceived as operating in a context of uncertainty in which there is a statement of multiple options, which can be affected by multiple stake-holders in education and in society at large, and with no certainty as to which group has the final say.[6]

Five specific themes, illustrative of the trends and pressures of the time, were covered in this phase of the programme, each resulting in a major report, as follows:

  i) lengthening the time perspective for educational planning;[7]
  ii) responding to the demand by various groups in society to increase their participation in the decisions affecting them;[8]
  iii) recognition of the growing inter-relationship between education and other sectors of policy, leading to the need for more inter-sectoral approaches to educational planning;[9]
  iv) improving the capacity of decision centres to respond more effectively to local needs and aspirations;[10]
  v) better understanding of the way in which the demand for education operates at the level of the individual and of the factors which influence this demand and its variations.[11]

It is extremely difficult to summarise the results of this work or assess its impact. It reflected an attempt to respond to *ad hoc* issues and pressures emanating from both inside and outside the educational system rather than any deliberate or systematic effort to provide guidelines for the development of educational planning as such. Inevitably, the work was influenced by changes in broader socio-political thinking, most prominently exemplified by the participatory movement, as well as by the special interests of those who at one time or another headed educational planning offices.[12] Much of what was done also derived from purely academic interest and was never intended to become part of educational practice. On the whole, its function was essentially pedagogical rather than prescriptive.

In this sense, its cumulative effect on the concepts of educational planning was considerable. In its advocacy of improving the "thinking capacity" of educational systems by enriching the information base on which decisions are made; in stressing the need to take into account existing conflicts and uncertainties in the pursuit of multi-value social objectives; in breaking down the notion of "programme autonomy" in such a large sector of social policy as education; and in demonstrating the intricate relationships between planning, decision-making and implementation at all levels, the work brought new insights into the inherently political nature of educational planning in which the restrictions which were often put on it in the past to operate on given policy objectives seemed entirely artificial. As a consequence of this, planning structures and procedures needed to be thought anew.[13]

Such rethinking of educational planning was undertaken by OECD in the early eighties.[14] By that time, however, the policy context for education had considerably changed as a result of the rapid decrease in economic activity consequent on the successive oil-crises, rise in unemployment, particularly youth unemployment, drastically contracting public budgets and profound demographic changes resulting in decreasing school populations. This was accompanied by a re-ordering of social objectives and priorities with education losing its previously privileged social rank – problems which we shall discuss in greater detail in the next chapter. Educational planning was thus confronted with a new challenge of how to reconcile the features described above to the need to respond to pressures from acute conjunctural problems, *i.e.* of how to establish realistic links between short/medium and long-term educational objectives. An empirical analysis of how different countries were handling this dilemma pointed to the clear conclusion that because of resource constraints, nearly all planning decisions were becoming politically charged policy decisions, implying that successful planning needed to be even more closely integrated than previously with the policy-making process. Within this reality, however, it was important that opportunities be provided for policy options to be presented for informed debate amongst all the interest groups. This would facilitate public participation in the planning process, while leaving it to democratically elected governments to determine their policy targets and tactics. In this, public access to information beyond that generated or controlled by governments was an essential requirement; and this led to the recommendation that at least some educational planning activities should be undertaken in centres of expertise that are independent of government.[15]

Education and social indicators

As already noted, the need for closer attention to be given to the evaluation and measurement of educational outcomes, particularly in relation to broader social objectives, was one of the more precise recommendations of the 1970 Conference on Policies for Educational Growth. Work on this was followed-up within the OECD programmes, parallel to the work on educational planning described above. Pedagogical aspects of evaluation were briefly dealt with in CERI as part of the more general concern with innovation.[16] Work on educational indicators, which was to be vigorously taken up by CERI some ten years later, was initially handled within the Education Committee programme in the context of the broader attempt within the Organisation to develop "social indicators".

The ideology which underlay the wave of interest in social indicators which emerged in the early seventies was the belief that it would be possible to extend the politically effective system of national accounting to a system of data on the "quality of life".[17] Partly inspired by the "programme budgeting" movement in fashion at that time, the effort was directed at establishing "output measures" in relation to clearly defined objectives in different sectors of social policy. Education was one of these sectors so far dominated by elaborate "input" statistics and indicators. The work was entrusted to the Working Party of the Education Committee on Educational Statistics and Indicators which, in a fairly short time, was able to present an agreed framework of educational statistics related to the main policy concerns of Member countries.[18]

To a large extent this framework was concerned with measuring the impact of education on society. Fully accepting that education serves many objectives and that indicators of performance must be multidimensional, the framework found it necessary to reduce the number of dimensions to six pragmatic categories, as follows:

i) Contribution of education to the transmission of knowledge.
ii) Contribution of education to equality of opportunity and social mobility.
iii) Contribution of education to meeting the needs of the economy.
iv) Contribution of the educational system to individual development.
v) Contribution of education to the transmission and evolution of values.
vi) Effective use of resources in pursuit of the above policy objectives.

Under each of these categories a series of relevant indicators was identified, amounting to a manageable total of 46. A subsequent and more analytical report by the Secretariat provided a slightly revised version of the categories and considerably expanded the number of indicators – to about 150 – geared more directly to the contribution of education to the achievement of social objectives.[19] This latter report, particularly in its discussion of the theoretical and technical problems surrounding the definition and compilation of output indicators, still remains a useful source of reference which has also inspired subsequent work on this subject within OECD.

That there was no immediate follow-up to these reports was due to two reasons. While it was fairly easy to reach agreement on the broad categories of policy objectives, these remained, by necessity, selective, representing the minimum level of generality on which countries could agree. In addition, most goal dimensions were dependent on each other, so that no weighting could take place independent of the level of goal achievement in most other dimensions. Secondly, educational statistics were traditionally input-oriented and no country showed enough interest in gearing up the necessary research effort to relate them to output indicators. As with planning, the ultimate value of this work was pedagogical rather than policy and practice oriented. But at least it did lead to greater awareness of the need to reform educational statistics systems and improve their international comparability basis.

Education and social concerns: the operational dimension

The policy/planning work described above was, during the seventies, accompanied by a substantial series of more operational activities, mostly within CERI, designed to explore pragmatic applications of the interface between education and social policies and concerns. The revised mandate of CERI, and its ability to attract additional outside funds, lent itself to this task. The primary motivation remained the role which education could play in the distribution of opportunity and the elimination of social and cultural inequality. Previous work had demonstrated the limited extent to which education by itself could contribute to this objective and that wider support systems had to be developed if the needs of various groups of individuals were to be met. At the same time, the emergence of new community concerns, such as health and the environment, and of new perceptions in social policy of the scale and significance of poverty in contemporary societies, led to increasing demands being made on education by other social institutions in attacking these problems. This in turn demonstrated the need for closer consultation and co-operation between educational and these other institutions. If education was to play a pro-active, rather than merely re-active, role in the solution of these inter-disciplinary problems, it could not avoid getting involved in the formulation of policies in these other sectors, or, at least, in the shaping of inter-sectoral policies in relation to the problems in question. The work on recurrent education, described in a previous chapter, set a good example for this.

In the account which follows no attempt will be made to give a detailed description of the large variety of activities that were undertaken in this area, or to impose an artificial pattern on the *ad hoc* evolution of this work. Much of it had its origins in earlier activities on the role and functions of schools and universities and on compensatory education and equality of opportunity. It ranged from analyses of the general problematique of education/community relationships to the study of the special needs in specific sectors and of individual groups in society, continuing in the case of the latter well into the eighties and beyond.

School and the community

The widespread interest in, and experimentation with, innovative schools which marked the early seventies, partly fanned by the "de-schooling" movement, led to new questioning of the structure and functions of the school as a community institution. The debate was as refreshing as it was inconclusive. It was dominated by the theoretical analyses of social scientists which were in no way matched by the more terre-à-terre views and interests of educational practitioners and administrators. At stake was the dilution of the monopoly of the educative role of the school, implying, on the one hand, a broadening of its function to include social and community service and, on the other, close involvement by other social agencies and institutions in the exercise of this role and in the use of school resources for broader community purposes.

That these were complex issues not amenable to generally acceptable interpretations, let alone solutions, became clear at a first OECD/CERI conference on this subject in 1973.[20] Three different kinds of school and community interaction were identified: a) *School and place of work,* raising profound questions about how the school could combine responsibilities towards the local and national economy with responsibilities towards the individual; b) *Schools for minority groups within the community,* with all the problems that this raised in the creation and operation of "alternative" schools outside the main body of publicly-provided and administered schools; c) *Community schools,* in the sense of the large and heterogeneous category of developments which were taking place within public education systems aimed at exploiting the mutual dependence of the school and the community in the interest of both good education and the health of community life; *i.e.,* attempts to make schools more responsive to their neighbourhood communities as a whole, including the sharing of resources in the overall interest of community development.

Discussion of these forms of school/community interaction, nourished by specific country examples and experiments in each of the three areas, inevitably raised the politically sensitive question of the *participation* process in decision-making: what is the dominant aim and by whom is it decided? What are the respective roles of the politicians and other interest groups, on the one hand, and of professionals, on the other? – questions which could only be answered in the context of specific national situations and politics.

Though no conclusions were reached, the discussion ended on a note of scepticism as to the feasibility, and indeed the desirability, of any radical change in the traditional status of the school in the community. While recognising the general need for closer links between the two, the feeling was that any such radical change, largely ideologically driven, could well vitiate the fundamental purposes of schooling without leading to corresponding advantages in terms of overall community development. Even in the concrete case of the joint use of educational building and facilities, subsequent work by PEB showed that this could not be considered as an ideal or a panacea to the problem of more economic use of public resources, not least because of the difficulty in setting up effective management systems to co-ordinate the interests and roles of the disparate agencies involved. This conclusion was not seriously affected by the growing move towards decentralisation of educational decision-making and the devolution of responsibilities for the management and maintenance of educational facilities from central to local levels, as further PEB work in this area domonstrated. Indeed, such devolution did enable needs to be met more rapidly and stock to be better maintained, but the problem of overall co-ordination remainded unresolved.[21]

But at least in one area the conference conclusions were positive: the importance of integrating education and other community services – health care, welfare and those that promote cultural or recreational activities – to meet the problems of groups in the population with identified special needs, *i.e.* disadvantaged groups, whether urban or rural, ethnic and cultural minorities and those with physical disabilities. This provided a rich agenda for fruitful subsequent OECD work, of which only broad indications can be given here.

A first next step was to look at significant innovative programmes in Member countries specifically designed for this purpose and try and draw out of this experience a structure to guide future policies for the further development of such integrative or collaborative approaches.[22] This was followed by parallel in-depth studies directed at: *a)* education policies for *rural* populations, resulting in a comprehensive analysis of the problems posed for rural education beyond the needs of special populations and of the contribution which such education could make to the revitalisation and development of rural areas;[23] *b)* the role of education and other services in meeting the needs of *urban* populations, with a strong accent on the disadvantaged and the contribution which local initiatives could make to improving their educational and economic perspectives and, more generally, to urban development[24]; *c)* a ''mapping'' and examination of current practices and policies in fifteen Member countries of *educational provision for special populations,* particularly linguistic and indigenous cultural minorities, and analysis of the key issues pertaining to such provision, namely identification, rationales, autonomy, service delivery and costing.[25]

Out of this work also grew the longer-term CERI studies on *Early Childhood* (discussed below) and on *Multicultural Education* and on the *Handicapped* which were carried over into the eighties and which we shall consider in another chapter.

Early childhood

If the integration of educational and social/community services at the level of formal schooling remained problematic, and often controversial, the need for such integration at the preschool level came to be much more readily accepted, by both policy-makers and practitioners. The early seventies witnessed a rapidly growing interest in policies for early childhood education, partly as a result of the comparatively recent recognition of its crucial impact on lifetime chances and partly because of its role in widening opportunities for women. The fact that preschool education differed from the other sectors of initial education in not functioning through well-established institutional structures facilitated its merge with child care policies and programmes, the need for which had already been documented by previous studies of compensatory education. This escalation from problems of preschool education as such to overall policies for early childhood, including the role of the family, is well illustrated by the evolution of the OECD activities in this area during the seventies.

The initial step in this direction was a review of recent developments and trends in the Member countries, discussed at an OECD conference in late 1973.[26] More than demonstrating the limited scope of provision in most countries, and the wide variations among countries in the nature and administration of this provision, the conference provided a research-based justification for an expanded role for early childhood for economic and social reasons as well as for its contribution to the cognitive and affective development of children. This was an agenda-setting event and a number of specific issues were identified as deserving further attention: *a)* supply and demand questions, and the arguments and evidence for or against universal preschool education; *b)* problems arising from changes in the perception of "compensatory" education, reaching beyond geographical designations of disadvantage to include disadvantage deriving from social background and other individual circumstances; *c)* the need for early childhood intervention to be effectively co-ordinated with broader social, housing, health and welfare services; *d)* the need to take account of the transition from pre-primary to compulsory school provision; *e)* parental involvement, all the more important where both parents worked; *f)* specific problems of the proper training of staff and the relative amount that should be devoted in pre-primary education to the cognitive and to the social-emotional development of children.

Clarification of these questions, involving as they did the interplay between education and other social policies, on the one hand, and between the fast moving research on early childhood development and its practical applications on the other, was seen as an urgent need at a time when countries were still groping with the definition of overall policy stances on early childhood. The importance which child-care questions came to occupy in the newly established OECD programme on the *Role of Women in the Economy* gave additional impetus to the search of solutions, as reflected in the considerable number of experimental projects mounted in Member countries. Over the next few years, the CERI activity on early childhood education, expanded to include early childhood care, provided a forum for the continued analysis of significant policy developments and experimentation in this area.[27] The high level of country participation in these discussions, at the level of both policy makers and researchers, was indicative of the importance which Member countries attached to this work.

It was becoming clear by the mid-seventies that the rapid quantitative expansion of preschool provision, extending now to children of all social classes from their birth to the age of formal schooling, and encompassing a wide variety of programmes and services, raised new questions about the quality and effectiveness of these services. Attention thus shifted to the need for organisational reform of these services. This in turn called for a more "ecological" approach to the problems of childhood in order to arrive at a better understanding of the many tightly interwoven factors that constitute the child's environment and affect the use of services. Central to this approach were the changes taking place in family patterns and structures in industrialised societies and the diversity of "family realities" that children experience from their birth – meticulously analysed in a special study, drawing on demographic data to describe, among other things, the changing composition of households and families and its implications for the educational role of the family.[28] Account needed also to be taken of the different, and often conflicting, interests involved before the objectives and instruments of early childhood policies could be defined.[29] It was to these problems that the concluding phase of CERI work was addressed, culminating in an Intergovernmental Conference on Policies for Children, in March 1980.[30]

What in essence emerged from this work, and from the conference itself, was a strong political plea for the formulation of *explicit policies for early childhood* to give purpose and coherence to the wide range of fragmented and dispersed programmes that were proliferating in Member countries at that time. Preschool education could no longer be conceived in isolation of other social and economic measures addressed to children and their families. Such policies were in fact seen as inseparable from overall *family policies,* with all the sensitive issues that these policies raised in safeguarding the freedom of parental choice and avoiding the imposition of normative values through undue State intervention – policies, in other words, which fully recognised the plurality of objectives in democratic societies and allowed families to function effectively in all their diversity. To the extent that the family environment remained the dominant feature in the child's development, attention shifted to how families could be helped in their educational role, taking into account the changed family circumstances resulting from the increased incidence of divorce, single-parent families and the amount and quality of time which parents spent with their children in situations where both parents were working, while recognising at the same time the need for improved professional guidance in the upbringing and education of young children.[31]

Higher education and the community

The exploration of new education/community relationships at the level school and preschool provision, as described in the two previous sections, was accompanied by parallel investigations into the problems which these relationships posed for higher education institutions, particularly the universities. Here, the overall problematique was how these institutions could become more responsive to the needs of the communities within which they operated and more generally contribute to the solution of emerging problems in society. This raised questions not only of curriculum content and teaching methods and of the objectives of courses provided, but also of the structure of institutions and their links to the outside world.

The original impetus for this work came from the earlier study of *Interdisciplinarity.*[32] The application of the concepts and strategies which had been clarified there needed to be tried out in specific fields chosen for their inherently interdisciplinary character and being sufficiently broad for the various functions of interdisciplinarity to be empirically tested. Two such test areas were identified – *Environment* and *Health* – both also representing problems of growing concern to society and to governments. Beginning with the identification of educational objectives and study models common to both areas – a broad interdisciplinary base for all students, subsequently narrowing down to allow for specialisation and then widening out again at interdisciplinary level, with close links throughout to local or regional communities[33] – the work led to a rethinking of the institutional structures for the training of professionals in these two sectors, with strong implications for the redefinition of policy approaches to them. This is an interesting example of the pro-active role which education could play in the formulation of policies in other sectors, as already mentioned.

The *Environment* was the first area to be tackled starting with a review of general trends in environmental education and of specific experiments with interdisciplinary environmental studies in a number of countries in Europe and North America. The results were discussed at a conference in Tours (France) in April 1971 which led to the formulation of a series of recommendations addressed to governments and to higher education institutions respectively, with a separate set of recommendations for continued international co-operation in this highly volatile area still characterised by diversity of approach, of organisation, of rationale and of future expectations, and influenced more by theories, plans and proposals rather than by concrete, systematised action.[34] Much remained to be done in the way of the revision of curricula, teaching methods and university structures, one of the main conclusions of the Tours conference being that ''since it breaks new ground on every count, environmental education means that knowledge must be reorganised in terms of present problems and needs of the community''.

Though it was not to be expected that such a radical departure from epistemological traditions would meet with ready acceptance by universities and the academic establishment, the educational implications of the new environmental awareness were increasingly recognised to be profound, and significant programmes were being established in higher education institutions across the OECD membership. The next phase of the work, therefore, concentrated on deeper enquiries into the nature of these programmes directed at the training of professionals, both generalists and specialists, as well as educators and decision-makers dealing with environmental questions.[35] Based on this comprehensive review, a high-level evaluation conference was held at Rungsted (Denmark) in 1974.[36]

By that time, the wave of environmental concerns that had been sweeping over industrialised countries seemed to have somewhat lost its earlier passion, with evidence that governments had been responding to public anxiety by the setting up of Ministries of Environment and through significant innovations in policy, legislation and environmental management programmes. The international organisations had also been responding, notably the OECD with the creation of its Environment Committee and corresponding Directorate, and the United Nations with the creation of its Environment Programme following the major World Conference on Human Environment held in Stockholm in 1972.

The mood at Rungsted therefore was one of consolidation and maintaining the momentum rather than of exhortation and experimentation, even though a great deal of attention was paid to the organisation and detailed content of interdisciplinary courses and programmes and to the research requirements for environmental studies.[37] Two general recommendations stand out: Governments were urged to encourage and support the establishment of National Councils for Environmental Education to promote such education at the pre-primary, primary, secondary and post-secondary levels; higher education institutions were urged to assume leadership roles in establishing forums to formalise communication between interdisciplinary teams and decision-makers on community and regional environmental problems.[38]

The Rungsted conference marks the conclusion of OECD work on higher education and the environment. Environmental education was to be taken up again in the late eighties, driven by the resurgence of the environmental imperative. But this time the focus was the school rather than the university and the concern as much pedagogical – developing dynamic qualities in pupils through active pedagogic strategies, including action research, around environmental problems in their local setting – as with promoting deeply rooted environmental awareness in pupils, teachers and members of the community around them.[39] The ultimate objective of this work, which is still in the process of development, is how present episodic environmental education initiatives at the school level can be transformed into an integral part of school policy, permeating the curriculum and its pedagogy.

Work on the *Education of the Health Professions* proceeded in parallel with that on the environment. It was both more extensive and intensive, aided by a generous grant from the Joseph T. Macy Foundation, as well as more prescriptive in its approach, using education as an entry point into reform proposals for rapidly expanding health care system. The links between such systems and the education of health professionals were, of course, well established already, but clear discrepancies were emerging between the two in their respective rates of advance, with education lagging behind the new objectives and delivery methods of health care systems brought about by social and economic changes. The movement towards self-care and health education provided additional impetus to closer co-ordination between the two sectors and their interaction with other social sectors.

It was to look into these problems and their implications for future policies that a prestigious Group of Experts, under the chairmanship of Bror Rexed, Director General of the Swedish National Board of Health and Welfare, was set up by the OECD, under CERI initiative, in 1973. The Group had a broad mandate: "to identify major needs and possibilities for innovation in health education in the OECD countries, in the context of the organisation and management of health care systems" and make appropriate recommendations for further action by Governments and appropriate international organisations. The group reported in 1975.[40]

The recommendations which emerged from the Group's wide-ranging enquiry were as sharp as they were far-reaching. They were as follows:

i) Clearly expressed national health policies should be developed, preferably by permanently established planning mechanisms in which providers and consumers of health care play a participatory role.

ii) National health care policies should foster education/health action at the regional level, and institutions at that level should establish mechanisms to implement such action.

iii) Permanent means of co-ordinating and integrating government action in health care and education of the health professions should be established.

iv) Government agencies, educational institutions and professional organisations should encourage innovation and experimentation in different health care systems and make adequate provision for research into and evaluation of these programmes.

v) Health care systems should join with educational systems in mounting comprehensive continuing education programmes for all practising health professionals, managers and teachers.

A concluding recommendation stressed the need of continued international cooperative efforts in the above areas and, more particularly, in establishing a sound database about health care personnel and expenditure.[41]

In summary, the Group held the view that future health care should have a much stronger orientation to individualised, community-based health care. This reorientation would require professional personnel with new understanding and skills in social, psychological and management areas. The effectiveness and speed of the re-orientation hinged on new partnerships between education and health care – partnerships forged at the regional level and fostered by national and international policy clarification.[42]

Within OECD, the group's recommendations were immediately followed up along two lines of further enquiry. The first of these was directed at exploring models of education/health care interaction at the *regional* level, based notably on country material prepared for the Group's investigation. The results were discussed at an international conference at the end of 1975.[43] Underlining that the supply of health must be dynamically balanced against the demand, the conference concluded that the optimum operational unit would be the region, the objective being a better quality and more accessible type of health care, as well as the control of health expenditure. The structure which would enable such a balance to be achieved – the Regional Health University – was seen as a post-secondary complex combining various preparatory courses for training doctors and allied health personnel in the traditional way with new forms of training which would supplement the former and enable all facets of the human personality to be dealt with. Complementing national requirements, such a regional complex would undertake research, information, health education and continuing training activities, as well as co-ordinate the services responsible for health and the delivery of health care.[44] A number of specific examples of such a model operating in different Member countries were made available to the conference.

The second line of enquiry, broader and more comprehensive in its approach, had as its objective to relate the recommendations of the 1975 report to the actual situation in individual Member countries. This was done through a series of national seminars, organised jointly by the health and education authorities in each country. Backed by Secretariat-based analyses and contributions by outside experts, these seminars did more than anything else to spread the message and influence policy thinking and developments at the national level in the directions suggested by the OECD Group of Experts. They were also useful in identifying emerging areas of concern and in monitoring policy approaches to them, reinforcing even further the need for closer co-ordination of health, education and broader social policies. The cumulative experience from these seminars was put together in a synthesis report[45] which marked the concluding phase of CERI work in this field – work which throughout all its stages had been carried out in close liaison with the World Health Organisation (WHO) and had contributed in no mean way to the broader treatment by OECD of the health sector as a major component of social policies.

"Communities have problems, universities have departments"

Health and Environment were but two concrete examples of how higher education institutions could respond to the increasing number of requests emanating from the community around them. Such requests were manifold and an adequate response to them called into question some of the fundamental purposes and functions of these institutions, their structure and organisation. Particularly for universities, the dilemma of how to forge closer links with their communities – local, regional as well as national – without sacrificing their independence and without loosing their objectivity in the pursuit of their regular academic functions, was especially sharp. Yet such were the pressures arising from the democratisation of higher education, from the consequences of the economic recession that set in around the mid-seventies and of rapid technological progress, and from the proliferation of social problems, that not responding to them could lead to the undermining of the social credibility of universities.

The search for a new social role for universities was best exemplified in the growing importance which their "public service function" was assuming side by side with their traditional institutional and knowledge-production functions. All over the OECD countries, various forms of "service to the community" was becoming a regular feature of university life, regarded with suspicion in certain quarters, encouraged by others, particularly local and regional authorities. It was a disorganised process, mostly generated by conjunctural exigencies, and there was a felt need for clarification and a spelling out of its significance and implications. To this end, a broad survey of universities in Member countries was carried out between 1976 and 1978, designed to identify the nature and extent of university/community links, their motivation and their impact, actual and potential, on university structures and purposes as well as their possible contribution to new ways of knowledge generation. The results were discussed at an international conference in February 1980.

The report which emanated from all this work was indeed an exercise in clarification.[46] Building on the empirical background provided by the survey it dealt in turn with the definition of the university's environment and the concept of "service"; the many forms of institutional and working arrangements by which university/community links were operating in Member countries; the consequences for the institutions, for teaching and for research; and the problems arising from the confrontation between university independence and the responsibilities entailed in full acceptance by the university of its cultural, social and economic role. The heading of this section, taken from a chapter of this report, neatly expresses one of the main difficulties in any university/ community partnership, which takes us back to the earlier discussion on interdisciplinarity.

Conclusion

This chapter has been essentially about the social role of education during a period in which education was witnessing a transition from constant growth to stagnation and then contraction. Social problems were growing in intensity at the same time as confidence in the "Welfare State" was waning.[47] For governments, and the public more generally, it was a legitimate expectation that the enlarged position which education had come to occupy in the social fabric should be reflected in its more direct involvement in tackling emerging urgent problems in society at a time when public resources were becoming increasingly constrained. For educators and educational institutions this presented a new challenge of accommodating external pressures, which they recognised and were ready to accept so long as fundamental educational purposes, as perceived by them, were not vitiated. It also gave them an opportunity to influence developments in other policy sectors for which an educational input was considered important. In both directions the achievements were modest, and one also had to reckon with the traditional inertia of educational systems. But at least one result of this movement was the evidence it provided of a change in the political climate within which education had henceforth to negotiate its status in the polity, a change which was to become even more pronounced in the period ahead, as we shall see in the next two chapters.

Notes and references

1. See, for example, the reports on *Fundamental Research and the Policies of Governments*, OECD, 1966 and *Fundamental Research and the Universities*, OECD, 1968, both prepared by the Science side of the Directorate, and the report on *Post-Graduate Education: Structures and Policies*, OECD, 1972, prepared by the Education side.

2. *Recommendation on Manpower Policy as a Means for the Promotion of Economic Growth*, May, 1964.

3. *Educational Policies for the 1970s: General Report*, *op. cit.*

4. *Ibid.*, p. 143.

5. For a brief summary of this work see *Educational Planning: An Historical Overview of OECD Work*, *op. cit.*, p. 15 ff.

6. *Education Policies in Perspective*, *op. cit.*, p. 21; *Alternative Educational Futures*, *op. cit.*

7. *Long-Range Planning in Education*, OECD, 1973.

8. *Participatory Planning in Education*, OECD, 1974.

9. *Inter-Sectoral Educational Planning*, OECD, 1977.

10. *Education and Regional Development*, OECD, 1979.

11. *Individual Demand for Education*, Vol. I: *Analytical Report*, OECD 1978, and Vol. II: *General Report and Case Studies*, OECD, 1979.

12. Kjell Eide, *Educational Planning in Perspective*, OECD, 1978 (mimeo).

13. *Educational Planning: An Historical Overview*, *op. cit.*, pp. 19-20.

14. *Educational Planning: A Reappraisal*, OECD, 1983.

15. *Ibid.*, pp. 359-360.

16. *Evaluating Educational Programmes: The Need and the Response*; and *Case Studies in the Evaluation of Educational Programmes*, OECD/CERI, 1976.

17. Eide, *Thirty Years of Collaboration*, *op. cit.*, pp. 33-35.

18. *A Framework for Educational Indicators to Guide Government Decisions*, OECD, 1973 (mimeo).

19. *Indicators of Performance of Educational Systems*, OECD, 1973.

20. See the report of the conference, *School and Community*, OECD/CERI, 1975.

21. *Building for School and Community*, Vols. I-V, OECD/PEB, 1978-80. *Decentralisation and Educational Building Management*, OECD/PEB, 1992.

22. *School and Community*, Vol. II: *The Consequences of Some Policy Choices*, OECD/CERI, 1980.

23. J. Sher, (ed.), *Rural Education in Urbanised Nations: Issues and Innovations*. An OECD/ CERI Report, Westview Press, Boulder, Col. USA, 1981.

24. *Education, Urban Development and Local Initiatives*, OECD/CERI, 1983.

25. *The Education of Minority Groups: An Enquiry into Problems and Practices of Fifteen Countries*, Gower, UK, for OECD/CERI, 1983.

26. *Developments in Early Childhood Education*, OECD/CERI, 1975.

27. See, in particular, *Early Childhood Care and Education: Objectives and Issues*, OECD/ CERI, 1977; and *Pre-School Education: Report from Five Research Projects*, OECD/CERI, 1978. A useful analysis of significant country programmes on child care, prepared for the OECD Working Party on the Role of Women in the Economy by the US Department of Health, Education and Welfare, can be found in *Child Care Programs in Nine Countries*, DHEW, Washington D.C., 1975, Publication No. (OHD) 30080.

28. H. Le Bras, *Child and Family: Demographic Developments in the OECD Countries*, OECD/CERI, 1979.

29. *Caring for Young Children: An Analysis of Educational and Social Services*, OECD, CERI, pp. 7-8.

30. *Ibid.*, and *Children and Society: Issues for Pre-School Reforms,* OECD/CERI, 1981. These two reports, together with the Le Bras study on *Child and Family*, constituted the background documentation for the conference. The conference proceedings as such were never published. For a summary and main conclusions see CERI/CD(80)11, mimeo.

31. Issues in this area were inconclusively pursued in a subsequent CERI project on the *Educational Role of the Family*, including a conference held in Japan, the results of which were unfortunately never published.

32. *Supra,* pp. 95-96.

33. *Environmental Education at University Level: Trends and Data*, OECD/CERI, 1973, pp. 43-47.

34. *Ibid.*, pp. 31-36.

35. *Environmental Education at Post-Secondary Level*, OECD/CERI, 1974.
Vol. 1 – *The Training of Generalists and Specialists*.
Vol. 2 – *Courses for Educators, Decision-Makers and Members of Professions Concerned with the Environment*.

36. The report of the conference was published in *Environmental Problems and Higher Education*, OECD/CERI, 1976.

37. *Ibid.*, p. 28 ff. (reports and recommendations of the nine Working Groups).

38. *Ibid.*, pp. 26-27.

39. See, *Environment, Schools and Active Learning*, OECD/CERI, 1991.

40. *New Directions in Education for Changing Health Care Systems*, OECD/CERI, 1975.

41. The study on expenditure data was subsequently carried out under the programme of the Committee for Manpower and Social Affairs, *Public Expenditure on Health*, OECD, 1972.

42. *New Directions*, *op. cit.*, preface by J.R. Gass.

43. *Health, Higher Education and the Community: Towards a Regional Health University*, OECD/CERI, 1977, and list of supporting monographs of the experience of individual countries.

44. *Ibid.*, pp. 7-8.

45. P.F. Regan and H.G. Schutze, ***Education for the Health Professions: Policies for the 1980s***. An OECD/CERI Report, Almquist and Wiksell International, Stockholm, 1983 – with accompanying list of country reports and experts' papers.

46. ***The University and the Community: The Problems of Changing Relationships***, OECD/CERI, 1982.

47. ***The Welfare State in Crisis***, OECD, 1981.

Chapter VIII

RECESSION AND ITS CONSEQUENCES
(mid-seventies – early-eighties)

It was becoming apparent by the mid-seventies that the educational euphoria of the previous decade was giving way to a growing sense of anxiety about future educational prospects. The transition was gradual, perceived more immediately by policy-makers and planners rather than by those who were concerned with the day-to-day business of education, teachers, pupils and parents. It was only towards the end of the decade that its effects began to be fully felt throughout the educational system, its operators and its institutions.

The turning point was the onset of the 1973-75 recession, consequent on the first oil shock. Overall educational expansion had been slowing down in many countries for some years, and this was perhaps inevitable after the hectic rate of growth in the fifties and sixties. The new economic situation sharply accelerated this process and its effects. Declining rates of economic growth and high inflation, leading to increasing curbs on public expenditure and on the rise of real incomes, were accompanied by steadily rising levels of unemployment affecting the most vulnerable groups, especially young people. Equally important changes were taking place in demographic trends resulting from the sharp drop in fertility rates which had set in around the mid-sixties, becoming much steeper in the early seventies.

This combination of resource constraints, high unemployment and demographic downturn had a direct impact on the demand for education as well as on the perception of its role and of its contribution to social and economic development. Coinciding with the advent of conservative governments in a large number of Member countries, it brought about a dramatic change in the political context of education. Continued growth could no longer be taken for granted either as a feasible or even a desirable objective. Constraints on public spending were particularly telling. As one of the major components of public budgets, education had to share the burden of restraint and became in fact a favoured target for ministries of finance engaged in the battle against inflation. Resource limitations raised new questions about the setting of priority objectives, in contrast to the earlier situation where a multiplicity of educational objectives could be pursued more or less simultaneously. This scramble for priorities among different interest groups sharpened the political conflict around education, its objectives and the direction and content of educational reform. The educational debate became increasingly politicised.

At the heart of this debate was the issue of how, in its constrained circumstances, education could adjust its role and functions to short-term exigencies without losing sight of its essentially long-term purposes and objectives; and how to do this against the background of growing uncertainties about the future economic and employment situation, also taking into account the new challenges and opportunities, arising from likely changes in modes of living and social patterns. If past strategies were no longer applicable, what new ones could be suggested? It was to this question that the OECD endeavoured to make a contribution from the mid-seventies onwards.

Searching for new policy directions for education: the first OECD Education Ministerial

It was recognised from the start that any attempt at redefining strategies for education in its new social and economic environment was an essentially political exercise which had to involve those with direct responsibility for educational policy making in the Member countries. The occasion for this was provided by the meeting of OECD Ministers of Education, held in October 1978. The very fact of this first ever OECD Education Ministerial (breaking with the tradition of resorting to the Standing Conference of European Ministers of Education) was indicative both of the political importance of the matter and of the interest which Member governments attached to the role of the Organisation in contributing to the elucidation of the complex issues involved and the search for appropriate solutions.

In typical OECD fashion, the Meeting had been well prepared, with the clear objective of enabling Ministers to arrive at an agreed set of conclusions to guide future educational policies. The ground had been softened up by two earlier reports – one on *Education and Working Life in Modern Society*[1] (of which more later on); and the other on overall *Education Policies and Trends*[2] – each prepared by a small group of eminent experts appointed by the Secretary-General. At the same time, the Organisation's Economic Policy Committee, as part of its general concern with containing public spending at a time of inflation and recession, picked the education sector for special analysis of past trends and estimates of future public expenditure. The general conclusion was that the proportion of GDP represented by traditional expenditure on education need not rise much in real terms above its level of the early seventies[3] – a conclusion which was questioned by the Education Committee. The Committee argued that future public expenditure on education could not be derived simply from an extrapolation of past trends and had to take into account new educational needs arising from social change as well as recognition of the fact that education is a good in its own right to which expenditure may be devoted without any ulterior justification. In the last analysis, decisions about resource allocation are political, depending on the choices of society, or rather of governments acting in its name.[4]

In endorsing this view, the Group of Experts on *Educational Policies and Trends* – all of whom, it should be noted, had strong affiliations to national Ministries of Education[5] – put forward two general considerations which guided their approach to the discussion of future educational policies: *a)* no valid projections existed as to the precise nature and pattern of the future development of the economies and of the employment situation in countries which could serve as a guide for the long-term planning of education. Education, therefore, could not be expected to adapt to economic cycles and, in particular, its long-term development could not be planned for a perspective other than one of full employment; *b)* the higher levels of educational participation and attainment among all groups of the population which had resulted from the massive growth of education in the post-war period represented a major social change of a secular nature, the consequences and irreversibility of which future policies for education could not ignore.[6]

Unrealistic as the first of these pronouncements may sound today, it should be remembered that the general expectation at the time was that OECD economies and labour markets would soon be reverting to their former vitality. The transient phenomenon of economic recession did not justify the severe attack to which many felt education was being subjected. The long-term role of education needed to be defended, even though it was recognised, as the Group made clear in its report, that important changes were required of established educational systems to enable them to better respond to new and pressing social and economic demands. Indeed, one of the main conclusions of the report was that, far from being a shrinking domain of public activity, education had to broaden its role in order to meet these expanded demands. In any case, the assertive line taken by the Group is illustrative of the cleavage in the educational debate that prevailed at that time and the difficulties of arriving at political consensus about future educational policy directions.

When the Ministers met, they had at their disposal a dispassionate analysis by the Secretariat of recent trends in education and of changes in the socio-economic variables that influenced the social demand for education as well as its supply, which taken together would largely determine the future quantitative and qualitative development of educational systems.[7] The conclusions which emerged from this analysis can be briefly summarised.

The drop in the birth-rate – with two-thirds of Member countries being already below the generation replacement threshold – was leading to a steady decrease in enrolments in compulsory schooling, estimated to reach up to 15 per cent by the mid-eighties. (Secondary and higher education would be affected in their turn, though not synchronically.) Diminution in enrolments was resulting in teacher surpluses and surplus school accommodation. This was seen as providing a golden opportunity for improving pupil/teacher ratios and the general quality of the service, with extra attention being paid to measures to expand and improve preschool education, combat school failure and meeting the special needs of the socially disadvantaged and those with physical disabilities. More generally, demographic changes were leading to the ageing of the population, altering the social environment in which young people would be living and increasing the social burden on the working population at a time when the supply of young people on the labour market would be decreasing. Education would have increasingly to compete with other social services, particularly health, for its share of public expenditure.

At the post-compulsory school level, the impact of the demographic decline would not be felt before the mid-eighties, and the strong growth which this sector had witnessed was expected to be maintained, supported by an increase in enrolment rates due, in part, to more young people choosing to prolong their education in the face of poor job prospects. Significant changes, however, were taking place in the demand for education at this level, in favour of the technical and vocational sectors, and also as a result of the increased supply of training programmes and other measures to ease the transition to working life. A different trend was evident with regard to tertiary education, where the growth in enrolments had been witnessing a marked slowing down since 1970, caused primarily by a drop in the transfer rate of secondary school leavers to universities as well as by a growing propensity by students to take short-cycle or vocationally-oriented courses in order to improve their chances on the labour market. This change in the social demand for higher education, attributable to the effects of the employment situation, was reinforced by the trend towards increased participation by adults, particularly for part-time courses, which in turn was reflected in changes in admission policies as higher education establishments sought to broaden their recruitment base.

Throughout the trends outlined above, concern with the changed relationship between education and employment was as pervasive as it was illusory. Slack labour markets were leading to a quantitative imbalance between labour supply and demand as well as to imbalances of a more qualitative nature, between the demands of the market and the output of the educational system. Job aspirations among young people were felt to be raised by their educational attainment above levels sustainable by the labour market. Conversely, the employment sector was not adequately responding to the rising levels of education among the working population, resulting in increased under-utilisation of the skills and capacities of the labour force. The forces at play were subtle and not easily amenable to diagnosis, let alone remedies. For governments, the main way by which they could intervene was through measures to improve the transition between school and working life, which explains the sustained policy attention which this matter attracted in the years ahead.

Finally, two salient features stood out in trends in educational resources. *Teaching personnel,* which had increased by about one-third during the sixties, was now in surplus, upsetting previous recruitment patterns and training policies. New solutions had to be sought, ranging from determined efforts in some countries to improve teacher/pupil ratios and raise the level of initial and in-service teacher training to a concern in other countries to cut down on recruitment and on the places available in training establishments, while recognising that a degree of surplus had to be tolerated to avoid the danger of shortages in the longer-term. The level of public *financial resources,* whose growth had markedly slowed down since 1970 – particularly reflected in cut-backs in primary education, in buildings and equipment and in teacher training – was increasingly squeezed by budgetary restrictions imposed since 1975. The planning hypothesis retained in the Secretariat analysis was that an increase in educational spending by one percentage point of GDP would be necessary by 1985 simply to meet the requirements of new programmes on preschool, compulsory and adult education.

Deriving from the above overall analysis, a clear set of issues were put for consideration by Ministers. These were:

– enhancing the quality of education;

- the pursuit of equality of educational opportunity;
- combatting the marginalisation of young people;
- the development of democratic and efficient management of the educational system.

(A separate item dealt specifically with the contribution of education to preparation for working life and the transition to employment, with which we shall deal in the next section.)

No doubt, the Ministers' discussion was both interesting and useful. It enabled Ministers to recognise the common problems confronting them and to benefit from the exchange about how solutions to these problems were being sought in the different Member countries. It would be fair to say, however, that neither in the analysis of the predicaments which educational policies faced nor in the options available for their resolution did the discussion break new ground beyond what had been put to Ministers in the Secretariat report. This was largely inevitable in view of the detailed consultations with the Member countries which had taken place in preparing the meeting. But at least in three respects the meeting was of particular importance.

Firstly, it was the first serious occasion which enabled educational politicians at the highest level, operating as they did within an OECD context, to confront their sectoral interests and ambitions to the stark economic realities of the time. In this sense, the meeting was an educational experience for many Ministers themselves. That it was appreciated was evident from the Ministers' decision to repeat the exercise at periodic intervals in the future. It set the pattern for similar meetings in 1984 and 1990. Secondly, while fully recognising the economic constraints and the need for education to respond to emerging social and economic demands, Ministers were able to re-asert in the most explicit manner the fundamental plural aims which education served in modern societies and from which it should not be allowed to be diverted in reaction to short-term external pressures. Thirdly, Ministers were able to agree on a clearly defined set of aims which deserved priority consideration in the formulation of educational policies to take account of the changing social and economic context. These priorities, (the "Ten Commandments", as they subsequently came to be referred to) and their underlying considerations, were embodied in a formal "Declaration", agreed by the Ministers and endorsed by the Council of the Organisation, something which in itself was without precedent in the OECD.[7] Though not binding on governments, the Declaration was to serve as a useful source of inspiration for the future directions of national policies and even more so for the definition of subsequent work within the OECD educational programmes.

The Education Ministerial can be seen as the *political* manifestation of the OECD response to the consequences of the recession and to the agonising process of the adaptation of education to conditions of contraction. Much of the educational work that the Organisation undertook in the years immediately before and after the Ministerial can similarly be seen as the *operational* response to the same problems. It was dominated, in a context of financial constraints, by employment concerns and their impact on both the supply of education and the social demand for it, particularly as it affected young people and adults and the institutions serving them.

The employment imperative

The relations between education and working life had been a constant preoccupation of the OECD educational programmes from their inception. That these relationships were undergoing severe strain was evident even during the happy days of educational expansion and full employment. The 1968 student revolt provided ample signals for this, particularly in highlighting the basic contradictions in modern societies whereby education for freedom, autonomy and individual fulfilment was followed, for many, by routine and boring work in hierarchic organisations: education could not fulfil its function of providing a basis for employment without a corresponding move in the other direction to adapt jobs to the aspirations of a more highly educated labour force. The old lines of division between education and work were themselves getting increasingly blurred. Taken together with broader contextual factors – the effects of rapid technological change; the questioning and, often, the rejection of the values, modes and structures of the past; and the questioning of many other social and political barriers in society – the relationship between education and working life inevitably merged into the larger question of how to equip people to play a useful role in society and to manage their own lives.

It was to look into these problems, and suggest co-ordinated approaches to their solution, that the Secretary-General set up a Group of Experts on Education and Employment, in December 1973. The Group's report,[8] completed within a year, was made available to the Ministerial Meeting on Education, as already mentioned. It was a pithy, policy-oriented document with a series of specific recommendations covering social as well as economic objectives, which, though not particularly novel in themselves, as a total package went well beyond the current performance of any single Member country.

The main thrust of these recommendations was that the world of work and education had a joint responsibility in contributing to individual development and human satisfaction, thereby providing more equity in society as well as greater enhancement of all human resources and contributions. This called, on the one hand, for a "positive policy for working life", designed to promote and support action by the social partners to improve the quality of working life and to provide greater opportunities for the disadvantaged; and, on the other, for a more "integrative policy for education" of which recurrent education would be its core idea. "Continuing education for adults should become a major priority for government policy", with more flexible rules enabling individuals to move between (and within) education, work and leisure. "We favour more options for individuals in an increasingly "free-choice" society."[9]

Thus, the Group's diagnosis and recommendations were primarily *socially* driven. This was in line with the political climate which still prevailed then. However, by the time the Ministers of Education came to consider these problems, the climate had changed with youth unemployment constantly rising – reaching over 10 per cent in the OECD area as a whole and expected to get worse – and with clear indications that it represented a structural phenomenon with lasting consequences, strongly aggravated by conjunctural factors. The gravity of the problem was highlighted at the 1977 annual meeting of the OECD Council at Ministerial Level, where it was agreed that "in the efforts to reduce unemployment, particular attention should be paid to the unemployment of young workers''. Noting that a wide range of special measures were being taken in Member countries and that more might be needed, Ministers instructed the Organisation ''to strengthen its exchange of experience and organise urgently a ference for this purpose''.[10]

It was inevitable that Ministers of Education, while endorsing the social stand in the Experts Group's report, would feel under pressure by the employment imperative to give more attention to the ways in which education and training could help alleviate the dramatic situation of young people in the labour market. This they did by giving detailed consideration to two strategic areas: *a)* better preparation for working life during *compulsory schooling*; *b)* measures designed to ease the *transition* of young people to employment at various exit points from the educational system, *i.e.* those entering the labour market before completion of upper secondary education, those entering after completing upper secondary education and those graduating from higher education, and the implications that such measures carried for the reform and reorganisation of studies at these various educational levels, including improvements in career education and occupational guidance.[11] These themes were to dominate the continued discussion of the relationship between education and working life for many years to come, with employment considerations taking precedence over social concerns.

In these discussions, and the substantive work behind them, the point of departure was recognition of the reality that youth unemployment resulted from low levels of economic activity and job availability: ''when there are not enough jobs to accommodate the supply of labour, it is youth who bear a disproportionate share of the burden''.[12] There was no question, therefore, of education being responsible for youth unemployment or that it could provide the overall remedy. What it could do was to improve the chances of individuals in the waiting queue for jobs, by building up their competences and skills more in line with the demands of the labour market – hence the importance which was attached to the revamping of vocational education and training. It is important to underline this because of the tendency observed on the part of certain economic and employment quarters, unable themselves to raise the general level of employment, to look on education and training as the panacea to youth unemployment – a view which often led to friction between the education and the employment constituencies.

Within the Organisation, the approach taken was that the two sides had a shared responsibility in tackling youth unemployment, the main problem being how to bring the separate administrations in the Member countries to work together. As a first move in this direction, the unprecedented step was taken of organising a joint meeting of the Education and the Manpower and Social Affairs Committees to discuss the conclusions of the Expert Group's report on *Education and Working Life in Modern Society.* (It was interesting to note that a number of national delegates to this joint session were meeting their opposite numbers within national administrations for the first time!) The practical outcome of this meeting was the setting up of a Joint Working Party of officials from Member countries representing the interests of the two sides ''to discuss and agree the objectives of public policies for education and working life and to consider how they can in practice be attained''.

In its report,[13] the Working Party dealt with two broad areas of policy: the transition from education to working life and the utilisation of education in employment. Within these areas a number of common thematic conclusions were identified to serve not as prescriptive policies, but rather as broad objectives agreed by all Member countries which could be attained through different country strategies according to national circumstances. These conclusions did not differ greatly from what had already emerged from previous work. Where they broke new ground was in explicitly linking educational initiatives to the need for parallel efforts on the employment side to improve the utilisation of the education and training of the labour force and in underlying the crucial role of the social partners therein. In addition, the process of joint deliberation which led to these conclusions initiated a habit of co-operation between the two sides within national administrations towards the co-ordination of measures and the identification of combined policy instruments in the fight against youth unemployment. Endorsed by the two Committees, these conclusions also provided the impetus for further joint work in this area within the Organisation.

Vocational education and training

The focus of this further work was on policies for *vocational education and training, i.e.* on an area where educational and employment interests come operationally together; an area, moreover, which, traditionally relegated to second place in terms of social status and prestige, was now surfacing as a major policy priority for governments because of its direct relevance to employment, a relevance which was also pushing up the social demand for this kind of education. Significant increases in public funds were being committed to it, both within and more particularly outside the formal education system, reflected in the vast array of training schemes by which governments sought to provide meaningful alternatives to the young unemployed and, incidentally, to define many of the 16-19 year olds out of the labour market; and this at a time when other sectors of public expenditure were being reduced in many countries.

Much of this expansion was taking place on an ad hoc basis and it was clear that the time was ripe to try and infuse some policy coherence into this disparate and rapidly expanding sector. Australia pointed the way in having its Educational Policy Review focus on the transition from school to work and further study.[14] Other countries sought inspiration from the apparent success of the Germanic *dual system* in keeping levels of youth unemployment down. Suddenly there was a resurgence of interest in apprenticeship, the corner stone of the dual system, and the OECD devoted a special, and critical, study to the development of apprenticeship schemes in the Member countries for the lessons that they could provide for the overall reform of vocational education and training.[15] The dual system, which in earlier times had tended to be denigrated because, among other things, of its assumed social selection bias, was now being rehabilitated as a model not necessarily for emulation, but as containing useful features more in tune with the new economic realities and on which other countries could draw.

The Apprenticeship Study was part of a more general review of how the various Member countries were trying to adjust their systems of vocational education and training to the economic and social changes of the seventies.[16] Even though these systems differed greatly, the general aim was strikingly similar: to promote economic recovery, to reduce unemployment and to help specific groups in the labour market obtain access to jobs. An Intergovernmental Meeting (1978), attended by senior officials from Ministries of Education and of Manpower and Employment, brought this clearly out, while also demonstrating the value which Member countries attached to comparing the different approaches they were using in trying to achieve this aim. To this end, the Joint Working Party of the two Committees was resurrected, entrusted with the task of reviewing the current state of policies for vocational education and training and identifying the options open to Member countries under their changed conditions of economic activity and the labour market and also having regard to their future economic, technological and social development. The Working Party reported in 1982 and its findings were adopted by both Committees.[17]

In its comprehensive coverage, the report stands out as a useful manual for all those dealing with the manifold aspects of vocational education and training. As its title indicates, it was concerned as much with the existing state of the art as with the future. This was particularly so in the attention it paid to the implications for vocational education and training at all stages of the widening applications of new technologies; and also in underlining the impact of the rapidly growing tertiary sector and its increasing share of employment as against that of the manufacturing sector with which vocational education and training was traditionally associated. Both of these questions were to acquire a dominant influence and consideration in the years that followed in the context of the restructuring of OECD economics.

Beyond that, the report spelled out in detail the changing role and status of vocational education and training in relation to general education as well as for economic, social, industrial, regional and local development. It included consideration of the institutional arrangements for the formulation of policies for vocational education and training, its quality and measures to bring vocational education in schools, initial and further training into a more coherent sequence of opportunities for individuals. It stressed the need for policies to place current short-duration work experience programmes for new entrants to the labour force within a longer-term strategy for the employment of less competitive groups; and discussed the distribution of responsibilities for training between the public authorities and employers, including the effectiveness of financial formulae and mechanisms. On this last point, the involvement of the social partners, through BIAC and TUAC, throughout the deliberations of the Working Party was of particular value. It demonstrated that, even if the interests of the two sides often compete in the labour market in the short run, they coincide on many issues when placed in a long-term perspective.

It is interesting to note that in this joint work of the two Committees the initiative and management of the activity rested with the Education side. This was in part due to the location of Secretariat capacity. But it also reflected the reality that it was education which was under particular pressure to respond, representing as it did a more clearly identifiable, and therefore more amenable to change, *system* than the labour market, if indeed one can speak of the labour market as being "a system". Moreover, many of the problems of the employment of young people were seen as having their origin in basic education and the way it fulfilled its function of equipping individuals with the minimum competences for entry into working life. Changes in technology and in the organisation of work necessitated a redefinition of these competences with direct consequences for the reform of curricula and teaching methods, particularly at the compulsory school level. An attempt at such redefinition was in fact undertaken in the follow-up to the Working Party's report, under three categories: *a) abilities and techniques,* covering reasoning, propensity for continuous learning, reading, writing, calculating skills, manual skills and elementary technology; *b) personal and social skills,* including work values, communicating skills and health and safety; *c) knowledge about working life,* including finding a job and survival and development in employment.[18]

But even here, responsibility was not exclusively with the education system. It was, therefore, felt necessary to try and delineate as clearly as possible how education and training could contribute to the employment of young people so as to avoid unrealistic expectations and unjustifiable blame. This was done through a formal Statement by the Education Committee, based on the results of all its work in this area.[19]

The immediate background to this Statement is to be seen in the high expectations that manpower and employment services had of education in relation to the labour market problems of young people, as underlined by the meeting of the Manpower and Social Affairs Committee at Ministerial level in March 1982. One objective of this Statement was to reduce these expectations to realistic levels. The general tone was set in the preamble to the Statement, which, because it encapsulates the essence of the problem, is worth quoting in *extenso.*

> "The Committee wishes to draw attention to the danger of three potential misunderstandings about the role of education and training in relation to the labour market problems of young people:
>
> First, education should not be diverted from the continuing purpose of helping all young people become mature and self-reliant adults, able to understand and contribute to the culture in which they live. Preparing them for life at work, important as it is, should be seen as part of this responsibility.
>
> Second, even though education and some training schemes withdrew many young people from the labour force so that they are not counted among the unemployed, unrealistic expectations should not be raised about the ability of education and training to resolve problems which are primarily the responsibility of other fields of policy, notably the creation of jobs through economic and employment policies. Whilst education and training cannot create jobs, the labour market problems of trained people are less than of those who have little or no training.
>
> Third, because the creation of jobs is beyond the scope of education and training systems, these systems and the resources devoted to them, should be judged, not by inappropriate criteria such as the reduction of unemployment, but by their effectiveness in qualifying young people for employment and in giving them the skills needed to contribute to production when they become employed or self-employed."

The main body of the statement dealt with an analysis of the labour market problems of young people, followed by a "balanced perspective" about the roles of education and training in relation to their current unemployment and their future employment. It concluded with the unavoidability of increased public responsibility for all young people beyond compulsory schooling, whether in the form of a "Youth Guarantee", of the kind explicitly adopted in some Nordic countries,[20] or more implicitly through the provision of a variety of measures – education, training, work experience and combinations thereof – applied in the majority of Member countries.

In this, an essential consideration was the need to offer young people *meaningful* activity so as to stimulate their interest in education and work and reduce their level of insecurity and confusion in an era of job scarcity. There was ample evidence to show that, contrary to what many people believed at the time, young people in general did not reject the traditional values of society and its institutions – family, school and work. What they did question was the *relevance* of the offerings available to them in terms of helping them establish a firm foothold as adults in rapidly changing, but job-poor societies.[21] The road to adulthood had indeed become much more complex and troublesome, and much less "visible" than in the past, and there were fundamental causes behind it of which employment was only one, even though a critical, aspect.[22] This was fully reflected in the variety of institutional innovations by which governments attempted to ease the extended transition process for many young people. Inevitably, most of these innovations were in the form of education and training programmes, many of which, however, were often no more than "parking places" for the young.[23]

Here we shall have to leave the vocational education and training story for the time being. Priority in subsequent work was given to its integration into comprehensive policies for post-compulsory education and training and to the further education and training of the adult labour force, before specific problems of vocational education and training as such were taken up again in the late eighties.

Higher education in crisis

In no other sector of education were the effects of the economic recession, and its accompanying changes in the social and political climate, more explicitly felt than in higher education. The promises held by the extended period of growth and diversification came to be stultified by the onset of stagnation which began to be felt from around the mid-seventies onwards. So much so that when, in 1981, the OECD reviewed the situation at an *Intergovernmental Conference on Policies for Higher Education* one could openly speak of higher education being in a state of crisis, a crisis which is still in the process of being resolved. The prevailing mood is aptly captured in the following extract from the Chairman's concluding remarks:

...at the beginning of the eighties the over-riding concern reflected in the Conference seems to be how to sustain public confidence in and support for a system which, in most countries, is no longer growing in such a way as to ensure its continued dynamic evolution ... In many countries there appears to be a crisis of confidence which is approaching alarming dimensions. Unless new policies are rapidly conceived and implemented there may be a real danger, over the longer term, that the potential of higher education for supporting countries' economic vitality and the welfare of their citizens, through cultural, scientific and technological development, could be seriously and perhaps irretrievably compromised.[24]

Many factors were collectively responsible for this dramatic reversal of earlier expectations. They were analysed in detail in the background documentation prepared by the Secretariat for the Conference.[25] Chief among them were finance constraints, at a time when higher education systems were under continuing pressures to assume new roles and meet new demands. In the majority of OECD countries, public expenditure on higher education ceased to grow by 1975 and in a number of them actually declined between 1975 and 1980, leading to a pronounced fall in expenditure per student.[26] On the whole, it was the higher education sector which bore the brunt of governmental budgetary constraints, which in essence amounted to a shift in political priorities, at least as far as traditional higher education was concerned.

In many countries, financial stagnation was accompanied by a levelling off in the demand for higher education, with the prospect of very slow growth in demand during the eighties. The high increase observed between 1965 and 1970 slowed down quite sharply in the ensuing five-year period and continued to drop thereafter, growth rates even becoming negative in some countries. It affected all categories of students, whether taking a first degree or engaging in post-graduate studies, and all types of higher education, whether university or non-university, though university enrolments were hit the hardest. Demographic factors – a shrinkage in the relevant age-groups – partly accounted for this decline. But even more important, and more disturbing, was a diminution of the proportion of secondary school-leavers proceeding directly to higher education, signalling a waning interest among young people in at least certain types of higher education.[27]

This waning interest was not unrelated to changed perceptions among young people about the social and economic value of post-secondary education. So far, higher education graduates had enjoyed a relatively privileged position in relation to their less educated contemporaries. However, their employment prospects were now becoming gloomier: curbs on public expenditure were resulting in less job creation in the public sector, traditionally the main employment outlet for graduates. Similarly, recruiting into teaching, their other major employment outlet, was also diminishing as a result of the stabilisation of school enrolment. In the prevailing economic climate it was unlikely that worthwhile alternatives could be provided by the private sector where the growth of qualified jobs had not kept pace with the supply of highly educated people. Inevitably, higher education graduates were seeing a relative decline in their private returns to education and of their overall status in society.[28]

Taken together, the factors outlined above – all external to the higher education system – largely explain the crisis of public confidence in the performance of higher education. But the crisis had another, internal and perhaps more fundamental dimension, one that touched on the very purposes of higher education institutions, their nature, their roles and functions and their place in the total higher education system. This was particularly true of the universities many of which had seen their mission diffused during the earlier period of growth and affluence and which found it difficult to sustain this role when additional resources were no longer available. They were also the ones to which public criticism was most frequently directed, in terms of lack of responsiveness to new demands, declining quality and vitality and inability to reconcile traditional values and functions with the requirements of mass education. They saw their strongly entrenched position as the guardians of academic standards and the pace-setters for the entire system seriously assailed for the first time. A reappraisal of the position of universities as an essential element in any reform of the higher education system emerged as an urgent need at the Intergovernmental Conference.

The internal crisis was also reflected in the upheaval which characterised the governance and power structures in higher education institutions. There was, firstly, a marked move in the seventies towards increased direct involvement of governments in the affairs of higher education – a move which was often resisted by the academic community as unacceptable interference with the freedom they traditionally enjoyed. Secondly, there were pressures towards more democratic or representative decision-making processes in the internal governance of institutions of higher education, and for the participation of external groups in the definition of institutional programmes and objectives to make them more responsive to the needs of the community – again raising questions about the dilution of academic freedom and the disinterested advancement of knowledge. All this, finally, raised the political question of who defines and controls the quality of higher education studies and evaluates their outcome. The dominance of strictly academic criteria in such assessments was thus being put into question, with the locus of judgement on the quality of the work of higher education institutions tending to shift outside the institutions themselves. All in all, the monopoly of academia was under attack.

All these questions were debated at length at the Conference, recognising that there was no easy way out of the crisis. Indeed, the crisis would deepen in the years ahead. But at least the main predicaments confronting higher education policies were clearly recognised[29] and these provided the recurring themes which nourished the OECD programme on higher education throughout the eighties. It will be convenient to deal with this important work at this point, even though chronologically it belongs to the next chapter.

Access to higher education[30]

From the point of view of the growth and vitality of higher education systems, access and admission policies was the central issue. It involved consideration of:

a) *The relationship between secondary and higher education,* particularly how to relieve the strain in countries, mostly European, where the trend was to set limits to the overall intake capacity of higher education; the balance to be achieved between the various self-sufficient objectives of secondary education and those which were more or less imposed by higher education institutions through their entrance requirements; the question of who should decide on the basic entrance qualifications to higher education and, when entry standards are not met, who should bear the main responsibility for remedial education; what should be the degree of uniformity of entrance requirements among and within different types of institutions and programmes; what value should be assigned to vocational and practical talents.[31]

b) Opening up the system to new or under-represented groups and to new forms of participation. Restrictive policies and cuts in student-aid schemes were leading to a stagnation in the proportion of higher education students from low socio-economic origins, and even to decline in some of the more selective and prestigious institutions. Though this deterioration was constantly deplored, nothing much was, or indeed could be, done about it; equity considerations were receding to the background and no sustained effort was made, including within OECD itself, even to monitor the evolution of socio-economic disparities in higher education – in striking contrast to what had been done in earlier times.

Instead, attention was targeted on two special groups – *women* and *adults* – both of which represented important, and well-lobbied growth potentials for higher education. In fact, it was these two groups from which higher education drew to make up for the decline in numbers coming from its more traditional clientele, male secondary school graduates.

Female participation in higher education had made spectacular progress in the decade between 1975 and 1985. It was part of the broader movement of equality between the two sexes in all economic and social spheres, marked by the UN's International Decade for Women ending with the Nairobi Conference in July 1985. The OECD contributed actively to the pursuit of this objective and to the monitoring of overall progress made in its Member countries.[32] It devoted a special study to its educational components.[33]

The study showed that, in terms of numbers, equality between male and female students had been achieved throughout the school system, including upper secondary education, and that in many countries the balance of women to men in the total higher education population was much closer to numerical equality than the one-third share common even as recently as 1970. Such aggregates, however, hid important inequalities between the sexes in terms of subjects studied. Fundamental divisions by gender were still apparent along the classic lines of women following courses in the humanities, arts and languages, with men predominant in the applied sciences. But even here there was evidence of some progress, women making increasing inroads into traditionally male branches, particularly in medical studies, law and architecture and in business management, commerce and administration. The one area where access of women still lagged well behind that of men was post-graduate education: women were, and still remain, heavily unrepresented in scientific research. And they continued, of course, to be discriminated against in the labour market: not only because the feminised faculties tended to be those where subsequent job opportunities were badly affected by the recession, but also because the technical and applied sciences, often highly valued on the labour market, remained, despite modest changes, male bastions, rendering still more imposing the task of eliminating employment and occupational segregation.

Adults in higher education were a relatively new group, despite a long tradition in some countries of extra-mural part-time studies. Though still marginal in numbers, they were particularly welcome to higher education institutions struggling to maintain their viability; and many of these institutions, and in some cases governments themselves, were willing to adjust their admission policies and modes of instruction to facilitate effective access by these non-traditional students. They were a heterogeneous group, with different motivations and objectives:

- those who entered or re-entered higher education in order to pursue mainstream studies leading to a full first degree or diploma;
- those who re-entered to update their professional knowledge or acquire additional qualifications;
- those without previous experience in higher education, enrolling for specific professional purposes, especially in short duration courses;
- those, with or without previous experience in higher education, who enrolled for courses with the explicit purpose of personal fulfilment.[34]

The growing incursion of these categories of adults into higher education provided the spearhead for the development of policies, at governmental and institutional levels, to promote *continuing education,* as distinct from traditional adult education discussed earlier, through the higher education system. Such policies necessitated organisational changes designed to remove barriers to adult participation, such as open admission in some countries (US) or recognition of work or life experience as a equivalent to entry qualifications in others (Sweden). Of even greater importance was the availability of part-time modes of study in order to permit adults to combine study and work. Other organisational options included distance study – and not only through "Open Universities" – facilitated by the rapid advance in telecommunications and information media permitting interactive modes of communication; credit transfer; modular courses; and the provision of suitable information and counselling facilities.

These developments were still fairly new to most higher education systems. Their pace depended on the degree of flexibility with which individual systems were endowed; it was more rapid, for example, in the US and Canada, as well as in Australia and New Zealand, than in most European countries. In all cases, however, as the numbers of adults in higher education increased, and as they gradually came to be integrated into the mainstream of institutional provision, so did continuing education come to be recognised as a genuine mission of higher education, side by side with initial education and research. During a period when such innovation as existed in higher education was primarily concerned with reacting to contraction and budgetary constraints, the advent of mature students provided a new and refreshing impetus not only for growth, but also for change.

Universities and their alternatives: a reappraisal

The need for a re-examination of the purposes and functions of higher education institutions, and more particularly of the position of universities, emerged as a clear recommendation from the 1983 Intergovernmental Conference. Sustained attention was given to this question in the OECD programmes throughout the eighties, resulting in three major studies covering the university and non-university sectors and post-graduate education.[35] It was a daunting task to undertake internationally, not least because of the pronounced differences – historical, legislative, administrative and social – which characterise higher education systems across the OECD membership. That countries were willing to support such an enterprise, and to contribute specially prepared analyses of their respective situations as a basis for such a review, is nevertheless indicative of their recognition of the commonality of the problems afflicting their higher education systems and of the importance they attached to a sharing of experience with regard to the options available for tackling them. Particularly with regard to universities, one had the feeling that their sacrosanct position could be more conveniently attacked internationally rather than within specific national contexts.

The detailed findings of these studies provide very useful insights for an understanding of contemporary higher education policies. Perhaps the most striking feature of the overall picture which emerged was the contrast between the security, prestige and credibility which the non-university sector had succeeded in establishing for itself over the past fifteen years or so, on the one hand, and the uncertainty with which much of the university sector was still struggling in its efforts to adapt to new demands and outside pressures, on the other. This was a reversal of the situation which had prevailed in earlier times, when the non-university sector was searching for an identify. In terms of numbers, growth patterns between the two sectors had been largely similar even though in some countries the expansion of the non-university sector had been quite spectacular. In terms of clarity of purpose, service to the community, the employability of graduates and innovative approaches to teaching methods and course content and design, the non-university sector had moved ahead – so much so that many universities were now seeking to appropriate at least some of the attributes which had been specific to their sister institutions.

Differences, of course, still remained, particularly in the employment conditions of teaching staff and in the location of research, though these varied from institution to institution and from country to country. On the whole, however, parity of esteem had been largely achieved. Universities themselves were becoming increasingly differentiated, so that the question was no longer one of the traditional distinction between the two sectors, but rather of a new kind of differentiation among institutions across both sectors, leading to new types of prestige hierarchies and "pecking orders". The binary divide became increasingly blurred and the recent decision in the United Kingdom to confer university status on all Polytechnics marks the logical recognition of this development.

The strain on universities had indeed been considerable as they struggled to adjust their instructional and scholarly functions to expanded societal demands and to basic changes in the very nature of knowledge, particularly in the natural sciences. New, and more heterogeneous, student populations necessitated a greater diversity of programmes and of organisational arrangements, raising questions about how the demands of equity could be reconciled to the need for maintaining academic standards and quality. Pressures for career-oriented courses of study, at both the first degree and the post-graduate level, led to the danger of over-vocationalisation of study programmes at the expense of their general education component. The decline in the employment value of the social sciences and the humanities tended to undermine the standing of these disciplines in which the bulk of the student population was still to be found. Those among universities which had formerly flourished on their "liberal arts" orientation found themselves particularly vulnerable to the effects of these trends.

All of this pointed to the need for serious rethinking of the structure and purpose of undergraduate studies, particularly in the "soft" sciences which came increasingly to be seen as basic preparation for further, more specialised, studies leading to employment, rather than as terminal courses. The problem was exacerbated by the fact that, within faculty, the dominant interest and skills were in research rather than in teaching and pedagogy.

A similar state of crisis was evident at the *post-graduate level,* where professional concerns were taking precedence over academic interests and pursuits and the pedagogical value of research. This was reflected in the growing demand for an intermediate post-graduate degree between the first degree and the doctorate, such as the terminal master's degree in the US. The majority of students in such degree courses were employed adults enrolling on a part-time basis. There was also an increasing interest for practice-oriented doctoral degrees different from those preparing for an academic career and also for non-degree post-graduate study, such as specialisation courses, often sponsored and funded by employers for their employees, or by unions and professional organisations for their members.

In addition, the position of *research* within universities had been seriously altered by a combination of economic imperatives and resource limitations. Research in science and technology was given prominence to the neglect of the arts and the humanities. Most of this research was of an applied nature, directed and utility-based rather than curiosity-driven, dominated by industrial R & D models which were not necessarily relevant to the broader purposes of universities. There was a tendency, moreover, for the location of research to shift to bodies outside higher education, thereby impoverishing teaching. This had serious consequences for faculty renewal, accentuated in many countries by the departure of researchers to the private sector or to other countries where pay was better. In some countries with high adult enrolments, the research potential among students themselves had also diminished. When to all this is added the ever-increasing rate of specialisation and the fragmentation of knowledge among and within individual disciplines, one can readily appreciate the pervasive sense of confusion and uncertainty which prevailed with regard to the structure and content of post-graduate education.

The above summary review of the condition of higher education pointed to one clear question: how are the various and expanded missions of higher education to be distributed among its various institutions, recognising that these functions represent a continuum which cuts across the categorical distinctions of the past? The trend was clearly towards a new polarisation based on institutional and programme differentiation: a prestigious group of institutions, on the one side, selective and well-resourced to ensure academic excellence and high quality research; and, on the other, a larger number of a variety of other institutions, more popular in their intake and less resource intensive, catering to the manifold learning needs of society. This trend was most eloquently exemplified by the California hierarchical model, with the nine campuses of the University of California, the State University with its nineteen campuses, and its one hundred and six Community Colleges, as recently reviewed by the OECD[36] – even though the rationale behind this model is much more explicit than many of the European countries would care to admit or follow.

The financing of higher education

Not surprisingly, many of the questions discussed above were, in one way or another, related to one central issue: the level, sources and methods of higher education financing – an issue which by and large coloured the changed relationships between governments and higher education institutions. This was only natural in a situation of budgetary constraints and where higher education in the vast majority of OECD countries continued to be viewed as a public service, largely publicly financed. (Only in Japan and the United States did private institutions constitute a substantial part of the total higher education provision. An important difference between the two countries, however, was that, in the US, average expenditure per student in private universities was 60 per cent higher than in public institutions, whereas in Japan it was 50 per cent lower.) It would not be an exaggeration to assert that governmental policies for higher education in the eighties were predominantly finance-driven: containing levels of expenditure and using financial schemes and incentives to steer the development of the higher education system and its institutions. This emerged clearly from a special study with which the OECD wound up its analysis of higher education problems, as discussed above.[37]

In the majority of countries, the financial stringency which had set in in the early seventies was maintained, and in some cases increased throughout the eighties. (Only Finland and France reported the likelihood of increased public funding for higher education towards the end of the decade.) There was growing interest, therefore, in finding additional sources of funding while focusing public funds more explicitly on what governments perceived to be national needs. This led to changes in institutional funding, often side by side with similar changes in the financial aid to students. This had increased massively during the 1960s and 1970s. Initially in the form of grants, it was gradually being replaced with loans, or combinations of the two, accompanied in many cases by a trend towards charging fees to students as a way of contributing towards the costs of higher education.

The main features of these changes can be summed up as follows:

– more sharply-focussed targeting of central core funding of institutions out of public funds, with an increased proportion of public funding to be "bid for" by institutions;
– increased sophistication of the formulae used in the allocations to each institution, designed to provide institutions with efficiency incentives, such as ensuring that students completed their courses within the prescribed period;
– this was accompanied by greater financial autonomy for the institutions once they had received their funding;
– sharper distinction between funding of research and of teaching;
– increased proportion of institutional income deriving from student fees and from contracts with employers and commercial organisations.

Taken together, these changes represented a move towards the use of market-type approaches to the funding of higher education institutions, designed to provide incentives for institutions to improve their efficiency. The increased financial autonomy accorded to institutions put an imperative onus on each one of them to demonstrate that the resources allocated to them were in fact used efficiently, *i.e.* to become more *accountable.* The emergence of the accountability movement was something new in the ethos of higher education institutions. It had important implications for their internal governance as they struggled to develop appropriate evaluation schemes, performance indicators and management structures and techniques to respond to accountability pressures.[38] In fact, such was the force of these pressures that in many cases one could observe a marked shift in the balance of power from the academic towards the administrative branches of institutions.

Indeed, to many academics, the notion that "efficiency" could be evaluated on the basis of primarily finance-driven criteria, notably of input measures, was anathema. The very concept of "efficiency", as against that of *effectiveness,* with the economic connotations that it carried, tended to distort performance, particularly in teaching which was much more difficult to evaluate than research. It could not, thus, be used to evaluate quality or as a basis for decisions about the setting of priorities. Accountability was seen as part of the design for justifying financial cut-backs and for increasing the interventionist role of governments in the internal affairs of higher education, particularly of the universities. In this lay the germs of the political conflict which was generated between governments and institutional leaders, using finance and academic freedom as their respective platforms.

This conflict is still far from being resolved, though there are signs of a growing recognition that the two sides have more in common than often seems apparent. No government can substitute, nor would it want to, for the professional competence of faculty or undermine the freedom of universities in advancing the frontiers of knowledge, in providing independent critique and new ideas. Equally, academia is becoming increasingly sensitive to the legitimate concerns of governments for accountability as to how public resources are used and also to the need to respond to new collective needs. There are already examples of constructive dialogue between the two sides, within which the thorny questions of funding, evaluation and accountability can be settled in a framework of broader purposes and objectives, one that resolves the present schizophrenia between funding and control and gives individual institutions a more creative role in making use of the increased financial autonomy which has devolved on them.

An essential element in this dialogue is mutual recognition that the public budget alone will not be able to support the enormous costs of ever expanding higher education needs in industrialised societies. Redeployment of resources within either the educational budget or the total public budget has not proved feasible[39] and alternative sources of funding need to be found. These can only come from individuals and the private sector, leading to systems of mixed financing. Devising such systems, such that do not distort the public service character of higher education, is becoming the accepted common challenge for the future development of higher education.

Postscript

The latest phase of OECD work on higher education, concluding with an international conference in 1992, has focused on relationships to employment, with special reference to recent developments in continuing professional education, the employment situation of humanities and social sciences graduates, and an overall analysis of the flow of students from higher education and their entry into working life. The reports emanating from the last of these three items, in providing a full and up-to-date picture of the situation in individual Member countries, constitute a useful source of reference, statistical and otherwise, for any discussion of future policies in this area.[40]

Notes and references

1. OECD, 1975.

2. OECD, 1977.

3. *Public Expenditure on Education*, OECD, 1976.

4. Report of the *Ad Hoc* Working Party of the Education Committee, OECD, 1976 (mimeo).

5. The Group was chaired by Reimut Jochimsen, Under Secretary of State in the German Federal Ministry of Education and Science, the other members holding equivalent positions in France, Norway, Sweden, the United Kingdom and the United States. They, of course, acted in their personal capacities rather than as governmental representatives.

6. *Future Educational Policies in the Changing Social and Economic Context*, OECD, 1979. The analytical report by the Secretariat, and its statistical annex, is contained in Part two, p. 39 ff.

7. *Op. cit.,* pp. 27-29, for the full text of the Declaration. Within the OECD statutes a Council "Declaration" falls just short of the binding authority carried by a "Recommendation".

8. *Education and Working Life in Modern Society*, OECD, 1975. Chaired by Clark Kerr, who was at that time Chairman of the Carnegie Council on Policy Studies on Higher Education, the group included Jacques Delors, Diez-Hochleitner, John Hargreaves, Torsten Husén and Sylvia Ostry.

9. *Ibid.,* pp. 8-9.

10. The Conference was held in December, 1977. See *Youth Unemployment*, OECD, 1978. Vol. I (General Report of the Conference) and Vol. II Inventory of Measures for Youth in Member Countries). For an analysis of the respective weight of structural and conjunctural factors see, *The Entry of Young People into Working Life: General Report* and accompanying *Technical Reports,* OECD, 1977.

11. *Future Educational Policies*, *op. cit.,* pp. 21-29.

12. *Youth Employment, op. cit.,* p. 25.

13. *Education and Working Life*, OECD, 1977, and accompanying document on relevant Innovative Measures adopted in Member countries.

14. *Reviews of National Policies for Education: Australia*, OECD, 1977.

15. *Policies for Apprenticeship*, OECD, 1979.

16. *Report on Vocational Education and Training*, OECD, 1980, mimeo.

17. *The Future of Vocational Education and Training*, OECD, 1983.

18. *The Competences Needed in Working Life*, OECD, 1982, mimeo.

19. *The Role of Education and Training in Relation to the Employment and Unemployment of Young People: Statement by the Education Committee.*

20. Subsequently analysed in detail in a special CERI project. See, *Towards a Guarantee of Youth Opportunities*, OECD/CERI, 1984, mimeo.

21. See, on this, *Education and Work: The Views of the Young*, OECD/CERI, 1983, bringing together the main findings from surveys of youth attitudes in a large number of OECD countries. A representative example of these national surveys can be found in A.G. Watts, *Work experience Programmes: The Views of British Youth*, OECD, 1980, mimeo.

22. J.S. Coleman and T. Husén, *Becoming Adult in a Changing Society*, OECD/CERI, 1985 – a comprehensive survey of the research literature covering all aspects of the transition from adolescence to adulthood, with the main accent on problems of youth socialisation. Its findings pointed to a less conventional picture of the position of young people than the one depicted in the previous report, calling for even more radical changes to their education and training and to overall public policies to facilitate their social insertion.

23. For a description of such innovations and their relevance to the overall youth problematique, see: *Facets of the Transition to Adulthood: Report of a Project of Enquiry*, OECD/CERI, 1986 (mimeo). The empirical analysis in this report complements the research-oriented analysis embodied in the two preceding publications.

24. *Policies for Higher Education in the 1980s*, OECD, 1983, p. 8.

25. *Ibid., passim.*

26. *Higher Education Expenditure in OECD Countries*, OECD, 1981 (mimeo).

27. *Policies for Higher Education in the 1980s*, *op. cit.*, Statistical Annex.

28. The complex issues in an analysis of the economic benefits of education are discussed in G. Psacharapoulos, *Earnings and Education in OECD Countries*, OECD, 1975. On the employment issue see: *Employment Prospects for Higher Education Graduates*, OECD, 1981, mimeo.

29. For an overview of these predicaments in their historical evolution, see: G.S. Papadopoulos: "Higher Education Predicaments: What Can be Said About Them That Is New?", *Higher Education Management*, Vol. 3, No. 2, OECD/IMHE, 1991, pp. 184-190.

30. For an exhaustive discussion of this issue see: *Policies for Higher Education in 1980s*, *op. cit.*, Part two, p. 73 ff.

31. Discussed in *Education and Training After Basic Schooling*, OECD, 1985; and *Pathways for Learning: Education and Training from 16 to 19*, OECD, 1989.

32. *The Integration of Women into the Economy*, OECD, 1985.

33. *Girls and Women in Education*, OECD, 1986.

34. *Adults in Higher Education*, OECD/CERI, 1987. See also, *Adults in Higher Education: Policies and Practice in Great Britain and North America*, Almquist and Wiksell International, Stockholm, 1987. Both these studies incorporate the results of a CERI project on this subject.

35. *Universities Under Scrutiny*, OECD, 1987, with list of country reports.
    Alternatives to Universities, OECD, 1991, with list of country reports.
    Post-Graduate Education in the 1980s, OECD, 1987.

36. *Higher Education in California*, OECD, 1990.

37. *Financing Higher Education: Current Patterns*, OECD, 1990, with list of Country Reports on which the study was based. For a documented analysis of the historical evolution of higher

education expenditures, see, *Educational Expenditures, Costs and Financing: An Overview of Trends, 1970-1988*, OECD, 1992. For an earlier description of student aid policies, see, M. Woodhall, *Review of Student Support Schemes in Selected OECD Countries*, OECD, 1973.

38. Much of the work of the OECD IMHE programme in the eighties was devoted to these problems and reported in successive issues of *Higher Education Management*. See also *The Concept of Productivity in Institutions of Higher Education* (report of an IMHE Conference held in Quebec, 1987), Presses de l'Université du Québec, 1988; and *Dimensions of Evaluation: Report of the IMHE Study Group on Evaluation in Higher Education*, Jessica Kingsley, London, 1992.

39. *Educational Resources and Problems in Resource Redeployment*, OECD, 1983, mimeo.

40. *From Higher Education to Employment*, OECD, 1992:

 – *Vol I – Australia, Austria, Belgium, Germany*.
 – *Vol. II – Canada, Denmark, Spain, United States*.
 – *Vol. III – Finland, France, Italy, Japan, Netherlands, Norway*.
 – *Vol. IV – Portugal, United Kingdom, Sweden, Switzerland*.
 – *Synthesis Report*, 1993.
 – *The Case of the Humanities and Social Sciences*, 1993.

Chapter IX

EDUCATION AND STRUCTURAL CHANGE
(the eighties)

With this concluding chapter we move into the contemporary scene where the perspective is necessarily descriptive rather than historical. This is not to underestimate the gravity of the new dilemmas and challenges which education had to face in a decade dominated by structural change, economic, but also social, and in a political climate marked by the rise of aggressive neo-conservatism on both sides of the Atlantic and in the Pacific region. Many of these dilemmas and challenges are still being played out in the current decade, and this also goes for much of the OECD work which was initiated in response to them.

In this work, more than in any other period, the perennial question of how education could contribute to new economic imperatives while also help improve the position of the less privileged groups in society and, at the same time, pursue its own intrinsic objectives, surfaced in *operational* terms. It was the question that dominated the discussions at the second and third OECD Ministerial Meetings on Education, in 1984[1] and 1990.[2] Theoretically, the answer was simple: education had to improve its *relevance* and its *quality,* a view with which no-one could disagree. In practice, particularly in a situation of financial stringency and of sharpened differences in political ideologies, both within and across countries, the question brought out more conflict than consensus – conflict about the setting of priorities and how such priorities related to differing views about the long-term purposes of education in society. How the OECD activities endeavoured to steer a pragmatic course through this thorny field is the main theme running through this chapter.

It would be convenient to deal with these activities under three main headings, recognising however that the three are inter-related:

– Catering to the needs of the disadvantaged;
– Education and economic restructuring;
– Quality in education.

The disadvantaged: the push for integration

Though it is largely true that the 1980s saw a continuation of the tendency for economic imperatives to take precedence over questions of equity, it is equally true that the educational situation of disadvantaged and under-represented groups could not be ignored or wished away. In fact, the process of economic restructuring carried with it painful social consequences which both sharpened disadvantage and extended it to new groups. What was at stake was the cohesiveness of democratic societies, seriously threatened if significant minorities in them remained segregated because of their social, cultural or ethnic handicaps, usually going together with educational disadvantage. To the social and political implications of segregation, serious enough in themselves, had to be added the economic costs – to the individuals themselves and their families, to the taxpayer and to the community as a whole: particularly at a time of emerging labour shortages, insufficient use by a country of its human potentials and skills was likely to prove an expensive waste.[3]

Integration thus surfaced as the guiding principle underlying policies to combat educational inequality. Added weight was given to this principle by a growing volume of research evidence pointing to a more positive role of schools in overcoming social and economic disadvantage, in contrast to the pessimism which had prevailed at the time of the Jencks study on *Inequality* in the 1970s.[4] In the United States itself, the Republican Administration had come, by the mid-eighties, to give new attention to measures directed at the integration of underprivileged groups into the mainstream of society. The integration objective was pursued at two levels: that of general policies directed at the reform of mainstream provision, and that of special programmes targeted at clearly identified groups. The two often went on concurrently all the evidence pointing to the conclusion that initiatives directed at specific groups are most effective when part of coherent "whole school" policies. They were also seen to involve co-operation between educational authorities and institutions and other policy agencies, as well as the active support of local employers and the community as a whole.

A good illustration of this is provided by the OECD project on *Disadvantaged Youth in Depressed Urban Areas,* an attempt to bring together the perspectives of education authorities and those of local programmes for economic and social renewal in four cities, Barcelona, Hamburg, Glasgow and Metz.[5] Similarly, the ongoing CERI project on *Children and Youth at Risk* is directed at enabling Member countries to identify those among their young populations who, because of their socio-economic or personal circumstances, remain educationally disadvantaged and to suggest integrated measures, both preventive and remedial, which can reduce their vulnerability and bring them closer to the mainstream of educational, social and economic participation.[6]

But it is above all in relation to *minority* populations and those with *disabilities* that integration has been most explicitly set in the past decade and to which the OECD activities made a special contribution. In the case of minorities, the question was squarely one of combating disadvantage, educational, social and economic, *i.e.* of equality. In the case of the disabled, it was also one of equality, but equality in a broader sense, of assimilation into the normal stream of humanity. In both cases, there were limits to integration, but for different reasons.

Minorities

In no area of its work did the OECD touch on more politically sensitive issues as in the education of ethnic and cultural minorities. Even finding a title for the CERI project on this subject acceptable to all Member countries proved difficult. The one finally agreed – *Education and Cultural and Linguistic Pluralism* – was a compromise. Countries like Australia, Canada and the United States could readily accept multiculturalism as a feature of their societies. Most of the European countries and Japan were more reticent; and some of them, with indigenous groups or regions claiming distinct identities, were downright hostile. To the majority of European countries, the only such minorities they could recognise were the immigrants and their children, the legacy of the large influx of foreign workers during the earlier period of labour shortages in Northern Europe. But even on this issue there were conflicting views and interests as between the sending and the receiving countries, the former clamouring for special educational provision by the host countries such as to enable their ''nationals'' to maintain their linguistic and cultural identities. The one common denominator in all this was general recognition that it was among these ethnic and cultural minorities that educational disadvantages were most concentrated.

In these delicate circumstances, the OECD contribution had to be carefully orchestrated so as not to appear to be interfering in countries' internal affairs. The work, therefore, over a period of about ten years, was organised around theoretical analyses of the concept of multiculturalism and the role of education therein, statistical analyses of the educational situation of minority groups, and cross-country exchange of their approach to and experience with multicultural education policies and programmes. The starting point was the general review undertaken in the late seventies of the funding, organisation and administration of schooling for special populations.[7] Linguistic and indigenous minorities surfaced as one of the categories concerned and a special study of educational programmes for these groups was carried out.[8] The results of this study showed how the development of multicultural education was conditioned more by the laws governing educational systems than by cultural, social and economic factors outside education.

However, a survey of the conditions that allowed multicultural education to emerge brought out clearly the influence of the political and economic context. A series of subsequent country reports specially prepared for the CERI project demonstrated the growing dominance of political considerations in the multicultural education options adopted in various countries. Driven primarily by pressures from ethnic minorities, several governments were gradually led to relax their attitude towards the aspirations of minority groups and introduce changes in their educational systems which allowed a strengthening of the cultural and linguistic rights of such groups. But this is still a long way from the institution of coherent policies for multicultural education. By and large, the initiative was left to the schools, which, in response to the needs of their local environment – cultural conflict, glaring inequalities, ethnic ghettos in major cities – came up with ad hoc solutions, such as bilingual programmes in the United States, the inclusion of ethnic courses in curricula and the creation of special classes for minority groups. Even with such programmes, however, the integration at school and work of children not belonging to majority cultural groups was far from being achieved.[9]

This absence of integration, with its accompanying educational disadvantages for minority groups, remained most manifest in the case of immigrants' children. A statistical analysis of their situation in seven European countries showed that:

- by the mid-eighties over two-and-a-half million foreign pupils were attending schools, the highest rate of growth being in pre-primary and primary education in line with the higher fertility rates of foreigners than among nationals;
- immigrants' children were over-represented in special education;
- proportionately, there were more young foreigners than nationals in short duration courses or in the less difficult cycles of secondary education and a higher percentage of them failed to acquire a solid general school grounding;
- differences between foreigners and nationals were not so great where the foreign children's families had been resident in the host country for a long time.[10]

Though these conclusions were somewhat attenuated by special surveys in a number of countries, *e.g.* the Swann Report in the United Kingdom (1985), which stressed that social background was a more determining factor than nationality, the fact remained that being of foreign origin or belonging to an ethnic minority group were factors that could accentuate educational inequality.

Thus, a main conclusion from all this work was that multicultural education policies, in spite of the lip-service paid to them in a number of countries, had by and large failed to materialise. Education systems and schools were still struggling to respond to the challenges raised by cultural and linguistic diversity. This conclusion notwithstanding, some progress had been made and there were examples of countries and schools which were succeeding in providing rich inter-cultural education experiences for all children. In the US, for example, significant gains had been experienced for Black and Hispanic students, even if these groups still lagged behind. Other countries could also boast of similar examples, and these were reviewed in the concluding phase of the CERI project for the lessons they could provide to guide policy-making in this area.[11] A key finding from this review was that successful innovations in culturally and linguistically diverse settings could not be implemented without developing stronger, meaningful involvement of minority students, parents and communities in educational decision-making and processes.

This underlines, once more, the controversial and political nature of the debate about multicultural education. Contrasting concepts are at play, in terms of the role of the mother tongue, and of cultural separateness, integration or assimilation, that touch at the heart of to-day's societies and the relations between the different groups which comprise them. At least, the OECD work helped in the dialectical clarification of this debate, essential to the development of a conceptual framework for multicultural education policies,[12] and in providing empirical examples of ''good practice'' in this direction.

The disabled

Unlike the minority groups discussed above, the disadvantages suffered by children and young people with disabilities do not derive primarily from their socio-economic circumstances: the incidence of disability cuts across all layers of society. This is reflected in the composition of pressure groups militating in favour of the disabled, more clearly identifiable, better resourced, and more articulate and politically influential than in the case of other minority groups. Moreover, disability in its diverse forms – ranging across many degrees of physical and mental handicap – is a highly personalised matter which carries humane and compassionate resonances in society; and this has added force to the push for change in public attitudes and policies towards the disabled, change which eventually led to a general acceptance of the principle of integration, *i.e.* recognition of the *entitlement* of disabled persons to participation, educational, social and economic.

Progress along this road has been consistently monitored, and to a no modest extent facilitated, by the CERI project on the education, training and employment needs of children and young people with disabilities. Drawing inspiration from the spate of national reports which saw the light of day in the late seventies – of which the Warnock report in the United Kingdom (1978) is a typical example – the project was launched in 1978, with substantial financial support by the Bureau of the Handicapped in the US Department of Education matched by corresponding contributions from other countries. Still in progress, the project has provided a forum for the identification and analysis of innovative policies and practices in individual countries and their dissemination to other countries, the development of a framework for the discussion of common issues and the setting up of networks of dedicated specialists across the OECD membership. It has dealt successively with problems of definition and legislation, integration in the school, transition from school to working life and to adult status, and the need for co-ordinated policies to achieve the objective of integration. The results are embodied in an impressive series of reports and publications, listed in the bibliographical references to this chapter. Their titles speak for themselves.[13]

It would be useful, nonetheless, to indicate, and comment on, the main policy conclusions which can be drawn from this work as these emerged from the discussions at a high level conference in December 1986, attended by Ministers and senior officials from the Member countries.[14] Based on in-depth reviews of policies for the disabled in three countries, Australia, France and Sweden, the discussions drew on the totality of past CERI work in this area and also on the experience of all the twenty-one countries represented at the conference. Not all of these countries had of course reached the advanced level of policy thinking, let alone practice, reflected in the conference conclusions. These nevertheless stand as testimony to the remarkable progress which had been made in the direction of integration and to the significant impact on the policies of Member countries which CERI work in this area has had.

Their point of departure was that the attribution of handicap as an individual characteristic was unacceptable. ''The degree to which disability becomes handicapping depends on interaction with the environment, other people and the organisation of society – hence the over-riding importance of the acceptance of the integration principle in school as well as in work; the problem then becomes one of how to overcome the difficulties in the practical application of this principle."

Integration within the school was recognised as the first essential step; and there were examples, particularly in Italy and the Scandinavian countries, to show that this was possible. But this could not be achieved without additional resources, changes in curricula, pedagogy and classroom organisation, and, above all, in teacher education. It is these difficulties which many countries, even among those who fully accepted the principle of integration, found insurmountable. Special schools for the disabled remained the norm in many countries.

Beyond schooling, paid employment was seen as the main objective and as the only means by which the right of the disabled to adult status could be given substance. But here, again, there were limits to integration, depending on the degree of individual handicap and on the availability of jobs. Sheltered employment and other forms of useful work and valued activity could not therefore be excluded; they continued, in fact, to be extensively used in many countries. But this did not absolve governments from their role of stimulating employment opportunities for the disabled, within both the public and private sectors. Specific legislation to this end was essential, as was the setting up of intermediary services to link the disability milieu to that of work. There was a need, above all, of sustained, government-sponsored strategies to change public attitudes, particularly those of parents and employers. And there was an equal need "to involve the disabled themselves in schemes and decisions affecting their future and creating an environment in which they could develop their self-esteem, independence and capacity to cope, and this could best be done if they were to be involved in actual work situations".

All in all, these conclusions amounted to the reaffirmation that disability could no longer be regarded as a peripheral issue, one that could be left to the compassion of society. It was an integral part of educational and social policy. This explains the assiduity with which the principle of integration was advocated as the corner-stone of policies for the disabled. Any deviation from it was regarded as heresy, even though the difficulties of its application in practice were fully recognised. Not the least among these difficulties was the co-ordination of policies and services among the various ministries and government departments concerned – a point which was firmly driven home by OECD by bringing the conclusions of the conference to the attention of governments through the Education and the Manpower and Social Affairs Committees and the Council itself.

Education and economic restructuring

Alongside with curbing inflation and improving public sector efficiency, economic restructuring came to dominate governmental concerns in the eighties. This had significant effects on the political position of education: whereas formerly the educational sector tended to be primarily looked upon for the savings it could contribute to public spending, there was now a more positive attitude to it in a rediscovery of the economic importance of education.

The argument can be simply stated. "Human resources" occupy a crucial place in the economic vitality of advanced industrialised countries and their capacity to compete, both with one another and with the rest of the world. In this, education plays a leading role: it provides and updates the skills and competences of individual workers, which is an essential requirement for the development of flexible labour markets capable of responding to the continuous changes that result from economic restructuring, itself strongly propelled by rapid technological change. It also ensures the advancement of scientific knowledge, through research, and its application in production.

The argument was not in itself new. It is, in fact, reminiscent of the sixties. What was new was the force and urgency with which educational change was *politically* advocated to respond to the new economic imperative, marked by growing country inter-dependence and competition in the global economy. It was given additional acuity by the weight which was attached to education in the explanation advanced of the differences in economic and employment performance between OECD countries and the emerging dynamic economies in South-East Asia, and between OECD countries themselves, partic-ularly between Europe, Japan and the United States. Both the total volume and the quality of education and training were implicated in this line of reasoning, at the level of formal schooling as well as at the work place.

Comprehensive policies for post-compulsory education and training

Up to about the mid-eighties, priority continued to be given to the situation of young people in the 16-19 age group. Persisting high levels of youth unemployment, combined with larger cohorts of young people and rising aspirations was leading to a growing number who had reached the statutory school leaving age to remain in education and training – in upper secondary schools, in apprenticeship schemes and in the growing variety of less formal programmes which combined education, training and work experi-ence, as we have seen in an earlier chapter. The result was a very rapid expansion of education and training opportunities immediately after compulsory schooling, leading many European countries to approach the pattern of quasi-universal attendance already established in the United States and Japan. The need was to bring this wide variety of opportunities within a comprehensive policy framework. This was the purpose of the discussion of this topic at the 1984 OECD Education Ministerial, based on the conclu-sions of a special Secretariat study analysing recent trends and policies in the Member countries.[15]

Three distinct organisational approaches were identifiable in the policies adopted by different OECD countries for the expansion and diversification of education and training provision for 16-19 years old: the "schooling model", with schooling on a full-time basis for the majority of the age group (Japan, the United States and the Scandinavian coun-tries); the "dual model", characterised by a strong apprenticeship sector (the Germanic countries); and the "mixed model", such as it existed in the United Kingdom, whose main distinguishing feature was the importance assigned to training outside the formal education system and beyond the scope and control of education authorities. Aspects of these three settings, of course, co-existed in most countries and there were signs that they were becoming increasingly blurred.

Whatever the setting, a number of problems were common to all Member countries. Firstly, there was the problem of a significant minority of youngsters who, even though they might have completed basic schooling successfully, failed to benefit from upper secondary education and left either prematurely or without obtaining a vocational qualification. This was a feature common to all systems, those countries closer to the "dual" model tending to achieve better results than those where full-time schooling predominated. Educational disadvantage translated into employment disadvantage – all the more dramatically so because of the competition for scarce jobs and in a situation in which educational qualifications remained an essential, though no longer a sufficient, condition for access to employment. A variety of imaginative innovations, involving education, work-experience and community service, were introduced in different countries to ease the transition stage for these and other youngsters with similar difficulties;[16] but these remained episodic rather than generalisable practice.

Secondly, the educational situation of young women still left much to be desired. True, overall participation rates between girls and boys had become evenly balanced, but sharp differences persisted in terms of types of study pursued, the majority of girls being concentrated in general subjects or in vocational streams leading to traditional female occupations. They also had greater difficulties in finding apprenticeship places and opportunities for work/study arrangements or part-time studies of the type available to young men.

Thirdly, little progress had been achieved in bridging the traditional distinctions between general, technical and vocational education and between education and training. Most European countries had seen a rapid increase in the scale of vocational education and training, contrary to Japan and the United States where the expansion had been mainly in academic/general education. But everywhere the expansion and greater diversity of the student body, together with changes in entry requirements to higher education and to employment, had led to more, rather than less, differentiation of programmes. Gradually questions of integration/differentiation came to replace institutional considerations as the centre of the debate on policies for post-compulsory education.

In essence, the question was one about the curriculum, *i.e.* the content and structure of studies, which was addressed in a follow-up OECD report based on a series of country case studies.[17] Arguing that "the central task of post-compulsory education is to provide a preparation or foundation for a field of work or advanced studies", the report examined the curriculum implications of recent changes in the nature of that foundation. The simple dichotomy between "arts" and "sciences" was being challenged. The old, specific technologies were giving way to newer generic technologies of information and systems. The growth of service sector occupations was leading to a greater emphasis on organisational and interpersonal skills. The balance of occupations, and with it curricula, was shifting away from work with things towards work with information and with people, with an increasing element of "theory" entering in many fields, even in crafts. Greater emphasis was being given to the development of general analytic and problem-solving skills, and of attitudes and values, which would be useful in any kind of work or study.

Similar changes could be observed in the links between upper secondary education and higher education. The exclusive relationship which had formerly existed between general/academic streams and higher education was breaking down; formal opportunities were being created for students to enter higher education from a technical or vocational base ("second route"), and at a later stage ("second chance"). But it was also clear that the divide between the "transfer" and "terminal" functions of upper secondary education – transfer to higher education and direct access to employment – could not easily be resolved: the experience with many reforms of technical streams showed that efforts to strengthen their "transfer" orientations to higher education carried the risk of a declining employment value of their credentials. In addition, many higher education institutions, particularly universities, often appeared to be relatively monolithic in their access requirements; and the division between courses which led on to such access, and those which did not, remained a deep one in some countries.

The one general message which emerged from this analysis was that post-compulsory education had to be both *diverse* and *coherent*: diverse in terms of aims, content, levels, mode of attendance, teaching methods and learning environments, in line with the diversity of its student population and its closeness to both higher education and the labour market; coherent in terms of the need for a common, or commonly understood, currency of qualifications which would allow the various parts of the system to relate to one another and to the outside world. In this juxtaposition of diversity and coherence, effective systems of information and guidance had a central role to play.

In their discussion of these problems, Ministers by and large were in agreement with the above conclusions. Where differences arose was on the role and scope of the public responsibility for this age group and of education's role within it. Some (Australia, Canada, Finland) saw the role of post-compulsory education as preparation for adulthood interpreted broadly, and hence arguing that education should not be over-responsive to economic requirements at the expense of educational and social objectives. Others (Germany, Netherlands, Switzerland) emphasised the primary responsibility of this level of education in equipping all young people with a recognised qualification to facilitate their transition to employment. While some Ministers (Scandinavian countries) advocated that responsibility for all young people up to the age of 18 should be primarily with the educational authorities, others argued in favour of a more diverse spread of responsibilities where training and work experience programmes were concerned – even though some among these (Germany, Belgium, the Netherlands) stressed the importance of all young people up to 18 being required by law to attend in education, at least on a part-time basis. Opposing views were also expressed with regard to the duration of formal schooling: Canada, for example, argued in favour of encouraging youngsters to stay in school for as long as possible, as a better alternative to unemployment, while the Danish Minister described as a "disaster" the tendency to keep young people out of the labour market until 18, 19 or 20 years old.[18]

The 1984 Ministerial meeting was the last occasion on which the education/employment problems of young people were politically discussed within OECD. Thereafter, interest shifted to the education and training of the adult labour force and the broader question of human resource development. Not that the problems of young people had been solved. But these problems, and the options available to tackle them, had already been exhaustively discussed and little that was new could be expected from further discussion or analysis. In addition, the unemployment of school age youngsters had lost some of its drama as in most countries their quasi-totality was being drawn into various forms of education, training and work-experience programmes. Their labour market predicaments were thereby postponed to a later age.

The rediscovery of human resources

Inelegant as the phrase may be, "the development of human resources" aptly captures an essential requirement for the vitality of modern economies: the availability of an adequate level, and the right kind, of knowledge and skills in the labour force without which the potential benefits from other forms of economic investment cannot be fully realised. Propagated in the sixties, in the wake of the discovery of the "residual factor" in economic growth, the importance of "investment in human capital" resurfaced in the eighties in the context of new economies dominated by technological change and fast evolving structures of occupations and work. Increasingly knowledge-based, these economies have to adapt more flexibly and more rapidly than ever before; and they have to do this on a *continual* basis. Education and training are thus seen as prime catalysts of successful change, economic as well as social.

At their 1984 meeting, Ministers of Education, while reiterating that "education cannot be a substitute for economic and labour market policies", nonetheless recognised that the rapid pace of economic change and spread of new technologies called for a re-examination of the role of education in preparing the young for working life. How to do this, however, came up against the difficulty, indeed the impossibility, of arriving at any precise forecasting of what "the jobs of the future" would be, even if some Ministers (Canada, Denmark, Germany) argued that some picture of future economic requirements, if only of a "broad-based" nature, must enter into educational planning. In their conclusions, therefore, Ministers, in agreeing on the need of further study of "the interaction between education and training and structural change in the economy and society", put the accent on the role of education in "developing the capacity of *individuals* for continuous learning, creativity and self-reliance, thereby promoting their quality and flexibility in the labour market.[19]

Central to the development of such quality and flexibility as no doubt the school system was, education could no longer be assumed to be synonymous with what went on in schools. Organised learning was increasingly taking place in settings outside the formal education system. In particular, training in enterprises had come to represent a sizeable component of the total learning resources of each country. Firms were themselves building up their own human resource strategies increasingly as part of their overall investment strategies and in a context in which, under the impact of new technologies, particularly information technologies, occupational structures were changing, with many of the established forms of work organisation and of skills structure and skill formation becoming obsolete. The educational implications of these changes were thus seen to encompass both school-based and enterprise-based education and training. A prerequisite to identifying and spelling out these implications was deeper understanding of the nature and extent of the labour market and work structure changes mentioned above. It is to this task that CERI devoted a great deal of its research effort throughout the eighties, resulting in a significant, and original, contribution to the state of knowledge in this area.

The originality of this work derived not so much from the nature of the subject under investigation – "Technological Change and Human Resources Development" – as from the research methods employed. The basic approach was through comparative analytical studies at enterprise level focusing on the education, training and skills implications of new technology and work organisation. Beginning in the early eighties with the automobile sector in five countries – the United States, Japan, Germany, France and Sweden – the study continued with a similar analyses in the financing and insurance sectors in the same countries, gradually extended to cover the service sector more broadly and in a larger number of countries, given this sector's growing importance in economic and employment terms. The empirical work in each country, carried out by a national team, covered both aggregate data on the service sector as a whole and detailed case studies, particularly in the retail and banking sectors. These national research efforts were complemented with a parallel series of international comparative studies focusing respectively on the interface between public and private education and training providers, on new employment patterns in the service sector and on a conceptual analysis of changes and innovation in skill formation at enterprise level. Results emanating from the various phases of the project were systematically discussed in a series of national and international seminars, culminating in a concluding international conference in November 1989, hosted in Utrecht by the Dutch Ministry of Education and Science.[20]

It is difficult to assess the impact of this extensive work. That it was generally supported by governments as well as the private sector is sufficient indication of the new recognition which human resource development had come to acquire as a factor of successful economic restructuring both at the macro level and within enterprises, in particular those facing strong competition. The pervasiveness of technology in the increasingly knowledge-based and service-oriented economy, together with new market demands for quality and flexibility in products and services, put a premium on human skills for the competitive vitality of enterprises. But it also changed the kind of skills required, in line with changes away from the rigidity of Taylorist forms of division of labour and work organisation towards more teamwork and greater decentralisation of control and responsibility. Particularly in the service sector, and service-type work in manufacturing, routine and low-skilled jobs were no longer in demand. The accent was on multi-skilling, on personal and customer-oriented skills within the work force.[21] These messages were fully incorporated in the subsequent broader work by the Organisation on the social and economic role of technology.[22]

Difficult as it seemed, identifying changes in skills requirements proved amenable to empirical analysis. Translating them into operational educational requirements was another matter. It raised complex questions about educational priorities, for example as between basic, youth and adult education, about changes in curricula and methods of teaching, particularly at compulsory school level, and about the relations between general and vocational education. It also raised questions of institutional organisation, i.e. the division of responsibilities for the provision of education and training as between the public and private sectors and between education and labour market agencies and institutions. Many of these questions, particularly as they affected the formal education system, were absorbed in the wider debate about the quality of education and will come up for consideration later.

Of more immediate relevance to the human resource argument was the prominence it gave to the need to review policies for *the further education and training of the adult labour force*. It is in this area where the links between education and the economy are clearest and most direct. It is also the area where the effects of the correlation between socio-economic status, lack of skills and high levels of unemployment become most dramatic. Preliminary analysis of the educational attainment of the labour force[23] showed that, in most OECD countries, a sizeable proportion of the working age population had less than an upper secondary education; and that it was those with the lowest levels of attainment who consistently faced the highest incidence and growing risk of unemployment. Low attainment was also shown to be one of the factors affecting the labour force participation of women: many women were in jobs which were lower in status than those held by men and when in comparable types of work did not enjoy comparable security or pay.

At a time when, because of demographic decline, the working population was ageing, it became imperative to ensure that the full potential of the adult labour force be utilised. This, in turn, called for more pro-active policies for further education and training for *all* groups in the labour force, all the more essential because of the continual obsolescence of skills brought about by technological change. The nature of the basic skills needed to function effectively in the economy were themselves changing, giving rise to the phenomenon of "functional illiteracy" which, combined with persisting traditional forms of illiteracy, came now to be recognised as a serious problem in many advanced countries.[24]

But to speak of policies in the field of adult training and retraining, at least in the sense of *public* policies, is somewhat of a misnomer. Though such policies do have a role to play, it was generally accepted that primary responsibility lay with individual firms and, as we have seen, individual enterprises were developing their own strategies in relation to their work force. This was in line with the equally generally accepted notion that the work place provides the environment within which training in specific job-related skills can be best obtained. However, not all firms are sufficiently equipped, or have the skills and capacity, to undertake the required training themselves. Moreover, not all adults are in the workforce, nor are those who are in the work force equally amenable, or adequately prepared, to receive training. Thus, patterns of provision differed widely between firms, regions and countries, as did patterns of participation, levels and methods of financing and the role of the social partners. The level of overall investment, however, remained well below what was needed; and no country, except perhaps Australia, had as yet developed a comprehensive strategy for adult training and skill formation.[25]

Most countries saw the role of public policy as essentially one of a catalyst – in providing incentives to firms for expanding their training provision; in ensuring the more equitable functioning of "training markets" across regions, firms and individuals; and in facilitating better co-operation between enterprises and education and training institutions. The one area where governments had main responsibility was the training of the unemployed or those at risk of being displaced from employment through structural and technological change. In this, governments worked mainly through their employment and training agencies, in co-operation with both firms and educational institutions as part of overall labour market policies. A central challenge to such policies remained how to design schemes for a more constructive use of unemployment benefits, with efforts increasingly directed at associating these benefits with the provision of training opportunities for the unemployed.

The desirability of working towards more comprehensive policies was, however, generally recognised, and much of the OECD work in this area was directed to this objective.[26] In this respect, five specific issues can be singled out for comment, as they emerged from the 1991 Phoenix (Arizona) conference organised jointly by OECD and the US Department of Education.[27]

Firstly, the *links between training policies and other policies,* particularly employment and industrial policies. The effectiveness of training policies is very much conditioned by policies concerned with the industrial structure of a country, the laws governing wages and employment, and business policy in the sense of how firms organise work. Such co-ordinated policies also have to have a strong regional dimension and take account of regional particularities of industrial structures, values and needs. Establishing such links, however, calls for integrated approaches at policy-making level throughout a variety of departments and agencies for which governmental machinery does not exist in most countries.

Secondly, *the centralisation/decentralisation dilemma.* The desirability of moving toward greater decentralisation in the design and implementation of training policies is generally recognised and a marked move in this direction is evident in most countries. But it is one thing legislating for comprehensive policies, quite another co-ordinating such policies among the various interest groups concerned and at the various levels of regional and local responsibility where these policies are applied. Even the most rationally legislated national policies will remain ineffective unless they are accompanied by a meticulous process of dialogue and negotiation designed to ensure their social acceptability. This permeability between local and national interests finds its full expression in the need to maintain nationally recognised standards in skill achievement and qualifications, essential to facilitate worker mobility in highly volatile economies and labour markets. Increasingly, this need is being seen as ever more cogent in view of the growing internationalisation of labour markets, particularly among European Community countries.

Thirdly, *the role of the social partners.* This is as crucial as it is complex. There are various types of employers and unions. Enterprises may be privately owned, in the public sector, large corporations, but also small and medium-sized ones with fewer resources. On the unions side, these may be craft-based or industry-based. Enterprise unions, as in the case of Japan, have different incentives and responsibilities from unions organised along industrial lines, as in most other countries. In addition, in many countries unions are split according to political ideologies. In all cases, the roles that employers and unions can play depend on the nature of interaction not only between themselves, but also with other actors and stakeholders in society, at both national and local levels. These complexities determine the various forms of co-operation that can be envisaged: *a)* partnerships between business and education, on a bilateral basis and operating mostly at local level; *b)* collective bargaining agreements, primarily between employers and employees, but also involving a role by the State, in which training is becoming an increasingly important component; *c)* tripartite agreements among employers, unions and the State under which the social partners are systematically consulted and involved in policy-making, in setting standards in training and in monitoring the process and outcomes of training provision. A typical case of such tripartism is Germany, where the roles and responsibilities of the various actors are statutorily set out.

Fourthly, and related to the above, *credentialling*. This is recognised as part of industrial relations and tripartite agreements, the objective being to ensure the transparency of qualifications, wherever they may have been acquired, as an essential component of "training markets". At present, credentialling is heavily influenced by educationally-derived practices and standards, which may not always be appropriate to the assessment of competences and qualifications deriving from the work environment. There is need for such credentialling to be matched by industry-based credentialling, towards the development of a common currency of qualifications, combining the two, and one which would be increasingly internationally oriented.

Finally, the *policy process* itself. The choice here is between policies being generated through a series of initiatives and well-conceived experiments around specific problems, *i.e.* an evolutionary approach, as is the case in the majority of countries, or through a more systemic approach, as is the case in Australia, France and, until recently, in Sweden. Whatever the approach, one of the principal objectives remains of how to develop a robust and comprehensive framework of incentives designed to enhance the motivation of *all* people in the labour force to participate in the opportunities offered to them by training policies, on which the success of such policies ultimately depends.

The 1989 Education and the Economy Conference

Structural change, as we have seen already, dominated OECD economic thinking throughout the latter half of the eighties. It was seen, and analytically treated, as a "horizontal" issue, covering many sectors of policy and calling for more effective co-ordination of these sectors, among which education and training received privileged attention. A special chapter was devoted to education in the general report which the Organisation submitted to the OECD Council at Ministerial level on this subject.[28] Even more privileged attention to education and training was given in the analysis of labour market policies and the search of solutions to the employment/unemployment situation, as reflected in the Organisation's manifesto on a "New Framework for Labour Market Policies".[29] It was only natural that economic and employment considerations should dominate the approach to education in these reports at the expense of its more general and long-term objectives. But, as on previous occasions, to the educational bodies of the Organisation this approach seemed somewhat simplistic, carrying the risk of reducing education to a mere instrument of economic and labour market policies – reminiscent of the situation a decade earlier. Again, the Education Committee felt the need to "put the record straight" and issued its own *Statement on Education and Structural Change*.[30]

There were two central points of disagreement. Firstly, the Committee saw structural change as a much wider phenomenon than that perceived by economists. It was intimately related to changes in life styles and in dominant values and expectations attached to work and leisure, to social structures, the community and the family. Secondly, the interaction between education and social and economic restructuring was not a simple process of merely adjusting education to meet social and economic needs. It was rather one which underscored the role of education itself, through its direct impact on individuals and the multiple objectives which it serves in highly industrialised societies, in influencing the pattern and direction of social and economic change. Over-emphasis of immediate economic returns of education could lead to short-sighted and narrow definition of educational objectives, to the detriment of personal development and self-fulfilment of individuals, but also at the cost of social development, cultural enrichment and the advancement of knowledge for its own sake. "Far from prescribing unilateral educational adaptation to economic "requirements", structural change thus draws renewed attention to the multiplicity of educational objectives, and to the need for integrated policies, recognising that the well-being of individuals and the further development of societies depend on creative interaction among different spheres of human activity".[31]

That these were more than fine words was shown by their practical educational implications which were spelled out in the main body of the Statement and which were discussed in further detail at the Intergovernmental Conference on "Education and the Economy in a Changing Society", in March 1989. Chaired by John Dawkins, the then Australian Minister for Employment, Education and Training, and attended by a number of ministers from other countries, the conference was the culminating event in the work which OECD had done in this area during the eighties. Its report, together with the analytical papers by the Secretariat, stands as a useful summing up of a comprehensive view of the economic and social circumstances of education in their radical evolution since the Washington Conference some twenty years earlier.[32]

For a detailed account of the Conference proceedings and its conclusions the Conference report itself has to be consulted. Its great merit lies in bringing together, within a structured framework, the wide, complex and often confused set of issues that link education to its economic and social environment and in detailing their implications for both policy and practice. But at least three of its features are worthy of note.

Firstly, as regards the *political nature* of the event. This was the nearest thing that the OECD ever came to a tripartite discussion in this area, involving governments, employers and employee representatives. The tone of the discussions was in fact set by initial presentations of their respective viewpoints by the three sides, a Minister of Education, a Trade Union leader and an industrialist. That the latter was none less than Akio Morita, President of Sony Corporation, added spice to the occasion because of the interest which other countries had in understanding the causes behind Japanese industrial success and the lessons which they could draw from this experience. BIAC and TUAC were also actively involved in the discussions and used this occasion to sort out their own agreements and differences, reflected in the joint statement they submitted to the conference.[33]

Secondly, with regard to *context*. The conference was seen as a clear expression of the policy pressures that were common to all OECD countries: pressures for continual structural adjustment and social change; for micro-economic policy measures to complement traditional demand management policies; for further improvements in productivity performance; and pressures associated with changes in demographic structure, technology and the organisation of work. The challenge was how education systems could become more responsive to these pressures and at the same time contribute to the process of change. *Change* was, in fact, the pervasive theme running through the conference discussions, itself dominated by the realisation that it was as unprecedented as it was *unpredictable*. The broad implication of this was that individuals should be equipped with the flexibility and adaptability they require to cope with and contribute to change. In turn, these qualities of flexibility and adaptability had to be reflected in the ways in which education and training themselves are organised and made available to individuals.

Finally, in what concerns the *coverage* of the conference. The point of departure was a redefinition of the relationships between education and the economy, based on detailed consideration of the contextual factors, with the accent on structural change and unemployment, along the lines already discussed. Perhaps the most innovative idea that emerged here was a new role for education in societies where the traditional sharp division between the "active" and the "non-active" population was breaking down because of structural unemployment, with the notion of "active life" being extended beyond paid employment to include other socially-desirable activities. The concept of the "Active Society" was in fact put forward by the Secretariat, Ron Gass in particular, in a valiant, but desperate effort to establish a basis for getting as many people as possible into an active role in society and thus break through the harsh and demoralising effects of unemployment. There was considerable subsequent discussion within the Organisation of how this concept could be operationalised, but it fizzled out with Ron Gass's departure the following year.[33a]

On the basis of this initial analysis, the conference then proceeded to consider, in turn, the implications for initial education, secondary school education and training, the further education and training of adults and higher education, concluding with a discussion of strategies for bringing about change. The succinct Secretariat issues papers on each of these topics, reproduced in the conference report, represent, at least in the author's opinion, the most authoritative, balanced statement of the problems anywhere available. It is significant that they provided the platform from which the OECD subsequently endeavoured to transfer its experience on education and the economy to the newly liberated central and eastern European countries.

The debate on education and structural change was long and often contentious. Yet, in the end a surprising degree of consensus prevailed as to the general objectives and expectations of education and training systems, along the following lines:

- Recognition of the primordial importance of a solid and extended initial general education for all children, equipping them with a broad base of skills needed for their subsequent education and employment careers.

- Beyond compulsory schooling, the availability of extensive and flexible education and training opportunities – often in combination with work experience and involving closer co-operation between schools and the world of work – with special attention to the needs of socially and educationally disadvantaged groups.
- Improved systems of educational and career guidance to enable young people to make informed choices among the diverse options available to them.
- Review of the content and structure of studies in upper secondary education towards a better balance between general and technical/vocational studies and the training for specific job-related skills increasingly deferred to the work-place.
- Wider and more flexible opportunities for access to post-secondary studies for both qualified school-leavers and adults, including arrangements for this to take place on a recurring basis for those who choose to do so.
- Greater responsiveness of higher education institutions, without impinging on their autonomy or on their longer term objectives, to national and regional economic and social needs and, in co-operation with Government and industry, to enhancing the adequacy of continuing education and training for adults.
- Contributing to the development of an articulated set of national arrangements for the assessment, certification and accreditation of skills, wherever these may have been acquired, thereby improving the portability of qualifications and the mobility of workers in the labour market.
- The need, at all levels of the education and training system, to manage resources effectively and ensure high standards of quality; the crucial role of teachers, trainers and instructors in this.

Back to basics: the debate on quality

The politics of the "human resource development" argument were nothing compared to those which surrounded the "quality in education" debate, the other dominant theme of the eighties. All, of course, were in favour of quality; but wide divergences existed as to is precise meaning, how it could be judged and the means by which it could be achieved. Behind these divergences lay more fundamental differences, political and ideological, themselves reflected in differences about the aims of educational policy in relation to which the quality concept has to be seen.

Broadly speaking, there were two opposing camps: on the one side, the neo-conservatives, dominated by Reaganite and Thatcherite views of society, and on the other, the "egalitarians", largely represented by the Scandinavian model of society – even though Sweden, under its new conservative-led coalition government, has since forcibly moved into the other camp.[34] Within OECD, it was the Americans, and more specifically the US Department of Education, who pressed, powerfully and persistently, for quality to become a top priority in the Organisation's work, drawing inspiration from the 1983 report of the National Commission on Excellence in Education, *A Nation at risk: The Imperative of Educational Reform*. Comparisons with the apparent superior performance of the Japanese educational system, the evidence for which was seen in the higher scores of Japanese pupils in international tests, served as a constant incentive to this educational crusade.

The debate focused primarily on the quality of *school* education; but it also extended to the post-secondary sector, particularly in the case of the US with its wide variety and disparate quality of higher education institutions. (In the case of European countries, with their more uniform pattern of provision at this level, the concern was with increasing the *efficiency* of higher education institutions rather than with quality as such.) Reduced to its essentials, the debate was about the fundamental purposes of schooling: the one camp seeing them as essentially concerned with learning outcomes, assessed in terms of subject matter mastery, particularly in the traditional basics; the other viewing such outcomes within a broader social educative role for the school aimed at leading every child into a balanced and many-sided growth. These differences were, in turn, extrapolated into differing perceptions about the core curriculum, pedagogy and the instruments and processes of improving quality, with the accent on choice, competition and privatisation, *i.e.* the application of market principles, on the one side, and, on the other, on more child-centred approaches, emphasising co-operation rather than competition, ensuring a pleasant learning environment for children and safeguarding the sanctity of public provision – with resulting disagreements on such matters as school organisation, the role and nature of examinations and the bases for assessing teaching performance.

There were also different interpretations about the causes which gave rise to the concern for quality. Both elitists and egalitarians would agree that education was failing to meet some of its general aims, *e.g.*, equality of opportunity, and that many teachers, particularly among those recruited during the period of expansion, were not as competent as they ought to be. But while the former would play up evidence that educational standards had fallen, blaming it on the permissive pedagogies of the sixties, and that academically gifted pupils were being swamped by mediocrity, the latter would argue that children from disadvantaged groups were being sold short because educational expansion had not carried with it the additional resources that were required to enable traditionalist school systems to become more responsive to the needs of these groups. In the economic climate which prevailed at the time such additional resources were even less likely to be forthcoming and this added to the strain put on individual schools in their efforts to sustain quality.[35]

These contrasting viewpoints on the quality question came out clearly in the country submissions to an international conference on the subject, held in Washington D.C. in May 1984 at the invitation of the US Department of Education. It was essentially a clarifying exercise around the concept of quality and its dimensions, covering goals and expectations, content, the organisation of schooling, teaching and assessment policies. The report of the conference[36] provided the basis for the discussion of "Quality in Basic Education" as one of the three themes of the 1984 Ministerial meeting on Education.

Concern for the quality of compulsory schooling was no stranger to the OECD activities. Already in the late seventies a systematic survey had been carried out of how different countries' educational financing practices related to the achievement of policy goals for primary schools. It is significant that such goals, as defined by the countries themselves, were still primarily seen as relating to the equalisation of opportunities, across areas and localities and between social groups, but also to the extent to which parents felt that they had real, practicable options to choose among different styles of schooling for their children, *i.e.* the goal of diversity and choice. The results of this comparative analysis showed that: *a)* the furthering of the quality objective did not call for any radical re-casting of a country's educational financing system; *b)* differential educational provision for certain groups could only be effective if accompanied by concomitant organisational and governance arrangements; *c)* increased local autonomy, more feasibly achieved through less categorical financial transfers from central to regional and local jurisdictions rather than on non-centrally generated revenues, was an essential, but not in itself a sufficient means for ensuring diversity in, and choice among, educational offerings; *d)* "financing arrangements that affect the nature of the teacher work-force appear to be pivotal in gaining policy leverage".[37]

Over the next four years, this line of investigation was broadened into a general review of recent tends, current problems and future prospects of the entire compulsory school sector, coinciding with the centennial of the inauguration of compulsory schooling in a number of Member countries. It resulted in a comprehensive report,[38] the nature and significance of which can be gauged by its contents: goals and functions; common or differentiated schools; the duration and continuity of schooling; school and class size, and patterns of attendance; curriculum issues; equal opportunity and special groups; preparation for working life; children, students, parents and families; new roles and training programmes for teachers; control, accountability and evaluation; and ending with a summary of main problems and options for the future. It was essentially a report about the quality of schooling, forestalling the emergence of this concern on the national and international scene. Ominously, its concluding paragraph reads as follows:

> The burden of this report is that priority for the next ten years will be improvement of the quality of compulsory schooling. All OECD countries have made tremendous economic efforts during the past twenty years to invest in the material provision of schools and to carry out sweeping structural, organisational and curricular reforms... So far, however, success has been measured in largely material terms. The next phase will call for emphasis on less tangible improvements which will necessarily prove more difficult to achieve than fulfilment of quantitative targets. It will require education authorities at all levels to consider now what compulsory schooling should look like in ten or twenty years' time. What will society then be wanting from the schools and what will schools be wanting from society? (p. 145)

When, in 1984, OECD Ministers of Education picked up this challenge it was easy enough for them to endorse the general proposition that improving the quality of basic education was a high priority; and that in the pursuit of quality effective teaching and school leadership were crucial. But the consensus stopped here, and, unusual for this kind of meeting, the lively debate which ensued brought out all the controversy on quality which we have already mentioned. The summary record of the meeting makes interesting reading.[39] Led by Sir Keith Joseph, with his rich UK experience in educational reform projects, the conservative camp argued in favour of a more concentrated core curriculum, stricter forms of examinations to provide a more absolute, rather than relative, assessment of pupil performance, and for regular evaluation of teacher performance, which, as further expounded by the US representative, should lead to performance-based yardsticks to determine teacher pay. To this was added the argument put forward by the Danish minister on how parental choice should be exercised, drawing an analogy with enterprises in a free and competitive market whereby products and their quality derive primarily from the exercise of consumer choice – a view strongly contested by his other Scandinavian colleagues, among others.

Similarly contested were the proposals for performance-related teacher salaries, both of the general principle and the practicalities involved. Nor was there agreement on what a "core" curriculum would consist of and on the role and objectives of examinations and student assessment: the curriculum, the opposition argued, could not ignore its "soft" subjects and educational outcomes are much more than simply that which can be quantified; and examinations, though necessary, too often dominate the aims of schools at the expense of other aspects of school learning.

Inconclusive as the discussion was, at least the Ministers were able to reach agreement that the quality of basic schooling should be a priority for future OECD work, thus vindicating the American position. They also greed on the main parameters for this work:

> ...particularly basic education related to modern needs in increasingly pluralistic societies, including matters such as: better preparation for adult life; measures to improve the status, effectiveness and professional role of teachers; the organisation, content and structure of the curriculum and methods of evaluation; qualitative factors affecting the performance of schools, including school-based leadership; and programmes designed for the disadvantaged and the handicapped.[40]

All of these areas, many of which hark back to the sixties and seventies, were followed up in terms of specific activities within the OECD programmes, which will be briefly indicated later, alongside more general work on the further clarification of the concept of quality and its different interpretations as well as developments in those concrete policy fields most directly pertinent to the pursuit of quality. Member countries co-operated actively in this work, with Japan making a particularly significant contribution to the general debate. Paradoxically, it did this by casting doubts on the viability of its educational system as it had developed after the war, and whose success was so strongly admired in the West, particularly in the USA Initial signs of a change of mood were evident at an international seminar which the Japanese organised in 1985, ostensibly as a confrontation of the Japanese and US systems, but in reality as an occasion for drawing lessons for Japan of the educational reform experience of major OECD countries and of the Organisation itself.[41] Soon after this, at the instigation of Premier Nakasone, a National Commission was established to make proposals of how the Japanese educational system could be reformed to meet the needs of post-industrial society. The Commission came up with a devastating critique of the existing system for the very reasons for which other countries wanted to emulate it – too competitive and conformist, it did not encourage creativity, self-reliance and imagination, etc. "Desolation" was the evocative term used by the Commission to describe the effects of the system, and various reforms were suggested in a spirit of "liberation".

The Commission worked outside the structures of the Ministry of Education, and not all of its critique and recommendations met with universal approval. An international discussion of them, juxtaposing them to what other countries were doing, seemed useful to both sides. The OECD was invited to assist in the planning and organisation of such a discussion which took the form of an impressive high level OECD-wide seminar hosted by the Japanese in Kyoto in 1987, opened by Nakasone himself.[42] We are not here concerned with the politics behind this event, nor with its impact on the Japanese educational scene. In terms of the debate on quality, the seminar, by concentrating on the empirical approaches to educational reform strategies applied across the OECD membership, helped to attenuate the controversy on quality as such. It demonstrated that when it comes to practical implementation measures, countries face similar difficulties and have more in common, whatever their perceptions of quality may be.

This more relaxed and practical approach to the problem was reflected in the Organisation's work following he 1984 Ministerial, around the specific topics which had been identified by Ministers as having a direct bearing on the pursuit of quality. These were: teachers and teaching methods, particularly the educational uses of new information technologies; the curriculum; school organisation and school effectiveness; and assessment, evaluation and indicators. Practically all these areas treated of problems which had already been dealt with, but in a different context, during the seventies. Many of them are still under investigation and we cannot do more here than give a brief outline of what was done during the period under consideration.

Teachers

In education, teachers is the key resource. Concern with improving their effectiveness, professional roles and status, as a main requirement of successful educational reform, is a recurring theme in the educational policy discourse. This was so in the sixties and seventies, as we saw in an earlier chapter. It was even more so in the eighties, with the concern for teachers and teacher policies being fanned by the prominence given to improving the quality of education, and with no shortage of critics questioning the capacity of the teaching force either to maintain established standards or adapt to the modern world.

The nature of, and the factors behind this concern had, in fact, significantly evolved since the seventies. In the earlier period, the main problem was how to deal with teacher surpluses and how to get teachers involved in educational change, with all that this implied for the redefinition of their roles and tasks. Teacher surpluses were now giving way to shortages, particularly in mathematics and the sciences, different branches of technical and vocational education, and languages, the very disciplines that were accorded priority to realise the aims of economic adjustment and the promotion of international understanding. Though considerable improvements had been made to initial teacher preparation, through an upgrading of its status and the amalgamation of training for different levels of teaching, systematic policies for teacher *retraining* remained by and large glaringly absent. The innovation process itself had lost steam, with the cut-backs in resources and the ''back to basics'' movement in many countries. This was accompanied by greater demands, by both parents and public authorities, for improved learning outcomes predominantly associated with the performance of teachers, but in a situation in which the knowledge and attitudes of young people were increasingly shaped by media and peer-group influences often well beyond classroom control. The teaching profession itself was gradually ageing with inadequate levels of "new blood" coming in, even among women who in most countries had by tradition been attracted to teaching: persisting lack of promotion opportunities were increasingly forcing women to seek careers in other sectors of the growing service economy.

To all this must be added the gap which on the teachers' side was seen to persist between the higher expectations that society had of them, on the one side, and their own status and rewards, on the other. This dissatisfaction led the teaching profession to become more militant in pushing its claims, as demonstrated by the damaging disputes over pay and conditions of work in settings as diverse as Greece, Ireland, Italy, New Zealand, Norway, Sweden, the United Kingdom and some of the major city districts in the United States. In all countries, there was a strong move for the relationships between teachers and their employers to be put on a contractual basis, with clear definition of tasks and responsibilities in relation to pay conditions.

It is to these problems, as they affected teacher supply and demand and related questions of teacher selection, preparation and appraisal, that the Education Committee turned its attention in responding to the priorities set at the 1984 Ministerial. It set up a special *Working Party on the Condition of Teaching* with a wide mandate encompassing the variety of factors and developments affecting the situation of teachers and relevant to the formulation of teacher policies, supported by complementary work in CERI on teacher education and training, work which is still in progress. The Working Party reported in 1989. Its report,[43] on the findings of which the problems outlined above are based, was highly welcomed by both governments and teacher organisations, a tribute to the judicious mix of analytical insights and political realities which guided its preparation and conclusions. It provided a platform for the pursuit of social consensus, as against the damaging and educationally unproductive confrontation and distrust which characterised the teacher debate in the eighties. It was subsequently used by a number of countries for national discussions directed to this purpose.

Education and new information technologies

The rapid development of information technology since the early 1970s, when the "silicon revolution" began, and its inexorable pervasiveness of all spheres of society could not but leave its mark on education, its organisation and processes. Gone were the days – up to about 1975 – when, as we saw in a previous chapter, the educational impact of the computer was seen to be, at best, marginal. By the mid-eighties, and with the spread of the micro-computer, virtually every industrialised country had accumulated experience with the educational applications of the new technology, even though this was done in haphazard and uncoordinated ways.

At the origin of these confused approaches lies the fact that education was late to enter the new technology market; and when it began to do so in the early eighties, the content and conditions had already been set by powerful economic interests only peripherally related to educational preoccupations and needs. To the extent that educational policies were being devised towards the new technology, these were largely in response to the availability of hardware on the market, itself undergoing constant and rapid evolution. Many were the countries which saw their initial heavy investments in micro-computers for schools soon outdated, or found it difficult to exploit this investment because of the absence of educationally suitable software.

There was, thus, need for policy clarification and direction, and for a more realistic assessment of the potential held out by the new technology as between those who saw it bringing about a revolution in long-established habits and patterns in the organisation of learning and those who remained more sceptical as to its impact. CERI devoted substantial effort to this task during the latter half of the eighties, in which enthusiasm was tempered with sober analysis drawing on the best available policy thinking and research findings in this area.

The main stages in this work can be briefly recounted. A first requirement was to detect the strategy patterns which were developing in the different Member countries for the introduction of the new technology in schools. (The universities were a world apart, with computers coming into increasing, if uneven, use for both administrative and teaching purposes and with the rapid spread of computer science courses, particularly in engineering and business studies.) Four approaches to such strategies could be identified: the *vocational* approach, where information technology was introduced primarily as a response to the need for specialised manpower; *the comprehensive* approach, where information technology was regarded as part of general education for all; the *equipment* approach, where priority was given to generalising the provision of micro-computers to schools; and the *curriculum* approach, dominated by purely educational concerns, especially the inclusion of information technology in overall curriculum development.[44] In all cases, priority was given to secondary rather than primary schools – micro-computers in the latter case being used mainly for teaching traditional subjects and basic skills, whereas, in the former case, they led to the creation of new subjects such as computer awareness at junior levels, and computer science at senior secondary levels and in vocational schools.

This, of course, did not exhaust the range of possible uses of micro-computers in education, constantly expanding with the development of new and more sophisticated products which could open up new approaches to the structure of learning itself. But for any of these applications to be effective, three conditions had to be met, each one of which was dealt with in subsequent CERI work. Firstly, they depended crucially on the attitudes and capacity of teachers. Particularly where micro-computers were used in applications more complex than simple drill and practice, teachers needed to become directly involved in applied research into what was taught and how it was learnt, learn new methods of classroom management, and become partners in curriculum development and the specifications of software. Many teachers remained ill-prepared for these new tasks and the structures for enabling them to adapt to the new technology, including systematic in-service training, were, as yet, largely non-existent.[45]

Secondly, equally crucial was the choice of good quality software, such that it could be imaginatively and coherently integrated into the curriculum. Educational software was flooding the market so that the problem was not one of availability, but rather of selection, an impossible task for individual teachers if they were unaided. Agencies and mechanisms were needed to evaluate the quality of educational software and provide teachers with information on which to base their selection of product that best suited their teaching requirements and the learning needs of their students.[46]

Thirdly, the role, and limitations, of the new technology in enhancing the effectiveness of the learning process itself needed to be elucidated. This was particularly important with regard to the basic skills taught at compulsory school level – reading, writing, science and mathematics – an area where considerable research and experimentation was already taking place, in conjunction with related research on how computer tools could lead to a better understanding of cognitive processes. Expert groups put together the most recently available research findings on each of these topics, and their implications for policy and instructional practice were discussed at an international conference in 1986, and widely disseminated thereafter.[47]

Changes in pedagogical practice and classroom organisation will necessarily have an impact on the way schools are designed and used. To complement the work of CERI, PEB has been trying to assess the way in which facilities may need to adapt. A first seminar, held in 1985, analysed the stages through which schools pass in integrating new technologies into their day-to-day operations, and offered practical advice to those starting out on the process. The greatest difficulty for planners and designers is to be able to see far enough ahead in a field in which both technical capacity and professional practice are moving rapidly, but according to different agendas. Business, telecommunications and mass entertainment define the directions taken by technological development, and their priorities are not necessarily the same as those of education. A second seminar held in 1989 therefore tried to take a medium- to long-term view, and without being prescriptive, set out to draw some general conclusions from societal as well as technological trends.[47b]

It is difficult to assess the cumulative impact of all this work on national policies or, indeed, on the functioning of educational systems. Certainly the expectations that the new technology, and the new forms of self-directed learning which it opens up, would improve the chances of the low achievers does not seem to have been fulfilled. Nor is the instructional process today, in spite of the growing presence of micro-computers in schools and classrooms, very different from what it was before. Even though computer literacy is now recognised as a phenomenon which has come to stay, few systems cater systematically to its school curriculum and teaching implications. But at least national administrations have become more conscious of the need of more coherent policies in this area and of new co-ordinating structures to ensure that teachers are trained in sufficient numbers in the educational uses of micro-computers with ready access to suitable hardware and software within the school. The fact that a number of countries volunteered to have their policies or plans in this direction reviewed by OECD is indicative of the benefit which they derived from this work.[48]

The curriculum

It was inevitable that the preoccupation with the quality of schooling would bring the curriculum, the ''stuff of education'', under the spotlight – in the same way as the preoccupation with scientific and technical personnel had done in the sixties. It was equally inevitable that the politics surrounding the quality debate would overflow into the curriculum itself, its structure, organisation and its very content. Significantly enough, it was the curriculum in basic schooling rather than at the post-compulsory level that roused the most heated controversy. The latter was dealt with more dispassionately, mostly in terms of subject content and changes in the balance among its three traditional sub-divisions – general, technical and vocational – towards their greater convergence resulting from changes in technology and the labour market and less rigidly defined access to higher education.[49]

At compulsory school level, as is the case with the debate on quality, the debate on the curriculum merges into the broader question of the purposes of schooling. All countries, whatever their political divide, adhere to the notion of a "national curriculum" as a main means by which the values and traditions of their societies are transmitted from one generation to another. Differences arise when it comes to defining this curriculum, in terms of the spread of subjects to be covered, the degree of local variation that can be allowed and the role it plays in the assessment of educational outcomes. In this, the central issue becomes the *core curriculum,* more narrowly defined by those who adhere to the "back to basics" movement than by those who take a more "progressive" view of educational purposes. These differences came out clearly at the 1984 Education Ministerial, as already mentioned. Clarification of what these differences really involve, and how the core curriculum, however defined, relates to subsequent learning designs, was seen as a prerequisite in the extensive new work on curriculum reform initiated by CERI in the late eighties.

Thus, the first phase of this work focused on a review of recent trends in curriculum reform in the Member countries. This was in fact a continuation and updating of the long line of curriculum concerns which had marked the CERI programme from its inception, as recorded earlier. The results were embodied in a report which places these trends in their historical perspective and discusses their implications for the central mission and purpose of the school in contemporary society.[50] This review also identified a number of key areas which emerged for more detailed investigation, and on which the current programme concentrates. These are: the teaching of thinking and reasoning as fundamental basic skills;[51] new developments in mathematics, science and technology; issues related to the humanities and values; the core curriculum; assessment, evaluation and learning. Work on all these topics is well advanced and initial reports are already available. (Final results were discussed at an international conference in mid-1993.)

Educational indicators

OECD has had a long tradition in the elaboration and compilation of internationally comparable statistics, dating back to the pioneering days of the sixties as described in previous chapters, and in the use of statistical analyses as the starting point for the discussion of specific educational policy issues and sectors. It proved feasible, in this work, to establish coherent statistical time-series which took account of changes over time in national educational structures and programme definitions,[52] as well as to explore, in the early seventies, the feasibility of moving from these statistics to the development of educational performance indicators, which proved at the time to be premature.[53] The Organisation was, therefore, well placed to respond to the mounting pressure in the late eighties for a new intergovernmental effort to develop such indicators. This pressure was, of course, directly related to the quality and accountability movements, but also to the prevailing fashion for international comparisons in an increasingly competitive world climate. The work of the International Association for the Evaluation of Educational Achievement (IEA), which was financially supported by a number of countries, provided additional inspiration for the launching of such an endeavour.

The pressure on the Organisation to embark on this work came heavily from the American side, with the US Department of Education being willing to make a special, if modest, financial contribution to help launch the activity. Extremely useful educational statistics were available for the US through the National Assessment of Educational Progress (NAEP) and there was growing interest in developing inter-state comparative indicators. Several other Member countries, even among those which were traditionally allergic to data collection, were establishing similar programmes for monitoring pupils' achievements. It seemed, therefore, only logical to add an international dimension to these national efforts, even though the difficulties, both conceptual and technical, of arriving at cross-national comparisons were fully recognised from the outset.

The work began cautiously, with an exploratory discussion at an international meeting in 1987, hosted by the Americans in Washington D.C., followed early in the following year by a similar one hosted by the French in Poitiers. It became clear from these meetings that, though countries differed greatly in their views and priorities on school quality and on how it could be assessed, there was nonetheless general agreement as to the need of improving the information and data base of the performance of their systems. There was still no question of the concrete specification of international indicators. Countries, however, agreed to provide a set of key indicators in use within their own systems as part of an exploratory phase designed to facilitate inter-country exchange on the problems surrounding the development of indicators. The work was seen essentially as developmental in nature and was entrusted to CERI. It was guided by a small group of expert advisers who played a key role in bringing the exploratory phase to a satisfactory conclusion and in ensuring country involvement and support for its continuation into the "production" stage, resulting eventually in the issue of a first set of OECD educational indicators,[54] accompanied by detailed analyses of the conceptual and technical problems facing the development of indicators and their possible uses and misuses in educational policy and management.[55]

Both aspects of this work – the developmental and the empirical – will continue in the future. The categories of indicators so far worked out cover the demographic, economic and social context within which education systems operate; costs, resources and school processes; and outcomes of education. Under each of these categories, specific indicators were inevitably determined by the availability of country data and the feasibility of converting these into internationally comparable data. Equally inevitably, the indicators lean heavily on input data and process data, but organised under carefully thought out policy-related clusters. That it was possible to reach agreement on all this by all the countries concerned is in itself no mean achievement. Equally important has been the light this work has thrown on deficiencies in existing systems of educational data collection, at both national and international levels. *Education at a Glance* will no doubt we used as a handy source of reference for cross-country comparisons of educational performance; but it is only the beginning of what could be a long and arduous process of developing a complete framework of international education indicators of the kind that operates in the economic sector. Whether this is at all feasible, remains an open question.

From educational reform to school effectiveness

The various components of quality which we have described above find their common denominator in the ways in which individual schools function. "School Effectiveness" thus comes centre stage and it should come as no surprise that much of the current effort directed at improving quality has this as its declared objective. This is also reflected in the evolution of the OECD programmes in this area, whether in terms of teacher quality, curriculum development, resource utilisation or school organisation and management. Presumably, the results of these various strands will be brought together one day in a concerted strategy for school improvement. But this is beyond the scope of our present concern.

As early as the late seventies/early eighties, there were clear signs in educational reform movements of more emphasis being placed on the local school setting as the locus of change. Three factors lay behind this move. Firstly, there was a slackening in the pace of centrally-initiated reform, partly as a result of resources drying up and partly because of the disillusionment with the practical effects of centrally conceived reform strategies. Secondly, and related to the above, but also to broader political considerations, education was affected by the general trend towards the decentralisation of public services and the evolution of decision-making to regional, local and institutional levels, with greater autonomy in the management of the resources made available to them. Thirdly, a growing body of research on educational change pointed to the importance of local factors in supporting or blocking implementation and institutionalisation of school improvement. "Top-down" approaches to educational reform were giving way to a "bottom-up" movement, even though the linkage between national and local initiatives was recognised.

It was in this context that the CERI "International School Improvement Project" (ISIP) was set up in 1983, as a decentralised activity to fill the gap created by the interruption of the general work on innovation. The initiative came from the Dutch, who provided substantial financial and organisational support without which the project could not have taken off. The Dutch educational system, with its "semi-autonomous" schools operating within separate denominationally-defined sectors, lent itself admirably to such a school-based approach. The project operated over a period of three years and was wound up at the end of 1986. Its accomplishments, both as a methodology and in terms of substantive outcomes, were by no means insignificant.

The organisation of the project and its methods of work would, in fact, make an interesting case-study in educational innovation. A core group of some fifty experts in educational research and administration, drawing on their own resources and what they could get from the institutions to which they were affiliated – only the Netherlands and Switzerland made formal matching grants to ISIP – managed the project, assisted by a small Steering Group and serviced by the CERI Secretariat. Participation in meetings organised under the project, hosted mostly by research institutions and local authorities, though rarely by governments, was much wider, both in numbers and in the attributes of the participants. The heart of the project were the area groups, one for each of the five substantive domains identified for analysis, with cross-country membership and led by a co-ordinator. The five domains were:

- school-based review for school improvement;
- principals and internal change agents in the school improvement process;
- role of support in school improvement processes;
- research and evaluation in school improvement;
- development and implementation of school improvement policies by education authorities.

A sixth, umbrella group was charged with the task of building the general conceptual framework for ISIP, drawing from the other groups. Around these topics a wide range of collaborative activities were developed (seminars, training conferences, co-development projects), which finally resulted in an impressive volume of reports; their titles speak for themselves.[56] They were used at a series of dissemination seminars in a number of countries. At its conclusion, the project undertook its own candid self-evaluation.[57]

The project had set itself a precise objective: to facilitate improved knowledge of and insights into the functioning of school improvement processes and to contribute to the development of relevant skills within the various levels of educational administration and decision-making. Its output testifies that this objective was largely achieved. Where it failed was in securing governmental interest and support. Working as it did outside governmental structures – even its links to the CERI Governing Board remained ambiguous – it was seen by many in official positions as a rival enterprise, neither amenable to public control nor reflecting the research priorities set by governments and, therefore, not entitled to a share of the limited financial resources which were available for educational research and innovation within the budgets of ministries of education. It was its distance from governments which led to its discontinuation – even though many of the issues it dealt with and the material it produced were to be subsequently taken up again within the programmes of the Organisation.

Schools and quality: a summing up

The reader may be reassured: no attempt will be made here to sum up the complex debate on school quality and the various factors that influence quality which have been the central concern of this chapter. Such a summing up has already been admirably done in a synthesis report which the OECD produced at the end of the eighties, bringing together the findings and insights from all its activities described above.[58] In its conclusions, the report draws attention to the *school* as "the heart of the matter". Research based on detailed school and classroom observation had in fact shown that pupil motivation and achievement were profoundly influenced by the distinctive culture or ethos to be found in each school; and that schools which performed well shared a number of identifiable characteristics. These are:

- a commitment to clearly and commonly identified norms and goals;
- collaborative planning, shared decision-making, and collegial work in a frame of experimentation and evaluation;
- positive leadership in initiating and maintaining improvement;
- staff stability;
- a strategy for continuing staff development related to each school's pedagogical and organisational needs;
- working to a carefully planned and co-ordinated curriculum that ensures sufficient place for each pupil to acquire essential knowledge and skills;
- a high level of parental involvement and support;
- the pursuit and recognition of school-wide values rather than individual ones;
- maximum use of learning time;
- the active and substantial support of the responsible education authority, including an adequate level of resources.[59]

This report, in turn, served as a basic document for the third OECD Ministerial Meeting on education, in 1990, the central theme of which, significantly enough, was *High Quality Education and Training for All.*

Agenda for the nineties

As on previous occasions, the 1990 Education Ministerial laid down an agreed set of aims and orientations for the future development of education. They amount to a formidable agenda for the nineties, rich in implications for action by individual member countries, but also for the future work of OECD. As usual, Ministers did this on the basis of their discussion of a Secretariat analysis of recent trends and future prospects, relating education to its political, social and economic environment. The proceedings of the meeting have been published[60] and need not be repeated here. What will be highlighted instead are some of the main distinctive features of the discussion and its conclusions.

Firstly, compared to its predecessors, the meeting showed a more relaxed, as well as a more cogent, attitude to the links between education and other sectors of policy. More readily than ever before, Ministers recognised both the constraints on education, but also the new possibilities opening up for it, by what was happening around it: the exponential growth of knowledge and rapid technological change; economic restructuring and changes in labour markets, jobs and skills requirements; the ageing of the population, often leading to labour and skill shortages; the emergence of new social concerns, such as the environment, health and drugs; the information glut and the pervasiveness of the media; changing attitudes to the role of public policy and to the administration and financing of public services; the reinforcement of civic and democratic values and the maintenance of social cohesion in competitive, market-driven and consumption-oriented societies; and the growing interdependence of countries, political, economic and cultural, within the OECD area, but also with the rest of the world.

Secondly, though quality remained at the centre of the debate, the approach to it was both more comprehensive and more pragmatic than the essentially academic interpretations which had characterised the rhetoric of earlier discussions. The very theme of the meeting – *High Quality Education and Training for All* – fully reflected this. The quality imperative applies not only to formal education and training, but also to the learning which takes place in other settings; not only to the academically gifted, but also to those who seek their personal development through the acquisition of practical or aesthetic skills; and not only to school achievement, but also to the whole role of education in preparing young people to manage their personal lives and function effectively in society as workers, but also as citizens, parents and their other capacities – recognising in all this that technology has become an integral part of contemporary culture and must be treated as such, towards the development of what may be termed ''a new humanism''.

Thirdly, and for many of the reasons stated above, Ministers readily agreed to endorse the notion that as OECD countries are moving ineluctably towards becoming ''learning societies'', some fundamental rethinking is necessary of the organisation, content and methods of education, at all its levels. New strategies need to be conceived which do not merely replicate existing structures and programmes, providing more of the same. Seeing that Ministers of education accepted that they no longer had the exclusive prerogative for all the educative activity in society, a first requirement in such strategies is a re-examination of the relative roles of formal and non-formal education and training, their co-ordination and consequences for the respective roles and responsibilities of the different authorities involved, the social partners and the individuals themselves.

If we now look at the specific priorities set out in the Ministers' communiqué,[61] many of them do not differ greatly from earlier stated desiderata: the need for a coherent and comprehensive curriculum; an adequate supply of good teachers; efficiency of pedagogy and work methods; and improved capacity in the management of schools and educational systems more generally. What makes the difference is the context within which these are placed. If the over-riding aim is to encourage all individuals to learn actively and continuously throughout their lives, this can only be done by giving reality to the concept of *life-long learning*. This, in turn, draws attention to the primordial role of a sound *basic education* so as to give all youngsters a solid start without which subsequent educational opportunities cannot be realised. It follows from this that effective ways of combating the persisting phenomenon of *school failure* become a *sine qua non* for the success of policies for high quality education for all. It is doubtful that this can be achieved within the existing level of resources, or without some fundamental rethinking of the traditional, classroom-based organisation of teaching designed to provide a more diversified and exciting learning environment for both teachers and pupils.

Thus, the commitment to *educational equality,* which had tended to be neglected during the eighties, reasserted itself as a major goal for the nineties. For economic as well as social and political reasons, societies could ill afford the continuing marginalisation and exclusion of those who remain educationally under-served because of their initial socio-economic circumstances. Similar arguments apply to the disabled, minority groups and the unemployed; bringing them into the mainstream of the social fabric calls for concerted action, involving education, social and labour market policies.

Finally, the meeting brought to light the need for national education policies to take into account the new *international dimensions* and perspectives which arise from the growing interdependence of countries. Knowledge of other countries cultures becomes essential to economic competitiveness, as does the mastery of foreign languages. Mobility of students and personnel across borders raises questions of equivalence of standards and qualifications, as well as of recruitment and access policies in higher education, as does the influx of students from developing countries.[62] New perspectives have also opened up for co-operation with the newly established democracies in Central and Eastern Europe following the demise of communism.[63] In yet another sense, growing internationalisation and the impact of media across national boundaries raise concerns, particularly for small countries, about how national cultural identities can be preserved.

The educational agenda for the nineties is thus both fresh and exciting. Implementing it will tax the political will of governments, their imagination and their organisational and policy/planning capacity, individually and collectively. It remains to be seen whether the Member countries can rise to the challenge. Certainly, the experience of the last thirty years, as recounted in this review, places the OECD in a unique position to continue its task of assisting them in doing so.

Notes and references

1. *Education in Modern Society*, OECD, 1985, and *OECD Ministers Discuss Education in Modern Society*, OECD, 1985.

2. *High-Quality Education and Training for All*, OECD, 1992.

3. *Ibid.*, p. 89.

4. Recent examples of relevant country studies are given in *High Quality Education and Training for All*, *op. cit.*, p. 97, Note 2. See also M.S. Smith, *Educational Reform in the United States*, OECD, 1986, mimeo.

5. *Disadvantaged Youth in Depressed Urban Areas: Final Report*, OECD, 1990, mimeo.

6. *Children and Youth at Risk: A Synthesis of Country Reports*, OECD, 1991, mimeo.

7. *Supra.*, p. 123.

8. Subsequently published in S. Churchill, *The Education of Linguistic and Cultural Minorities in the OECD Countries*, Multilingual Matters Ltd., Clevedon, USA, 1986.

9. For a summary of these country reports and of the general picture which emerged, see: *One School, Many Cultures*, OECD/CERI, 1989.

10. *Immigrants' Children at School*, OECD/CERI, 1987.

11. *Education and Cultural and Linguistic Pluralism: Effective Strategies and Approaches in the Schools* (provisional title), OECD/CERI, forthcoming.

12. See the collection of papers presenting different aspects and viewpoints in *Multicultural Education*, OECD/CERI, 1987.

13. The most important of these reports are:

    The Education of the Handicapped Adolescent: Integration in the School, OECD/CERI, 1981.
    Integration of the Handicapped in Secondary Schools: Five Case Studies, OECD/CERI, 1985.
    The Education of the Handicapped Adolescent: The Transition from School to Working Life, OECD/CERI, 1987.
    Handicapped Youth at Work: Personal Experiences of School Leavers, OECD/CERI, 1985.
    Disabled Youth: From School to Work, OECD/CERI, 1991.
    Young People with Handicaps: The Road to Adulthood, OECD/CERI, 1986.
    Disabled Youth: The Right to Adult Status, OECD/CERI, 1988.
    Transition of Disabled Youth from School to Working Life: The Genoa Experience, OECD/CERI, 1992, document on general distribution.
    Active Life for Disabled Youth: Integration and Practices, OECD/CERI, forthcoming.

14. A summary report of the conference was published in *Active Life for Young People with Disabilities*, OECD/CERI, 1987.

15. *Education and Training after Basic Schooling*, OECD, 1985. For the Ministerial discussion and conclusions see, *OECD Ministers Discuss Education in Modern Society*, *op. cit.*, p. 33 ff.

16. Representative examples can be found in *Facets of the Transition to Adulthood*, OECD/CERI, 1986, mimeo.

17. *Pathways for Learning: Education and Training from 16 to 19*, OECD, 1989. Country case-studies are listed in the Annex. They were published separately as "OECD Educational Monographs".

18. *OECD Ministers Discuss Education*, *op. cit.*, pp. 39-40.

19. *Ibid.*, pp. 44-48, reproducing the Press Communiqué of the Ministerial Meeting.

20. For the general report of the Utrecht Conference see, *Technological Change and Human Resources Development: The Service Sector*, OECD/CERI and the Dutch Ministry of Education and Science, 1990. Among the many reports which emanated from the CERI project and on which the Conference drew, the following are to be noted:

    Human Resources and Corporate Strategy: Technological Change in Banks and Insurance Companies, OECD/CERI, 1988.
    Changes in Work Patterns: A Synthesis of Five National Reports on the Service Sector, OECD/CERI, 1989, mimeo.
    The Evolution of New Technology, Work and Skills in the Service Sector, OECD/CERI, 1986, mimeo.
    New Technology and Human Resource Development in the Automobile Industry, OECD/CERI, 1986, mimeo.
    The Human Factor in Economic and Technological Change, OECD/CERI, 1987, mimeo.
    Towards an Enterprising Culture, OECD/CERI, 1989.

21. *The Service Sector*, *op. cit.*, pp. 5-6.

22. See, in particular, *New Technologies in the 1990s: A Socio-Economic Strategy*, (the "Sundquist Report"), OECD, 1989, and *Technology in a Changing World*, OECD, 1991.

23. In *OECD Employment Outlook*, July 1989, Chapter 2.

24. CERI has devoted a recent special study to this problem, its nature , causes and methods of combating it. See, *Adult Illiteracy and Economic Performance*, OECD/CERI, 1992.

25. For a general survey of the situation see, *Further Education and Training of the Labour Force in OECD Countries*, OECD, forthcoming, and its companion volume *A Comparative Analysis of National Strategies for Industry Training: Australia, Sweden and the United States*, OECD, forthcoming.

26. In addition to the studies referred to in the previous note, much interesting work on key components of such policies, particularly as they refer to school-based education and training, is being carried out under the current Education Committee activity on "The Changing Role of Vocational Education and Training". Parallel work in CERI has focused on empirical analysis of industry-education links. See *School and Business: a New Partnership*, OECD/CERI, 1992.

27. The report of the Conference – *Linkages in Vocational Education and Training* – is being published by the OECD in cooperation with the US Department of Education.

28. *Structural Adjustment and Economic Performance*, OECD, 1988.

29. *Labour Market Policies for the 1990s*, OECD, 1990.

30. *Education and Structural Change: A Statement by the Education Committee*, OECD, 1989, General Distribution.

31. *Ibid.*, p. 6.

32. *Education and the Economy in a Changing Society*, OECD, 1989.

33. *Ibid.*, Appendix, p. 117. Bilateral discussions between the two sides on these matters were pursued within the Organisation's Labour Management Programme.

33a. For a succinct statement of the concept and its implications, see J.R. Gass, "Towards the Active Society", *OECD Observer*, No. 152, 1988.

34. For an analysis of the educational policy of the new Swedish Government see the OECD *Educational Policy Review of Sweden*, forthcoming.

35. For a summary of these conflicting arguments see *OECD Ministers Discuss Education*, *op. cit.*, p. 24 ff.

36. *Quality in Education*, OECD, 1984, mimeo.

37. *Educational Financing and Policy Goals for Primary Schools: General Report* – and accompanying three volumes of *Country Reports* – OECD/CERI, 1979.

38. *Compulsory Schooling in a Changing World*, OECD, 1993.

39. *OECD Ministers Discuss Education*, *op. cit.*, pp. 28-32.

40. *Ibid.*, p. 48.

41. *Proceedings of the International Seminar on Educational Reform*, National Institute of Multimedia Education, Chiba (Japan), 1985.

42. *Proceedings of the Conference of High-Level Experts on Education*, Tokyo, 1987. Nakasone used all his authority to ensure high-level participation, particularly on the part of G7 countries. He had already raised with his G7 partners the need for concerted international action for educational reform. The conclusions of the Conference were transmitted to all OECD governments through the Education Committee.

43. *The Teacher Today*, OECD, 1990. The report drew extensively on country contributions and specially commissioned studies, as well as on the wider literature available. Not its least merit is the extensive bibliography which accompanies each chapter of the report. Recent developments in teacher training are covered in a separate report – *The Training of Teachers*, OECD/CERI, forthcoming.

44. *New Information Technologies: A Challenge for Education*, OECD/CERI, 1986. This report, and the international conference (July 1986) on which it was based, are an important landmark in the subsequent development of national policies for the introduction of information technologies in schools and the selection of criteria for national research priorities in this area.

45. *Micro-computers and Secondary Teaching: Implications for Teacher Education*, (Report of an international seminar by the Scottish Education Department in co-operation with OECD, October 1987), SED, 1988.

46. *Information Technologies in Education: The Quest for Quality Software*, OECD/CERI, 1989.

47. *Information Technologies and Basic Learning: Reading, Writing, Science and Mathematics*, OECD/CERI, 1987. The reports of the four groups stand as a major original contribution to the state of knowledge in these fields.

47*b*. *New Technology and its Impact on Educational Building*, OECD/PEB, 1992.

48. Examples of such country reviews are those of Norway and Spain. See, *The Introduction of Computers in Schools: The Norwegian Experience*, OECD/CERI, 1987; and *The Introduction of Computers in Schools: The Spanish Atenea Project*, OECD/CERI and the Spanish Ministry of Education, 1991.

49. *Pathways for Learning*, *op. cit.*, pp. 8-10.

50. M. Skilbeck, *Curriculum Reform: An Overview of Trends*, OECD/CERI, 1990.

51. Work on this topic was completed with an international conference in 1989. *Learning to Think, Thinking to Learn*, Pergamon press for OECD/CERI, 1991.

52. The most recent example of this is *Public Educational Expenditure, Costs and Financing: An Analysis of Trends 1970-1988*, OECD, 1992.

53. *Indicators of Performance of Educational Systems*, (1973), *op. cit.*

54. *Education at a Glance: OECD Indicators*, OECD/CERI, 1992.

55. *The OECD International Education Indicators: A Framework for Analysis*, OECD, 1992. This report also contains a description of the various stages of the CERI project, the methods used and the lessons that can be derived from the whole exercise so far.

56. The list of ISIP publications is as follows. (They were all published by ACCO, Leuven, Belgium, with French versions for some of them by ECONOMICA, Paris.)

ISIP Books:
W.G. van Velzen, M.B. Miles, M. Ekholm, U. Hameyer and D. Robin (eds.), *Making School Improvement Work: a Conceptual Guide to Practice*, 1985.
R.M. van den Berg and R. Vandenberghe (eds.), *Strategies for Large-scale Change in Education: Dilemmas and Solutions*, 1986.
R. Bollen and D. Hopkins (eds.), *School Based Review: Towards a Praxis*, 1987.
N.E. Stegö, K. Gielen, R. Glatter and S.M. Hord (eds.), *The Role of School Leaders in School Improvement,* 1987.
M.B. Miles, M. Ekholm and R. Vandenberghe (eds.), *Lasting School Improvment: Exploring the Process of Institutionalisation*, 1987.
R. van den Berg, U. Hameyer and K. Stokking (eds.), *Disseminsation Reconsidered: the Demands of Implementation*, 1989.
K. Seashore Louis and S. Loucks-Horsley (eds.), *Supporting School Improvement: a Comparative Perspective*, 1990.

ISIP Technical Reports:
D. Hopkins (ed.), *School Based Review for School Improvement*, 1985.
C. Hopes (ed.), *The School Leader and School Improvement: Case Studies from Ten OECD Countrie*s, 1986.
S. Loucks-Horsley and D.P. Crandall (eds.), *Analysing School Improvement Support Systems: a Practical Manua*l, 1986.
R. Blum and J.A. Butler (eds.), *School-Leader Development for School Improvemen*t, 1989.
D. Hopkins (ed.), *Doing School Based R: Instruments and Guidelines*, 1989.
L. de Caluwé, E.C.H. Marx and M.W. Petri (eds.), *School Development: Models and Change*, 1988.
U. Hameyer and S. Loucks-Horsley (eds.), *New Technologies and School Improvement, Support Policies and Practices*, 1989.

57. M.B. Miles, *International School Improvement Project: An Evaluation of the Methods of Work and Implications for Policy-Making*, OECD/CERI, 1987, mimeo.

58. *Schools and Quality: An International Report*, OECD, 1989. In addition to drawing on all relevant activities within the OECD programmes and on the vast output of research in this area, the preparation of this report involved a series of specially organised international conferences on the following topics: *Core Curriculum and Core Skills; School Leadership; the Vital Role of Teachers*; and *Evaluation and Monitoring of the School System*. Reports on each of these topics are available in mimeo form.

59. *Schools and Quality*, p. 141.

60. *High Quality Education and Training for All*, OECD, 1992. The analytical report by the Secretariat, including its statistical basis, is presented in Part Two of the volume. The Annex reproduces the joint statement submitted to Ministers by BIAC and TUAC, a remarkable document in its own right in indicating the high degree of agreement between the two sides on the diagnosis of the problems and on the general directions of policies to tackle them.

61. *Ibid.*, pp. 31-36.

62. The problems involved in the flow of foreign students have been under study within the CERI and IMHE programmes for some years now. They will be further developed in the future in the broader "internationalisation" context. See *Foreign Students and the Internationalisation of Higher Education*, proceedings of an OECD/Japan Seminar, Hiroshima University, 1989; and the selection of papers from the "German/OECD International Seminar on Higher Education and the Flow of Foreign students", edited by Alan Wagner and Klaus Schnitzer, in *Higher Education*, Vol. 23, No. 3, 1991.

63. OECD has already embarked on an active policy of co-operation with these countries, in education as well as in other fields.

Chapter X

CONCLUSION

The ambition set for this book has been quite modest. It is not to write the history of education during the last thirty years or so, nor to analyse the impact which the momentous changes which have taken place in education has had on OECD societies. This history and analysis have yet to be written. The objective has rather been to offer an informed commentary of the work of OECD in this area, of the factors and considerations which motivated this work and, to the extent that they can be identified, of the results achieved.

In terms of the substance of the work, a striking feature which emerges from this account is how constant the essential problems that face education remain over time. This is only natural, seeing that the plural objectives served by education – knowledge and culture, contributions to the economy and to social and civic development, among others – are also constant. So are the main parameters within which the pursuit of these objectives is played out: the student population, with its changing numbers, characteristics and age distribution; the availability of resources, both financial and human, with teachers occupying centre stage; content and pedagogy; educational institutions and the articulation, planning and management of the system within which they operate. What changes is the *context* within which perennial educational problems have to be tackled, particularly changes in the socio-economic and political context of education. These contextual changes eventually get reflected in policy decisions as to the choice of priorities among the various objectives of education and of the methods and means by which the favoured objectives are to be implemented – recognising of course that, in the last analysis, education is directed at the individual himself/herself, and that this sets an irreducible level of plurality in the choice of objectives at any given time.

In many respects, then, the history of educational policy developments in the Member countries during the whole of the period under consideration, at least as seen by OECD, can be interpreted in terms of shifts of emphasis among the various objectives of education generated by social, economic and political change. The process was neither easy nor smooth, and its impact often limited, because it had to struggle against the internal dynamics of well-established educational systems which see themselves as the professional guardians of the educative function entrusted to them by society and not readily amenable to outside interference. The gap between educational policy pronouncements and their translation into actual educational practice was, and remains, difficult to bridge. The selection of instruments – in the form of incentives, but also, and in some countries increasingly so, of measures of a coercive nature – to reduce this distance has in itself become an important, and often controversial, aspect of educational policy.

In the light of the above, and at the risk of over-simplification, two distinct epochs can be identified in the history of education at OECD as recounted in this book: one extending to the mid-seventies and the other from then onwards, with the onset of the recession in 1973-75 acting as the great divide. The main characteristic of the former period was *growth,* economic, demographic and educational. This made it possible for all educational objectives to be pursued more or less simultaneously, with particular accent on social and equality objectives, accompanied by a great deal of experimentation in structures, content and pedagogy, to ensure the relevance of education to the needs of the greatly increased and variegated school population. The importance of education for the economy was fully recognised but by and large, education was allowed to develop under its own dynamics, with governmental efforts concentrating on marshalling the resources and setting up the structures to meet the social demand for education.

The onset and gradual deepening of the recession, and the consequent constraints on public resources, dramatically changed the situation. Social and equality considerations receded to the background, giving way to economic ones, in terms of the allocation and use of educational resources as well as of the definition of educational purposes. What was formerly demand-led educational development gave way to one largely determined by supply; and factors exogenous to the educational system came to play an increasing role in the setting of educational targets and objectives – reaching down to the very contents of education and even its pedagogy – and in monitoring the performance of the system and the quality of its outcomes, leading eventually to the emergence of market approaches to the funding, organisation and behaviour of educational institutions.

The contrast between the two epochs outlined above is but one general illustration of how the approach to the problems facing education differs according to the prevailing socio-economic and political climate. Earlier chapters are replete with specific examples of how these ''educational cycles'' work: the same problems surfacing over and over again, even though under different circumstances and many of them remaining unresolved. Thus, to quote but a few examples, quality in education and human resource development were burning issues in the sixties as they were in the late eighties, even though then they were part of the general concern with the democratisation of education in contrast to their close association with the economic imperative of to-day. Present day concerns with teachers, their status, tasks and roles, do not differ from those raised in the seventies, nor are they nearer a solution. The concept of basic education and of the core curriculum remains a moving target; so does the role of the school vis-à-vis work-based training and life-long learning, as does the relationship between general education and vocational and technical education. Problems of interdisciplinarity and the delineation of the roles and functions of higher education institutions, particularly of universities, are still in search of solutions. Education remains the unfinished business.

This recurrence of themes, however, should not be interpreted as portraying a static situation; far from it. Education during this period witnessed unprecedented movement, at both the planning/policy and operational levels, matched by the vast volume of literature, in the form of research studies and policy analyses, which it has generated – and to which the OECD has made a contribution as shown by the bibliographical references which accompany the various chapters of this book. And in spite of the many problems which remain unresolved, we are now wiser in many respects as to both the possibilities and limits of what education can do as well as to how it works. We know, for example, that the high expectations of the sixties that education alone could bring about greater social equality were misplaced, as are current expectations that it could solve the unemployment problem. We understand better how the educational change process works and the fundamental role which grass roots initiatives play in this as against "top-down models". We have come to accept decentralisation of decision-making as an essential condition of effective educational innovation. We are more aware of the uncertainties surrounding educational planning and of how such planning feeds into policy-making. Above all, we have learnt to appreciate the changing nature of educational policy making itself and to recognise how deeply rooted this is becoming in the ideological panoply of the prevailing political power structure.

It is to problems of this kind that the OECD work recounted in this book has endeavoured to make a contribution. The impact of this work remains difficult to judge; and it varied from area to area, some "projects' being more successful than others. Certainly such influence as the OECD has had on national developments derives not so much from the generation of new ideas by the Organisation itself as from its ability to pick up new ideas, from research and political stances in the countries – the mix varying over time –, develop their potential for implementation and then bring them to bear more broadly on national policy agendas. Free of executive responsibilities in this field, the OECD was all the more equipped to exercise this catalytic and integrative function without which a number of developments in the countries would at least have taken much longer to occur.

MAIN SALES OUTLETS OF OECD PUBLICATIONS
PRINCIPAUX POINTS DE VENTE DES PUBLICATIONS DE L'OCDE

ARGENTINA – ARGENTINE
Carlos Hirsch S.R.L.
Galería Güemes, Florida 165, 4° Piso
1333 Buenos Aires   Tel. (1) 331.1787 y 331.2391
Telefax: (1) 331.1787

AUSTRALIA – AUSTRALIE
D.A. Information Services
648 Whitehorse Road, P.O.B 163
Mitcham, Victoria 3132   Tel. (03) 873.4411
Telefax: (03) 873.5679

AUSTRIA – AUTRICHE
Gerold & Co.
Graben 31
Wien I   Tel. (0222) 533.50.14

BELGIUM – BELGIQUE
Jean De Lannoy
Avenue du Roi 202
B-1060 Bruxelles   Tel. (02) 538.51.69/538.08.41
Telefax: (02) 538.08.41

CANADA
Renouf Publishing Company Ltd.
1294 Algoma Road
Ottawa, ON K1B 3W8   Tel. (613) 741.4333
Telefax: (613) 741.5439
Stores:
61 Sparks Street
Ottawa, ON K1P 5R1   Tel. (613) 238.8985
211 Yonge Street
Toronto, ON M5B 1M4   Tel. (416) 363.3171
Telefax: (416)363.59.63

Les Éditions La Liberté Inc.
3020 Chemin Sainte-Foy
Sainte-Foy, PQ G1X 3V6   Tel. (418) 658.3763
Telefax: (418) 658.3763

Federal Publications Inc.
165 University Avenue, Suite 701
Toronto, ON M5H 3B8   Tel. (416) 860.1611
Telefax: (416) 860.1608

Les Publications Fédérales
1185 Université
Montréal, QC H3B 3A7   Tel. (514) 954.1633
Telefax : (514) 954.1635

CHINA – CHINE
China National Publications Import
Export Corporation (CNPIEC)
16 Gongti E. Road, Chaoyang District
P.O. Box 88 or 50
Beijing 100704 PR   Tel. (01) 506.6688
Telefax: (01) 506.3101

DENMARK – DANEMARK
Munksgaard Book and Subscription Service
35, Nørre Søgade, P.O. Box 2148
DK-1016 København K   Tel. (33) 12.85.70
Telefax: (33) 12.93.87

FINLAND – FINLANDE
Akateeminen Kirjakauppa
Keskuskatu 1, P.O. Box 128
00100 Helsinki

Subscription Services/Agence d'abonnements :
P.O. Box 23
00371 Helsinki   Tel. (358 0) 12141
Telefax: (358 0) 121.4450

FRANCE
OECD/OCDE
Mail Orders/Commandes par correspondance:
2, rue André-Pascal
75775 Paris Cedex 16   Tel. (33-1) 45.24.82.00
Telefax: (33-1) 49.10.42.76
Telex: 640048 OCDE

OECD Bookshop/Librairie de l'OCDE :
33, rue Octave-Feuillet
75016 Paris   Tel. (33-1) 45.24.81.67
(33-1) 45.24.81.81
Documentation Française
29, quai Voltaire
75007 Paris   Tel. 40.15.70.00
Gibert Jeune (Droit-Économie)
6, place Saint-Michel
75006 Paris   Tel. 43.25.91.19
Librairie du Commerce International
10, avenue d'Iéna
75016 Paris   Tel. 40.73.34.60
Librairie Dunod
Université Paris-Dauphine
Place du Maréchal de Lattre de Tassigny
75016 Paris   Tel. (1) 44.05.40.13
Librairie Lavoisier
11, rue Lavoisier
75008 Paris   Tel. 42.65.39.95
Librairie L.G.D.J. - Montchrestien
20, rue Soufflot
75005 Paris   Tel. 46.33.89.85
Librairie des Sciences Politiques
30, rue Saint-Guillaume
75007 Paris   Tel. 45.48.36.02
P.U.F.
49, boulevard Saint-Michel
75005 Paris   Tel. 43.25.83.40
Librairie de l'Université
12a, rue Nazareth
13100 Aix-en-Provence   Tel. (16) 42.26.18.08
Documentation Française
165, rue Garibaldi
69003 Lyon   Tel. (16) 78.63.32.23
Librairie Decitre
29, place Bellecour
69002 Lyon   Tel. (16) 72.40.54.54

GERMANY – ALLEMAGNE
OECD Publications and Information Centre
August-Bebel-Allee 6
D-53175 Bonn   Tel. (0228) 959.120
Telefax: (0228) 959.12.17

GREECE – GRÈCE
Librairie Kauffmann
Mavrokordatou 9
106 78 Athens   Tel. (01) 32.55.321
Telefax: (01) 36.33.967

HONG-KONG
Swindon Book Co. Ltd.
13–15 Lock Road
Kowloon, Hong Kong   Tel. 366.80.31
Telefax: 739.49.75

HUNGARY – HONGRIE
Euro Info Service
Margitsziget, Európa Ház
1138 Budapest   Tel. (1) 111.62.16
Telefax : (1) 111.60.61

ICELAND – ISLANDE
Mál Mog Menning
Laugavegi 18, Pósthólf 392
121 Reykjavik   Tel. 162.35.23

INDIA – INDE
Oxford Book and Stationery Co.
Scindia House
New Delhi 110001   Tel.(11) 331.5896/5308
Telefax: (11) 332.5993
17 Park Street
Calcutta 700016   Tel. 240832

INDONESIA – INDONÉSIE
Pdii-Lipi
P.O. Box 269/JKSMG/88
Jakarta 12790   Tel. 583467
Telex: 62 875

IRELAND – IRLANDE
TDC Publishers – Library Suppliers
12 North Frederick Street
Dublin 1   Tel. (01) 874.48.35
Telefax: (01) 874.84.16

ISRAEL
Praedicta
5 Shatner Street
P.O. Box 34030
Jerusalem 91430   Tel. (2) 52.84.90/1/2
Telefax: (2) 52.84.93

ITALY – ITALIE
Libreria Commissionaria Sansoni
Via Duca di Calabria 1/1
50125 Firenze   Tel. (055) 64.54.15
Telefax: (055) 64.12.57
Via Bartolini 29
20155 Milano   Tel. (02) 36.50.83
Editrice e Libreria Herder
Piazza Montecitorio 120
00186 Roma   Tel. 679.46.28
Telefax: 678.47.51
Libreria Hoepli
Via Hoepli 5
20121 Milano   Tel. (02) 86.54.46
Telefax: (02) 805.28.86
Libreria Scientifica
Dott. Lucio de Biasio 'Aeiou'
Via Coronelli, 6
20146 Milano   Tel. (02) 48.95.45.52
Telefax: (02) 48.95.45.48

JAPAN – JAPON
OECD Publications and Information Centre
Landic Akasaka Building
2-3-4 Akasaka, Minato-ku
Tokyo 107   Tel. (81.3) 3586.2016
Telefax: (81.3) 3584.7929

KOREA – CORÉE
Kyobo Book Centre Co. Ltd.
P.O. Box 1658, Kwang Hwa Moon
Seoul   Tel. 730.78.91
Telefax: 735.00.30

MALAYSIA – MALAISIE
Co-operative Bookshop Ltd.
University of Malaya
P.O. Box 1127, Jalan Pantai Baru
59700 Kuala Lumpur
Malaysia   Tel. 756.5000/756.5425
Telefax: 757.3661

MEXICO – MEXIQUE
Revistas y Periodicos Internacionales S.A. de C.V.
Florencia 57 - 1004
Mexico, D.F. 06600   Tel. 207.81.00
Telefax : 208.39.79

NETHERLANDS – PAYS-BAS
SDU Uitgeverij Plantijnstraat
Externe Fondsen
Postbus 20014
2500 EA's-Gravenhage   Tel. (070) 37.89.880
Voor bestellingen: Telefax: (070) 34.75.778

NEW ZEALAND
NOUVELLE-ZÉLANDE
Legislation Services
P.O. Box 12418
Thorndon, Wellington   Tel. (04) 496.5652
Telefax: (04) 496.5698

OECD PUBLICATIONS, 2 rue André-Pascal, 75775 PARIS CEDEX 16
PRINTED IN FRANCE
(91 94 02 1) ISBN 92-64-14190-1 - No. 47275 1994